TABLE OF CONTENTS

Explore the World

SRI LANKA

Authors:
Elke Frey, Gerhard Lemmer,
Jayanthi Namasivayam

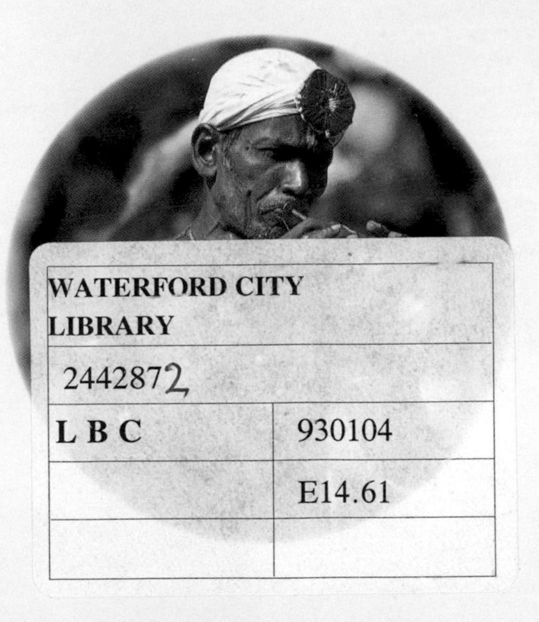

An up-to-date travel guide
with 157 color photos
and 18 maps

Dear Reader: Being up-to-date is the main goal of the Nelles series. Our correspondents help keep us abreast of the latest developments in the travel scene, while our cartographers see to it that maps are also kept completely current. However, as the travel world is constantly changing, we cannot guarantee that all the information contained in our books is always valid. Should you come across a discrepancy, please contact us at: Nelles Verlag, Schleissheimer Str. 371 b, 80935 Munich, Germany, tel. (089) 3571940, fax. (089) 35719430, e-mail: Nelles.Verlag@T-Online.de

Note: Distances and measurements, including temperatures, used in this guide are metric. For conversion information, please see the *Guidelines* section of this book.

LEGEND

Public or Significant Building

Hotel, Guesthouse

Restaurant

Market, Shopping Center

Church, Buddhist Temple

Mosque, Hindu Temple

Place of Interest, Ancient Site

Beach

National Park

A15 32 Route number

International Airport

National Airport

18 Distance in Kilometers

Koggala Place Mentioned in Text

Hakgala 2170 Mountain Summit (Height in Meters)

Provincial Border

District Border

Highway

Main Road

Provincial Road (partly paved)

Secondary Road (unpaved)

Cart Track, Path

Railway

SRI LANKA

Third Revised Edition 2001
ISBN 3-88618-229-0
Printed in Slovenia

Publisher: Günter Nelles
Managing Editor: Berthold Schwarz
Project Editor: Elke Frey
English Edition Editor: Kerstin Borch
Photo Editor: K. Bärmann-Thümmel
Translation: S. Bollans, L. Booth
Lithos: Priegnitz, Munich
Cartography: Nelles Verlag GmbH
Printed by: Gorenjski Tisk

- T05 -

FEATURES

GUIDELINES

MAP LIST

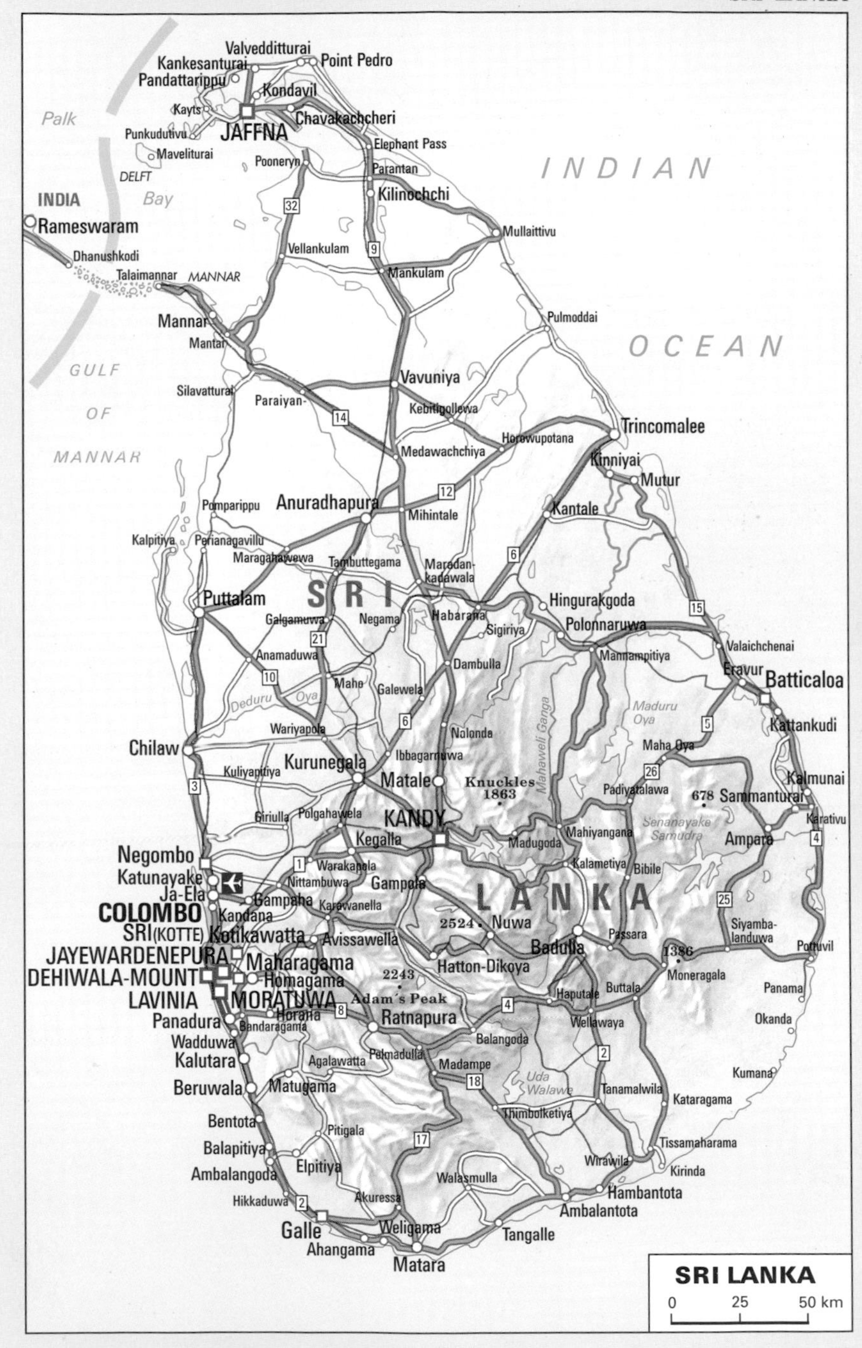
Valveddítturai
Kankesanturai
Point Pedro
Pandattarippu
Kondavil
Kayts
JAFFNA
Chavakachcheri
Punkudutivu
Mavelitürai
Elephant Pass
Palk
Pooneryn
Parantan
DELFT
Kilinochchi
INDIA
Bay
Rameswaram
Mullaittivu
Vellankulam
Dhanushkodi
Mankulam
Talaimannar
MANNAR
Pulmoddai
Mannar
Mantai
INDIAN
OCEAN
GULF
OF
MANNAR
Silavatturai
Vavuniya
Paraiyan-
Kebitigollewa
Trincomalee
Horowupotana
Medawachchiya
Kinniyai
Mutur
Pomparippu
Anuradhapura
Mihintale
Kantale
Kalpitiya
Perianagavillu
Maragahawewa
Tambuttegama
Maradan-kadawala
SRI
Puttalam
Hingurakgoda
Galgamuwa
Negama
Habarana
Polonnaruwa
Sigiriya
Anamaduwa
Valaichchenai
Dambulla
Manampitiya
Eravur
Batticaloa
Deduru Oya
Mahe
Galewela
Maduru Oya
Mahaweli Ganga
Wariyapola
Kattankudi
Chilaw
Nalanda
Ibbagamuwa
Maha Oya
Kurunegala
Kuliyapitiya
Matale
Knuckles 1863
Kalmunai
Padiyatalawa
678
Sammanturai
Giriulla
Polgahawela
KANDY
Senanayake Samudra
Karativu
Kegalla
Mahiyangana
Ampara
Madugoda
Negombo
Warakapola
Kalametiya
Bibile
Katunayake
Nittambuwa
Gampola
Ja-Ela
Gampaha
LANKA
COLOMBO
Karawanella
Kandana
2524
Nuwa
Siyamba-landuwa
SRI (KOTTE)
Kotikawatta
Passara
Avissawella
JAYEWARDENEPURA
Badulla
1386
Pottuvil
Maharagama
Hatton-Dikoya
DEHIWALA-MOUNT
2243
Homagama
Moneragala
Buttala
Panama
LAVINIA
MORATUWA
Adam´s Peak
Haputale
Horana
Ratnapura
Wellawaya
Panadura
Bandaragama
Okanda
Wadduwa
Balangoda
Kalutara
Agalawatta
Palmadulla
Madampe
Kumana
Uda Walawe
Beruwala
Matugama
Tanamalwila
Kataragama
Thimbolketiya
Bentota
Pitigala
Tissamaharama
Balapitiya
Elpitiya
Wirawila
Kirinda
Ambalangoda
Walasmulla
Hambantota
Hikkaduwa
Akuressa
Ambalantota
Galle
Weligama
Tangalle
Ahangama
Matara
SRI LANKA
0
25
50 km

THE GEOGRAPHY OF SRI LANKA

White sand beaches, dotted with palm trees, stretching along the blue sea: for many people, the island of Sri Lanka is the epitome of a tropical paradise. But while it boasts a coastline some 1,330 kilometers long, and a thin strip of sand beach runs around almost the entire island, this is only one facet of the island's legion idyllic natural landscapes.

Closer to the equator than to India, Sri Lanka lies only 30 kilometers southeast of its larger neighbor. It is a compact island state, some 65,610 square kilometers in area, which resembles a gigantic gem in the form of a teardrop. It is somewhat smaller than the Republic of Ireland, or the combined areas of the Netherlands and Belgium. Some 430 kilometers separate its northern tip from its southernmost point, while it measures 225 kilometers from east to west. The equator is located 650 kilometers further south, across the Indian Ocean; after that, there is nothing but endless sea between here and the Antarctic.

Two winds determine the annual seasons in Sri Lanka: the southwest monsoon, and six months later its pendant the northeast monsoon. The Bay of Bengal lies to the northeast of the island and the vast Indian Ocean extends to the south and southwest. Thus the strong winds can blast unchecked across the sea, picking up moisture in the process.

As a result, between May and September the surf crashes with particular intensity against the south and west coasts, and from November to May the east coast is similarly punished.

Preceding pages: More than 2,000 years of Buddhism have helped shape Sri Lanka. Idyllic beaches are a draw for tourists. Left: Underwater paradise along a reef.

At the onset of each monsoon period, the windward side of the island gets about one month of heavy rain, which abates gradually. The southwest monsoon generally lasts longer than its counterpart, and rainfall is higher when it holds sway. The weather is relatively settled in March/April and October/November, when the wind changes direction.

Just as farmers and fishermen are subject to nature's wiles, the tourist trade must likewise follow the dictates of the wind direction. Accordingly, the high season on the south and west coasts is between November and April, while March through October is the peak period on the east coast. Then again, some tourists prefer the off-season, and not just because it's cheaper. Not only are the temperatures consistently warm, but long, dreary days of endless rain are rare; rather, the rain comes in short, heavy bursts, followed by sunshine. The overcast sky tempers the heat of the sun, but not the strength of its rays, so that you can still get a fine tan. Unfortunately, during this period the sea is often too rough for swimming on the side of the island affected by the monsoon wind. The larger hotels have come up with a fine solution to this problem: no one need worry much about dangerous waves and currents when there is a hotel pool.

In the southwest, one bathing beach gives way to another in a quarter-circle around the island's edge: from Chilaw on the central west coast to Tangalla in the southern part of the south coast. Like a string of pearls, hundreds of hotels are lined up between these two towns, and they range from simple guest houses on the beach to five-star establishments. There are a large number of hotels in Negombo, Beruwala, Bentota and especially in Hikkaduwa, all on the west coast and less than three hours away from the island's only international airport at Katunayake. In other resorts the hotels stand in small groups or alone, particularly in

the south, where bays subdivide the coastline to a greater degree than they do on the west coast.

The southwestern section of Sri Lanka gets the most rain. This is partly because rainfall is higher during the southwest monsoon. In addition, in the remaining months there are refreshing showers and scattered thundershowers which replenish the water evaporated by the scorching tropical sun. Not surprisingly, the most lush tropical plants flourish here due to the higher rainfall. Some 500 years ago, the Portuguese discovered the wild cinnamon tree in this hot and humid jungle. By contrast, the area is today the home of coconut, rubber and cinnamon plantations, while every available piece of flat ground in the lowlands is taken up by rice paddies, where two harvests take place every year. The best yields are realized during the *maha*, the long, wetter season, while the *yala*, the second harvest of the year, usually produces lower yields. The majority of Sri Lanka's population, 19 million strong, lives in this southwest section of the island.

Above: Tropical rainstorms are short, but very heavy. Right: On the beach of Weligama after a monsoon rain.

Rice is also cultivated in the eastern section of Sri Lanka. However, though in places the rice paddies are much larger than in the west, all the paddies here need irrigation. None of the larger water reservoirs in the east was built until the second half of the 20th century; they enabled thousands of families who had moved to the area to establish new beginnings.

Bathing resorts on the east coast are few and far between. Three tourist centers have developed around very attractive stretches of beach located about 30 kilometers north of Trincomalee and Batticaloa, and at charming Arugam Bay south of Pottuvil – the only one which remained intact after the civil war. Though the east coast is subject to the influence of the northeast monsoon from November on, conditions are often suitable for ocean swimming by the begin-

ning of the year. The air here is less humid, and though the coastal beaches are lined with palms, the vegetation is not as dense or lush as it is on the hot, humid west coast. Population density is lower in the east, the region is less modern and the roads leading to the area are partly in poor condition. Moreover, guerilla activity by LTTE separatists have meant that at times tourism in the area has either been badly affected or has dwindled away altogether. Some people may find this off-putting, but during politically-stable periods this region attracts many independent travelers seeking tranquility, who appreciate the bonus of seclusion.

Both Sri Lanka and India lie on the same shallow continental shelf. No more than 70 meters deep, it surrounds Sri Lanka completely, extending no more than 19 kilometers from the coast. Like an extension of the island of Mannar, it continues towards India as a series of coral islands known as Adam's Bridge, which form a barrier to larger seagoing vessels. Other coral reefs, small islands, and sunken ships are strewn over the shelf area around Sri Lanka, all of them popular destinations for divers.

The best times for diving are the periods between the two monsoons, when there is relatively little wind. Hikkaduwa and Weligama are good diving bases, and both have acclaimed diving schools. The calm seas in April attract insiders to the two rock islands off the southeast coast. Called Little and Great Basses, they're best reached by boat from one of the bays close to Yala National Park, or from Arugam Bay. Both the coral reefs in front of the spit of land at Kalpitiya and the pearl banks in the Bay of Mannar – which have been exploited for centuries – are ideal destinations for independently-minded travelers; neither has much tourist development.

Wind conditions permitting, fishermen work along the entire coast, staying close to the shore as most of their boats are dug-out outrigger canoes or *kattamarans*, narrow rafts. Only a small number of the boats are modern and suitable for deep-

sea fishing. The richest fishing grounds are in the shelf area between Sri Lanka and India. On both the east and west coasts you can observe helpers on the shore, hard at work with the difficult task of hauling in the drag nets (some tourists like to lend a hand). Several places on the south coast are known for their "stilt fishermen" who, perched on poles, cast their lines into the surf (most tourists prefer to photograph this activity rather than to engage in it). Casting nets are used in shallow coastal areas and in lagoons.

Large areas of the hinterland adjacent to the coast consist of lagoons surrounded by mangroves. These are at their most impressive where thousands of migratory birds stop off to look for food during their wintering. The best-known bird preserves are Chundikkulam and Kokkilai on the northeast coast, and Kumana, Bundala and Wiraketiya on the southeast and south coasts respectively. In dry coastal strips the sea water in shallow bays tends to evaporate, so that setting up natural salt ponds proves a lucrative occupation.

Above: Dry zone in the north (near Mihintale). Right: The Randenigala Dam carries on the time-honored tradition of tanks.

The term "dry zone" is applied to the three-quarters of Sri Lanka in the north, east and southeast, adjacent to the hill country and wet zone. However, this designation is somewhat misleading: this is by no means a desert area. The term simply indicates that rainfall in the area is not constant and that there are fairly long rain-free periods. This in turn influences the vegetation which ranges from dense, extremely varied forest areas (jungle, monsoon forest), in which some trees lose their leaves during dry periods, to areas with sparse, low thorn scrub in the especially dry regions (savanna scrub).

Sri Lanka's driest regions are on the southeast and northwest coasts (Yala and Wilpattu National Parks), the island of Mannar, and the Jaffna Peninsula.

In the dry zone, there are a vast number of lakes of varying shapes and sizes. The

terrain appears flat, although gently undulating in places, and often does not exceed a height of 100 meters. At some spots, however, rocky promontories as much as 700 meters in height jut abruptly up from the plain. These are the resistant remains of a very old mainland area – most of which has eroded away over the years – which is also in evidence in India. This area of plains, crisscrossed by rivers, was probably largely forested when the Sinhalese began cultivating it two and a half millennia ago. They dammed up rivers, converted depressions into so-called *tanks* or reservoirs, and created an extensive irrigation system by building canals and making clever use of the rivers.

This system provided water during dry periods and ensured that the paddies could yield two rice harvests every year. But wars and the accompanying destruction of the irrigation system forced people to withdraw to the southwest part of the island after the 12th century, which was then relatively impenetrable. The jungle advanced and occupied the once-flourishing rice paddies; the tanks were left unattended so that some dried up, whereas the larger and deeper ones soon came to resemble natural lakes. This sparsely-populated jungle idyll became a playground for a rich variety of wildlife.

Not until the 19th century did people begin to realize the achievements of this early culture and make the first hesitant attempts to utilize the land in accordance with these early models. As Sri Lanka's population ballooned during the 20th century, the young country's government deemed it imperative to provide its people with farmland. In the thinly-populated dry zone, modern means were used to revitalize an irrigation system over a thousand years old. In the east, the Senanayake Samudra Reservoir was created; in the south, the Uda Walawe Reservoir; while a new, complex strategy was worked out for the northern half of the island where the heart of the old Sinhalese civilization once lay, involving not only the country's longest river – the Ma-

haweli Ganga, but also tanks, both old and recently built, as well as canals and other rivers. Known as the Mahaweli Program, the project is expected to reach completion in the 21st century.

Thanks to the Sri Lankans' remarkable nature conservation efforts, the dry zone is home to the island's two largest national parks, as well as many other nature reserves. And in some areas, behind dams and reservoirs, you'll see rice paddies and villages with lush gardens – just as there were during the region's century-long flourishing which ended in abrupt aggression over 700 years ago. In belts of land without irrigation, small farmers still cultivate land cleared by the slash-and-burn method, known as *chena*. Sometimes there are unexpected encounters with the animal kingdom, who cannot know where man has drawn the borders of the nature reserves. It isn't unusual to see elephants and other wildlife outside the reserves. And birds of all varieties are everywhere. Indeed, the dry zone is a veritable El Dorado for nature lovers.

Above: Terraced rice paddies in the hill country around Kandy. Right: Red rhododendron and remains of primeval forest on Horton Plains.

And there's more: this area is home to the ancient cities, monasteries, hermitages and irrigation systems of the ancient Sinhalese civilization, some of them excavated and visible once again, some of them swallowed up by the jungle. There are plenty of hotels within easy distance of these cultural sites, often surrounded by green forests, flowering landscaped areas and generally close to a tank.

The mountain country is an entirely different world. Located at the center of the island, it falls away sharply in the south, like a green carpeted wall, from a height of 2,000 meters. To the north it extends far into the forest and rice country characteristic of the dry zone. Southwest of the highest mountains lies the lower mountain area – Sabaragamuwa, boasting elevations of more than 1,300 meters. These cloud-enshrouded mountains are the island's rain-catchers. Yet it is the monsoons which determine when and where it rains: the stronger southwest monsoon brings rain to Sabaragamuwa, the south and west slopes of the hill country, from April through September; while the northeast monsoon is responsible for rain on the east side of the hill country from November onwards. The side not affected by the monsoon is generally blessed with clear, sunny weather. A famous demonstration of the reliability of this rule is the period designated for the pilgrimage to Adam's Peak, the holy mountain in the southwest of the hill country. The pilgrimage period begins with the full moon in December/January and ends in April.

All the island's large rivers have their sources in the mountains, from where they flow directly into the sea, so that they are all very short. The exception is the Mahaweli Ganga, which snakes its

way through the hill country: it begins in the southwest, close to Adam's Peak, and flows into the sea in the northeast of the island at the Bay of Bengal. Extending some 335 kilometers, Sri Lanka's longest river is an important lifeline for irrigation and the generation of energy.

After they had left the plains of the dry zone in the 12th century, the Sinhalese laid out their often tiny terraced rice fields in the steep, hidden valleys of the northern and eastern hill country. They did not, however, cultivate the impenetrable and densely-forested highlands themselves; these were cold (at higher elevations frost is not uncommon), very damp, and inhabited by wild animals, including elephants. However, the area was radically transformed within a few decades in the 19th century, when the English introduced plantations; initially coffee and later tea. Tea plantations are still a typical feature of the hill country today. The wild tropical mountain rain forest has been transformed into an intensively-cultivated man-made landscape, its breathtakingly steep slopes graced by orderly rows of pruned tea bushes. The area is so beautiful today that one almost forgets that it involved thoughtlessly ravaging the original countryside. This landscape can best be appreciated during a highland drive, from the window of a train, whilst on a canoeing or mountain biking trip, or on foot – though this is hardly the easiest option.

Meagre remains of the primeval forest land do exist, however, either as national parks (Horton Plains), or as nature reserves (Hakgala, Peak Wilderness, Sinharaja Forest). But to protect the flora and fauna, the parks here are only partly accessible to the very sparse numbers of tourists wishing to see them.

Anyone who has suffered for some time in the humid heat of the low country will breathe more easily in the pleasant, comparatively cool highlands. Some hill country resorts, such as Nuwara Eliya, Bandarawela and Ella, see themselves as places for relaxation and provide a wide variety of accommodation.

HISTORY

The in-flight attendants on SriLankan Airlines, the country's national airline, have to make all their announcements in triplicate: in Sinhala, Tamil and English. These are the three *linguae francae*, and a first-time visitor to Sri Lanka will realize on filling out his entry papers – at the very latest – that each language has a different written form. In the course of his journey he will be relieved to discover that he can generally get by with English, though only a fraction of the population speak it as their first language. Despite the fact that the majority of tourists won't need to become acquainted with Sinhala or Tamil, a brief look at the languages' histories and peculiarities reveals some interesting facts about the culture of Sri Lanka.

Mother of Indian Writing

Although the Sinhalese and Tamil languages have very different-looking letters, Sinhala being curved and rounded and Tamil tending to be upright and straight despite numerous rounded forms – they do have a common origin, namely the *Brahmi* alphabet. It is assumed that the latter originated in Mesopotamia and has been in use in India since the fifth century B.C., and from it the oldest verifiable examples of the script originated, which are preserved on the famous pillar edicts of the Indian Emperor Ashoka (ca. 273-227 B.C.). When the emperor decreed that Buddhism be spread throughout Sri Lanka, the *Brahmi* alphabet came with it. In numerous caves prepared for hermit monks, the name of the donor can clearly be seen scratched onto the walls of the cave.

Left: Who knows what the future will hold – young Sinhalese girl from Colombo.

It was from the angular, rune-like signs of the Brahmi alphabet that the complex, round letters characteristic of Sinhala developed. Specially-prepared strips of leaves from the talipot palm (*corypha umbraculifera*) were used as writing paper, and it was easier to score rounded letters than angular ones with the customary metal writing instruments.

The Brahmi alphabet was also the basis for the Tamil language used more than 2,000 years ago in southern India, and it influenced many other languages on the Indian subcontinent.

Two Languages, Two Literatures

Although the alphabets of Tamil and Sinhala have Brahmi as the same root, the two languages themselves do not share the same origin. Tamil, along with several other southern Indian languages, belongs to the Dravidian language family, which is said to be related to the Turkic languages. Sinhala, on the other hand, is an Indo-European language. The words for one, two, three – *eka, deka, tuna* – indicate a distant cousinship with European languages.

Tamil is considered to be the oldest literary language in the South Asian cultural sphere after the old Indian academic language, Sanskrit. Although there is no documentation of it, scholars believe that high-quality Tamil poetry was being written before the birth of Christ. Since the third century, at the very latest, there have been remarkable literary creations in the Tamil language, which since the seventh century, in keeping with religious developments, are largely devoted to Hindu subjects.

Both in India and Sri Lanka, written records were originally used for practical purposes only: business people noted down details of their transactions, while religious people recorded the good deeds they had performed in the course of their lives. This record of good deeds was duly

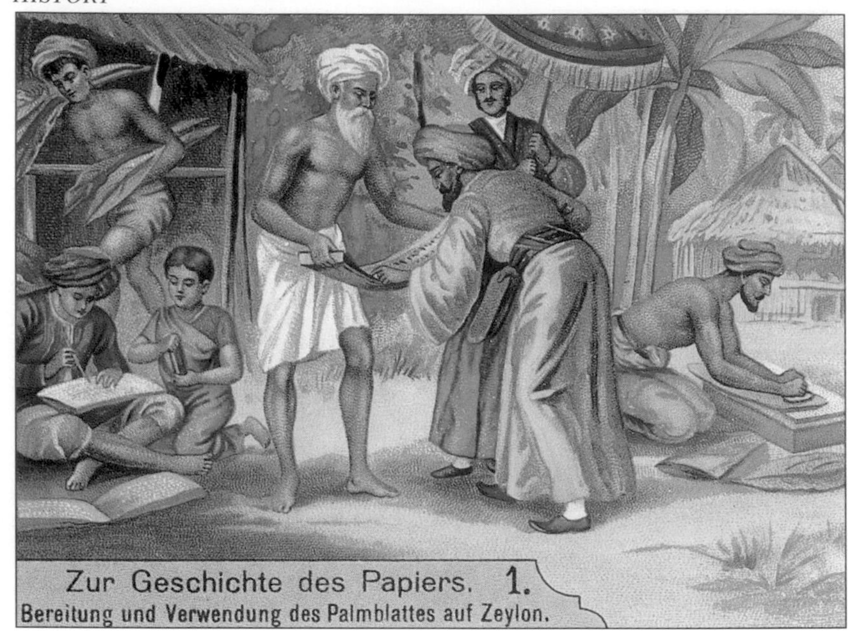

read out to those who were dying, so that they would be able to remember them clearly and recount them to Yama, the god of death, when they encountered him; this was supposed to help people secure a better reincarnation. However, important writings such as the old Indian epics or the teachings of Buddha were not initially written down but passed on by word of mouth.

Zur Geschichte des Papiers. 1.
Bereitung und Verwendung des Palmblattes auf Zeylon.

From the fourth century on, historical chronicles in Sri Lanka were recorded in Sinhala. Later, monks recorded them in the academic language of the day, Pali. The Buddhist academics in Sri Lanka thereby distanced themselves from the Hindu Brahmans in India, who continued to use Sanskrit.

Sri Lanka's chronicles may occasionally contradict each other, but they provide unique historical information about the island. The *Mahavamsa* ("Great Chronicle") and the *Culavamsa* ("Small Chronicle") recount the history of the Sinhalese people, especially the kings, starting with legends from before the birth of Christ and continuing up until 1815, when the last king of Kandy abdicated, thus covering a period of almost two and a half millennia. Other chronicles are devoted to specific themes, for example the story of the sacred bo tree, or that of Buddha's Sacred Tooth.

Above: Palm leaves are processed into writing paper (1905). Right: The three prevalent alphabets – Sinhala, Tamil and Roman.

A large proportion of Sinhalese literature is based on Buddhist writings. A famous example is the first written version of *Tripitaka* ("Three Baskets"), the central work of Buddhism written in 88 B.C. in the Aluvihara Monastery near Matale. A series of 550 legends known as the *jataka* tell of the exemplary behavior of the future Buddha.

An unusual example of early literature (dating from between the seventh and 12th centuries) are the graffiti visitors left etched on the walls of the rock fortress at Sigiriya, which was abandoned in the fifth century.

සමාධි බුදු පිළිමය
SAMADHI BUDDHA STATUE
(3-4 CENTURY AD) THIS IN MEDITATION POSE IS THE
BEST EXAMPLE OF I'TS KIND

Two Levels of Language

Even though Tamil and Sinhala developed differently, what they do share is the fact that in both languages there is a distinct difference between the colloquial language and the written or formal language. Mastery of both levels is necessary. The formal language is used for radio news, speeches, official letters, newspapers and most literature. For conversations, most of the country's movies, and similar instances, the colloquial is employed. However, while literature used to be written only in the languages' formal, written form, people today are making a conscious effort to use the colloquial language for literature as well, in both Tamil and Sinhala.

Who Speaks What in Sri Lanka?

Sri Lanka has a population of almost 19 million people. Some 74 percent speak Sinhala as their native tongue, 25 percent Tamil, and less than one percent English. While the *Sinhalese* are a fairly homogeneous group, the following distinctions are made with regard to the speakers of Tamil: about half of them belong to the group which has lived on the island for hundreds of years, if not more than a thousand years. These Sri Lanka Tamils are concentrated in the north and along the east coast of the island, but are also found in Colombo and other, generally larger, towns. The Indian Tamils, numbering fewer than a million, are based in the mountains. They were brought to Sri Lanka by the British in the second half of the 19th century to work on their plantations, and originally come from the South Indian state of Tamil Nadu. Following Sri Lanka's independence in 1948, they were not immediately recognized as Ceylonese citizens.

Tamil is also spoken by the Moors, of whom there are more than one million. These descendants of Arab traders first came to the island in the eighth century and have since intermarried with the local population.

Less than one percent of the population refer to themselves as *Burghers*; these are descendants of European immigrants, mostly of Portuguese or Dutch origin. They speak English.

The Early Inhabitants

The mosaic of cultures in Sri Lanka began with influences from the Indian subcontinent. Early, legendary accounts about the island of *Lanka* (land) all concur on the point that the island was already inhabited when visitors or settlers arrived from the Indian mainland. In the Indian epic *Ramayana*, the wild demon folk, led by their prince Ravana, carried off the noble Sita, wife of the Vishnu incarnation Rama. According to legend, Buddha, during his three visits, is said to have encountered the wild, warring *yakshas* and *nagas*, whom he was able to convert to his teachings. The northern Indian Vijaya, son of a prince and grandson of a *sinha,* or lion, conquered the hostile *yakshas* when he landed on the island with 700 men after his father banished him from northern India. Especially in the story of Vijaya, who united with a *yakkhini* (local woman) and had two children with her, it is clear that, although the inhabitants of the island are acknowledged to have some good qualities, the new arrivals from the mainland consider themselves superior. Vijaya abandoned his *yakkhini* in order to have a shipload of virgins brought in from southern India, with whom he and selected of his followers proceeded to sire the foundations of subsequent Sinhalese settlement.

It is still uncertain whether the *Veddahs,* who today live scattered in the eastern section of Sri Lanka, are descended from these legendary island inhabitants, or are even related to the Stone Age settlers who have been scientifically demonstrated to have lived on the island.

Above: Portrait of a Veddah – descendant of the island's Stone Age population? Right: The monk Mahinda is supposed to have landed in Sri Lanka on the Sila cliffs.

The Kingdom

There are no truly reliable historical sources which explain the details of how the northern Indian Sinhalese settled on the island. However, they are assumed to have arrived starting in around the fifth century B.C. in several waves, landing at various anchorage places (Mahatittha-Mantai near Mannar, Gokanna-Trincomalee), and proceeding to settle small areas of the dry zone in groups. They were accustomed to living with monsoon rains and lengthy dry periods; had experience cultivating rice in river valleys and were, furthermore, already experienced in building *tanks*, or reservoirs. Over the centuries, therefore, these settlers developed an admirable irrigation system; its enormous reservoirs and network of canals were able to provide water for extensive areas of rice paddies between the Mahaweli Ganga River in the east and the Dedura Oya in the west.

Anuradhapura was the location of the administrative hub for the whole complex network. This city was to serve as residence of the Sinhalese kings for more than a thousand years. Its territory, known as *Rajarata*, the "Royal Country," was destined to gain supremacy over the other sections of the country: *Malayarata*, the area south of the Dedura Oya, and *Ruhuna*, the remaining area in the east and south.

Buddhism

In the third century B.C., a decision was made which continues to shape Sri Lanka today. King Devanampiya Tissa (250-210 B.C.) made Buddhism the official religion in his state and its capital, Anuradhapura. In India during this period, the emperor Ashoka had created a large empire, from which he sent Buddhist missionaries to every known corner of the world. To Sri Lanka he sent his son, the monk Mahinda, who considered

the Lankan king worthy to follow the new doctrine. Not only was this an honor for Devanampiya Tissa, it also assured him of a new and powerful ally. Furthermore, he could, by making generous donations to the holy orders, ensure that his reincarnation would be a favorable one. He therefore founded the *Mahavihara*, or "Great Monastery," in Anuradhapura, the first such Buddhist monastic community in the country, which was to have a repeated decisive influence on the land's political fate, and also oversaw the chronicling of the country's history.

A United Country

The first person who managed to reign alone over the entire island was Duttha-gamani (161-137 B.C.), the son of King Kavantissa of Ruhuna. As prince, he experienced a situation which was a common occurrence in the island's history: the ruler in Anuradhapura was not Sinhalese, but rather the southern Indian Elara, who had seized the throne. While

Elara did conduct the affairs of Rajarata wisely, even in an exemplary manner, for several decades, the fact remained that he was a usurper and not a Buddhist. Dutthagamani reproached his father for tolerating this shameful situation and making no attempt to alter it. However, Kavantissa had no desire to expand his kingdom beyond the boundaries of Ruhuna; instead, he exiled his son and heir, who had already sent his father women's clothing as an expression of his contempt. After his father's death, Dutthagamani not only wrested his inheritance in Ruhuna from his brother Sadhatissa in battle, but he also went to Anuradhapura, where he fought and defeated Elara. He subsequently resided in the capital of Rajarata as king and ruler over the whole country. In order to increase his sum of good deeds, he donated several large buildings to the Mahavihara.

Above: The perahera (procession) in Kandy commemorates the legend of the victorious King Gajabahu in the second century A.D.

Wealth and Power for the Monasteries

According to orthodox Buddhist belief, only members of the *Sangha* (the order of the Buddhist monks) can attain nirvana – the ultimate aim of Buddhist existence – and thus avoid reincarnation immediately after their death. A king, on the other hand, is subject to the eternal cycle of death and rebirth. However, by giving generously and performing other good deeds during his lifetime, anyone can secure a favorable reincarnation. The Sinhalese kings, and others who could afford it, thus generally gave donations to the holy men of the *Sangha*. However, since individual monks were not allowed to have personal possessions, the monasteries amassed both land and goods, and gradually became wealthy and powerful.

The Classical Period

The following centuries, especially the first half of the first millennium A.D., are considered the classical epoch of Sinhalese civilization. Not that this was a peaceful period. It wasn't easy to impose central rule on this country: individual provinces often broke away, or disputes erupted over succession to the throne. Apart from internal conflicts, there was a constant threat from southern India, where the Pandyas, Pallavas and Cholas were always struggling for power. The group that happened to gain supremacy at any given time would then try to exert influence on Sri Lanka. In the fourth century, Hinduism gained in strength and largely drove Buddhism out of India. As a result, Sri Lanka saw itself as the keeper of true Buddhism, even though there had been no consensus among the *Sangha* since the first century A.D.

The following Sinhalese rulers played notable roles in the country's history: Vattagamani Abhaya (or Valagambahu) lost his land to the Panca Dravidians from southern India in 103 B.C. and had to go into hiding for 14 years. He spent part of this time in caves with the Dambulla monks. He owed his reinstatement in 89 B.C. to Mahatissa, a monk who had been excluded from the *Mahavihara*. In thanks, the king granted him a special place outside the old monastery. This led to a quarrel within the *Mahavihara*, which ended with 500 monks joining Mahatissa and moving to the new monastery, which was named *Abhayagiri Vihara*, after the king, its patron. This split effectively reflects the two branches of Buddhism current at that time: the *Mahavihara* remained faithful to the orthodox Theravada Buddhism, while the *Abhayagiri* monastery supported the modern Mahayana Buddhism.

The figure of King Gajabahu from the second century A.D. is shrouded in legend. He is said to have liberated 12,000 Sinhalese prisoners from India, as well as securing the relic of the gold ankle chain of the goddess Pattini, which had also been held in that country. The annual *perahera* (procession) in Kandy commemorates this event, as well as others.

Mahasena (274-301) is considered to be one of the great builders of tanks and irrigation systems. The Minneriya Tank, which dates from this time, is once again being used to irrigate rice paddies.

During the reign of his successor, Sirimeghavanna (301-328), the holy relic of Buddha's tooth was smuggled to Sri Lanka from India; it was considered to be in danger there due to the spread of Hinduism. Rather than being given to the brotherhood, the tooth was handed over to the king, who demonstratively entrusted the valuable relic to the care of the *Abhayagiri Vihara*. Historical records state that annual *peraheras* were held in Anuradhapura in honor of the relic.

The first task of Dhatusena (455-473) was to liberate his land from the Tamils, who had ruled it for almost 30 years. Like many leaders both before and after him, he had remained in the southeastern region of Ruhuna while mustering support against the occupiers. He, too, is remembered as one of the great champions of the irrigation system. The large Kala Wewa Reservoir, built during his reign, is still in use today. Dhatusena died under tragic circumstances: his son Kassapa (473-491), who had not been made heir to the throne, murdered his father and established his capital in the famous rock fortress at Sigiriya. His half-brother Moggallana (491-508), the rightful heir to the throne, succeeded in regaining the throne in Anuradhapura with the help of Tamil mercenaries.

On the one hand, then, the Tamils sometimes helped the Sinhalese, and many Sinhalese kings married Tamil women; but on the other hand, the number of attacks from southern India continued to increase. In 883, the Pandyas destroyed Anuradhapura. Although the Sinhalese were able to destroy the Indian city of Madurai as part of a successful retaliatory campaign, the Cholas had, in the

meantime, gained strength in southern India. In 1017, they took Sri Lanka and carried King Mahinda V off to India, where he died in exile in 1029. They also abandoned Anuradhapura as their capital. Polonnaruwa, close to the Ruhuna border, which had thereto served mainly as a hideout for rebels, was seen as a more strategically favorable location for government headquarters.

The Second Royal City

During its short period as capital, Polonnaruwa boasted three excellent Sinhalese rulers. Vijayabahu (1055-1110) succeeded in reconquering the country back from the Cholas. Parakramabahu I (1153-1186) repaired the irrigation facilities which had been destroyed and built new ones; he also, during a council, united the dissident chapters of the Buddhist brotherhood; furthermore, he attracted foreign ambassadors to the country, and is therefore justifiably referred to as "The Great." Nissanka Malla (1187-1196) was another outstanding figure; his legacy includes numerous buildings in Polonnaruwa and stone inscription tablets throughout the country.

Above: Statue of King Parakramabahu in Polonnaruwa. Right: Worshiping the relic of the Sacred Tooth (1890).

Towards the end of the Anuradhapura period, it had already become clear how important the relic of the Sacred Tooth was to the king: whoever possessed it was considered the rightful ruler of the country. In Polonnaruwa, the imposing Temples of the Tooth built by the three kings are evidence of its significance.

The monks responsible for guarding the relic saved the Sacred Tooth from Magha (1215-1236), the much-feared king of Kalinga in eastern India. His destructive actions, combined with the continuing quarrels among the Sinhalese over succession to the throne, so weakened the kingdom in the dry zone that large numbers of people left the area and made for the less accessible hill country

and the humid southwestern region of the island. Wars had badly damaged the irrigation system, thereby robbing the locals of their basic means of subsistence; the population was further diminished by the spread of malaria. In time, the once-majestic royal cities and temple complexes were reclaimed by the jungle.

Lack of Orientation

Almost four centuries passed before Sri Lanka's third and last royal city, Kandy, was established. In the meantime, the capital moved between various lowland cities: Dambadeniya, Yapahuwa, Kurunegala, Kotte and Sitawaka, finally ending up in Gampola in the hill country. These frequent changes of location between the 13th and 15th centuries can be seen as evidence of the Sinhalese kings' weakness in the face of the Tamils in the north. Since the island had been ununited save one occasion, it was not unusual for there to be several capitals at the same time. Possession of the Sacred Tooth relic remained vital for a ruler's acceptance by his people. Outsiders also wanted possession of the relic: Indian Pandyas and even, once, the Chinese, demanded its surrender.

Jaffnapatam

A Tamila kingdom was able to establish itself in the north of the island, on the Jaffna Peninsula. In the 13th century, the Pandyas handed the throne over to one of their generals, Aryacakravarti. When the Pandya empire on the Indian mainland was conquered by invading Muslims, he remained in Jaffna as an independent king. He and his followers subsequently made a concerted effort to bring the whole island under their control. The chiefs in the sparsely-populated areas south of Jaffna, known as the *Vanni*, had to pay him tribute. In the north the chiefs were Tamils, in the south they tended to be Sinhalese – generally former army commanders – who had established small autonomous areas of their own.

The only Sinhalese king who succeeded in conquering the Jaffna empire, Jaffnapatam, was Parakramabahu VI (1411-1466). He then put his adopted son Sapumal Kumaraya on the throne in Jaffna.

However, on his father's death Sapumal, not content with his small empire, fought for and won the Sinhalese throne in Kotte, which he ascended as Bhuvanekabahu VI. In doing so he lost control over his empire in the north, which became independent again under the Tamil king Pararajasekaram (1497-1519).

With the help of the *Vanniyars*, the local chiefs, the Tamil empire now had allies from Jaffna and Mannar in the west, and along the east coast as far as Yala. Even today, a disproportionate part of the population in these areas speaks Tamil.

Above: Galle – once an important fortified harbor for the Portuguese, Dutch and English.

Europeans on the Coasts

The chance landing of a Portuguese ship on the coast of Sri Lanka in 1505, just eight years after Vasco da Gama had dared to navigate a passage around the southern tip of Africa, was sufficient to awaken the greed of the Europeans for the island's valuable products, especially cinnamon. Sri Lanka's kings, for their part, were not disinclined to acquire foreign goods, and exporting cinnamon seemed a good way to get them.

However, the Portuguese saw their task not only as signing business contracts, but also as crusading against heathenism. Accordingly, they ruthlessly destroyed countless Buddhist and Hindu holy shrines, and scored particular success in converting the lower-caste fishermen living in the west and north of the country. Another notable missionary success was the baptism of the king of Kotte, Dharmapala, in the 16th century. The latter was so much under their influence that he turned the lands of

Buddhist monasteries over to the Franciscan order and appointed the Portuguese king as his own heir. Even before Dharmapala's death in 1597, the first Portuguese commander general took charge of the new colony. Because Sri Lanka was divided into several kingdoms, it was easy for the Portuguese to take the western and southern coastal regions so vital for their trade. In 1626, they also gained Jaffna. However, several attempts to take the kingdom of Kandy at the center of the island, founded at the end of the 16th century, ended in failure.

With the emergence of the United East India Company (VOC), which the Dutch founded in 1602, Portuguese fortunes began to wane. After negotiations with King Rajasinha II (1635-1687), this trading company had taken control of the Portuguese ports by 1658; a hundred years later, it had extended its influence throughout the island. The East India Company had to be more circumspect than the Portuguese in its dealings with the Sinhalese king, since they, unlike the Portuguese, had no claim to the throne, and the Kandy kingdom had attained a certain confidence over the years.

Meanwhile, Great Britain, Holland's rival, gained a strong foothold in India; thanks to political infighting in Holland, it was able to acquire Trincomalee, Batticaloa, Jaffna, Negombo and Colombo by 1796. Nineteen years later, the English captured Sri Vikrama Rajasinha, the last Kandy king, effectively securing control of the whole island.

The Mountain Kingdom

Of the eight kings who sat on the throne in Kandy between 1592 and 1815, Rajasinha II was the most determined to put up resistance to the Europeans. At the same time, it was during his reign that the coastal areas under the control of the Dutch East India Company encircled his highland kingdom in a ring that grew ever tighter. In accordance with tradition, Rajasinha's kingdom was divided into different districts, which were then split into sub-districts; and a horde of officials were responsible for administering them. The customs of the feudal agricultural society, thousands of years old, had continued to survive. Almost every family owned rice land, which they were obliged to work according to the rules governing the common irrigation scheme. Owning a piece of land brought with it specific duties, such as paying certain annual taxes, or providing the nobility with *rajakariya*, certain fixed services. A caste system regulated who could perform which task, and a *badda,* or overseer for the caste system, took great care not only that people married within their castes, but also that a family only carried out the services permitted to their caste. *Salagamas*, for example, could only peel cinnamon, while *dhobis* were only allowed to wash clothes. The most respected caste was that of the *goyigama* or *govikula*, the landowners, who made up about half of the population. Within this caste there were also strict subdivisions, ranging from big landowners, who had tenants do their work for them, to simple rice farmers.

The administration and maintenance of the royal court necessitated the creation of many honorable posts, whose holders presented themselves in society with great pride and appropriate pomp and splendor. Today, the famous *Kandy Perahera* procession gives some impression of this former grandeur.

Castes developed out of age-old traditions, rather than religion. The Buddhist orders were in a sorry state in the mid-18th century: while there were still monasteries, they were sometimes inhabited exclusively by secular residents, and celibacy was a thing of the past. There were no more monks capable of carrying out *upasampada*, or higher ordinations. This trend was reversed when the last king of

Sinhalese descent, Narendra Sinha, died in 1739 and the southern Indian Nayakkars ascended the throne in Kandy as his rightful successor. Under Kirti Sri Rajasinha (1747-1782), Buddhism enjoyed a renaissance in Sri Lanka.

British Rule

Though the inhabitants of the coastal region had been in contact with Europeans since the 16th century, the isolated kingdom of Kandy remained a traditional, feudal state until the 19th century. This contrast meant that there continued to be a distinction between lowland and Kandy Sinhalese into the 20th century (in censuses, for example).

Under British rule, agriculture, infrastructure and administration changed at breakneck speed, and by no means in keeping with the wishes of the Sinhalese. While the so-called Uva (province around Badulla) Rebellion was an organized uprising of the nobility against the new rulers, another revolt manifested itself in the unwillingness of the Sinhalese people to perform paid labor for their new bosses. Consequently, the British brought in Tamils from southern India as laborers, in particular for their tea and rubber plantations; by the time of the country's independence in 1948, their numbers had grown to about one million. In administrative positions, as well, the British tended to prefer the more pliant Tamils to the native Sinhalese.

Above: English colonial official with Sinhalese nobles, around 1875.

At the same time, Ceylon, as the island had been called since the advent of the Portuguese, developed into a model state for the Asian world – at least by European standards. The expansion of the plantations and the country's military defense necessitated the construction of railway lines and the extension of the road network. Ordinance surveys provided, among other benefits, knowledge on how to reclaim the dry zone for use as arable land for the growing population.

Thanks to its school system, Ceylon became a country with an above-average literacy rate, compared to other colonial countries. Steps towards political independence were evident in the formation of the National Congress in 1919, the introduction of the vote for women as early as 1931, and in the draft for a new constitution in 1944. Sri Lanka became independent on February 4, 1948.

The First Years of Independence

D.S. Senanayake had formed the United National Party (UNP) under British rule, and had served as Minister of Agriculture. He won the first elections and was Prime Minister up until his death in 1952. Senanayake did not implement any radical changes. Given the problems posed by rapid population growth, he concentrated his efforts on the agricultural sector. His tenure saw the start of the Gal Oya Project, which, through the construction of the large Senanayake Samudra Reservoir, helped to create new rice land in the eastern part of the country. He was succeeded by his son, Dudley Senanayake, but the island's economic problems forced him to implement unpopular measures, such as raising the price of rice, Sri Lanka's staple food, and reducing subventions to farmers.

Meanwhile, the Sinhalese had begun to realize that a disproportionate number of Tamils had been given administrative jobs during the colonial period (which they retained after independence), were generally better educated, and made up the larger portion of university students. And Buddhists criticized the government for failing to make the country the keeper of Buddha's true doctrine as the Enlightened One had commanded, according to the *Mahavamsa*.

In 1956, Buddhists around the world celebrated the 2,500th anniversary of their master's death. This *Buddha Jayanthi* was an occasion for widespread celebrations, in Sri Lanka as in other parts of the world, and it was also the year in which S.W.R.D. Bandaranaike and his Sri Lanka Freedom Party (SLFP) gained an overwhelming election victory. Bandaranaike had formed the party in 1951 after resigning from the UNP. The son of a well-to-do Sinhalese plantation owner, he had been discriminated against during his studies at Oxford; wounded in his pride, he left the Anglican Church and embraced Buddhism, and went on to take pains to erase all traces of colonialism. One of his demands was that people speak their native tongue, rather than English; soon, the slogan of this movement had become "Sinhala only," which excluded, of course, anyone whose native language was Tamil – Moors as well as Tamils. This nationalist-cum-religious battle over language led to an open conflict between Tamils and Sinhalese; the Moors cautiously abstained. But there were also enemies lurking in the ranks of those who had helped Bandaranaike to political victory: in 1959, the Prime Minister was shot by a Buddhist monk as he was bowing to him in reverence.

Asia's First Woman Prime Minister

After a brief period of interim government by the UNP, Sirimavo Bandaranaike (1916-2000), his widow, won the 1960 election to become Asia's first woman Prime Minister. Under her, the party swung clearly to the left.

There followed a wave of socialist-style nationalization. Government takeover of private schools especially affected Sri Lanka's many Catholics. The language conflict continued, and remained unresolved under the ensuing conservative UNP government, headed again by Dudley Senanayake (1965-1970). Senanayake also failed to solve the country's other pressing problems, such as unemployment, inflation and rising costs of food imports, which out-

paced revenues from agricultural exports, such as tea and rubber, whose prices were determined by the world market. In 1970, therefore, Sirimavo Bandaranaike was able to regain her post as Prime Minister thanks to the coalition support of a number of left-wing parties. The most important areas of the economy were nationalized: plantations, oil firms and other industries. Individuals were only allowed to own a few acres of land. In 1972, a new constitution established Sinhala as the national language, and the island was rechristened *Sri Lanka,* meaning "shining country." Increasing evidence of discrimination against Tamils gave rise to ideas about splintering off to form an independent, separate state. In 1974, some of the thereto stateless Indian Tamils were granted Sri Lankan citizenship; the remaining 350,000 or so were sent back to Tamil Nadu in southern India.

Above: S. Bandaranaike brings a Buddhist relic to Chiswick, England (1964). Right: The new Parliament Building in Kotte.

Seventeen Years of Conservative Rule

Sri Lanka was rocked by widespread strikes when, in 1977, the *UNP* led by J.R. Jayewardene won a convincing victory in the National Assembly, gaining 140 out of 168 seats. The constitution was amended, establishing a presidial government under Jayewardene.

The language conflict was defused by the recognition of Tamil as a national language, while Sinhala was retained as Sri Lanka's official language. The discriminatory distinction between Indian and Ceylon Tamils was abolished. In addition, 24 district councils were created in order to decentralize the administration and reduce ethnic discrimination. The abandonment of nationalization resulted in significant economic gains for the country, and in 1982 the President was reelected, an effective popular confirmation of the new political direction.

In the meantime, however, Tamil separatist groups had formed, and these were assured of support from southern India.

In 1983, popular fear of this threat exploded in the form of Sinhalese attacks on the Tamil civilian population.

Neither Jayewardene nor his successor R. Premadasa (1988) was able to bring about any form of reconciliation, and their efforts met with fierce opposition. The Liberation Tigers of Tamil Eelam (LTTE) demand the creation of an independent Tamil state in the north and east of the country, and use mainly guerilla tactics in the pursuit of their goal. A sigh of relief went up when the Indian peace troops, which had been stationed in Sri Lanka since 1987 by agreement between Jayawardene and Rajiv Gandhi, were withdrawn in 1990, but the UNP was unable to provide a lasting solution to the problem. Instead, it concentrated on improving the economy – with evident success. The privatization of companies that had long been under national control, and new income from foreign investors, more and more from East Asia, were clear factors in the country's economic improvement.

Bandaranaike's Daughter as President

However, the UNP remained powerless in the face of the Tigers, and towards the end of their 17 years in office their members had been charged with so many corruption and murder scandals that a political change was inevitable. In 1994, Chandrika Bandaranaike Kumaratunga, daughter of S.W.R.D and Sirimavo Bandaranaike, won a resounding victory in the parliamentary elections with her alliance of SLFP, Tamil and Muslim parties, and in the ensuing direct elections was voted President. Her scarce victory in 2000 mirrors her political and military failures. A potential guerilla war simmers in the background, regardless of Norwegian efforts to establish an agreement between the government and LTTE.

In the meantime, although the Sri Lankan military has established a foothold in Jaffna, the LTTE continue to hold up the country routes. Main tourist resorts remain unaffected by the civil unrest.

ONE COUNTRY – FOUR WORLD RELIGIONS

Sri Lanka's calendars sport more days marked in red than those of any other country. Apart from Sundays, there are 15 to 20 official public holidays, some of which, unfortunately for the working population, may fall on a Sunday. Every *poya*, or full moon day, is also a public holiday. On Fridays, many Muslim shops remain closed.

The majority of Sri Lankans agree that the most important holidays of the country's four major world religions should be enjoyed by everyone, regardless of their faith. Though there are certain deviations, the mosaic of the country's religious communities generally corresponds to that of ethnic groupings. Most Sinhalese, for example, are Buddhist (69 percent of the population), the Tamils are largely Hindu (15 percent), the Moors and the small Malay minority follow Islam (almost eight percent) and the remaining eight percent are Christians, mainly Catholics, comprised of Burghers, Sinhalese and Tamils.

Buddhism

The *Mahavamsa* ("Great Chronicle") states quite clearly that Buddha chose Sri Lanka as the country in which his doctrine should survive in its original form. The Buddha is said to have visited the island three times, and the 16 places where the Enlighted One stayed number among the country's most important pilgrimage sites.

Though it is fairly certain that Siddhartha Gautama – as the historical Buddha was called – never ventured beyond his main area of activity, which extended

Left: Ganesha, a Hindu god, is also worshiped by Sri Lankan Buddhists.

from southwest Nepal to the central Ganges Valley in India, his followers give greater credence to the legends surrounding his person than to actual historical fact.

Every Buddhist is familiar with the *charitha* – stories from the life of Buddha. Accounts and illustrations of the stories feature prominently in Sri Lankan literature and art, appearing in everything from valuable reliefs and colorful temple paintings to comic strips. The most commonly related events from Buddha's life include the following:

Before the birth of the future Buddha, his mother, Queen Mahamaya, had a strange and wonderful dream about his conception. A white elephant walked around her bed in the home of the gods in the Himalayan Mountains and penetrated her right side. The birth itself took place in a grove of flowering sal trees (*shorea robusta*), as the mother pulled a branch of blossoms towards her.

As the son of a king and member of the *kshattriya* (warrior) caste, the Buddha received a thorough education and led a life of great luxury. In spite of this, he was a thoughtful, meditative man, and the mere sight of a few people suffering made him ponder about the nature of life.

When Gautama was 28, he fathered the successor to the throne. At this point, he abandoned his worldly duties and gave up his home. Taking his horse, Kanthaka, and a servant, he secretly left his palace; once he had crossed the river Anona, he left them both behind, cut his hair, and exchanged his clothes with a beggar. From two holy men – there must have been thousands of these in India at the time – he asked for knowledge about the meaning of life; but their answers disappointed him. He then tried to approach the truth through self-castigation and fasting to the point of starvation. Five disciples so admired his steadfastness that they decided to follow him, but when after seven years Gautama, no nearer the

truth than he was before, gave up fasting, they abandoned him in disgust. Having experienced the extremes of great luxury and great poverty, the Buddha decided, at the age of 35, to pursue the "middle way." By eating normally he regained his physical strength; then, sitting down under a bo tree (*ficus religiosa*, a kind of fig tree), he vowed he would not get up until he had received enlightenment. While he sat meditating, his former life flowed past him and he understood that each new life brings new suffering. In order to avoid this suffering in the future, it is necessary to put an end to the *samsara*, or cycle of rebirths. Since anyone who has desires is plunged into suffering, the absence of desire not only means the end of suffering, but the end of the whole cycle of reincarnation. With this recognition, he became the Buddha, the Enlightened One.

Above: The bo tree, usually at the center of the sacred precinct, is adorned with colorful votive flags. Right: Teacher and pupil.

At this point, the Buddha could have acted selfishly by ending his own life in order to attain *nirvana*. Instead, however, he continued to sit under the bo tree, thinking about ways to spread this doctrine. Then Mara, the Evil One, summoned his army of demons and tried to distract him from his plans – but in vain. What is more, Buddha had helpers at hand. For instance, during a torrential downpour, a cobra reared up and formed a comfortable seat for the Buddha with its body, while its extended hood sheltered him from the rain.

The Buddha then went to Varanasi to convince his five former followers of his new doctrine ("The Setting in Motion of the Dhamma Wheel"), formed the *sangha*, or brotherhood, and took to the road for the next 45 years, wandering around the country in order to help thousands of people to find the right path. He must have hit a nerve in the contemporary psyche: the enlightened society 2,500 years ago was tired of hearing the formulaic utterances of the increasingly power-

ful priests of the Brahman caste. The Buddha brought them a doctrine which managed without gods, did not recognize a caste system, and promised redemption solely through personal engagement, one's own actions.

Buddha convinced his listeners by telling them realistic stories illustrating correct behavior. The 550 *jatakas* describe his own exemplary behavior as *Bodhisattva* (future Buddha); these are often illustrated in a series of images on the walls of Buddhist temples. Containing, as they do, elements of fairy tale, they have an innately memorable, symbolic character, and are ideal for pictorial representation. One famous story is that of the hare which springs into the fire in order to offer itself as food to a hungry begging monk. However, the monk is actually the god Sakra and is able to save the hare, a *Bodhisattva*, by placing him on the full moon. As a result, on every full moon holiday everyone remembers how the exemplary hare was willing to sacrifice its own life.

However, the doctrine of the order is much more abstract, and Buddha rightly selected new monks on the basis of their intellectual abilities. The *sangha* cannot exist without the secular population. A member of the order is supposed to concentrate solely on his own salvation, while the common men earn themselves points toward a better future life by providing him with clothing, food and accommodation. Even early on, monks criticized the fact that not everyone had an equal opportunity to attain *nirvana.* This and other points of contention led to splits in the brotherhood.

As early as 2,000 years ago, the views of *Mahayana* or "great vehicle" Buddhism became dominant and spread through central and east Asia: the Buddha became a god. People worshiped him and the countless saints, or *Bodhisattvas*, figures who have actually reached the stage of enlightenment, but voluntarily refrain from attaining *nirvana* until the rest of mankind has reached it as well.

In southeast Asia, Burma, Thailand, Cambodia and Laos, as well as Sri Lanka, the orthodox version of Buddhism, the *Theravada*, or "Doctrine of the Elders," is espoused. The alternative term *Hinayana,* meaning "small vehicle," is seen as being somewhat derogatory.

But in Sri Lanka, too, the Buddhist doctrine was strongly influenced by the ideas of *Mahayana* until the Council of 1160. This fact is evident from the dome-shaped *dagobas*, or reliquaries containing relics of the Buddha, the ornate pomp of monastery art, and the gigantomania evident in sculptures. The decline of classical Sinhalese civilization was accompanied by growing influence from the Hindu mainland; this left its traces in the art and architecture of Buddhist temples, even to the point of the inclusion of Hindu gods, for whom *devalas* (temples or shrines) were built.

Above: The Ruvanveliseya is one of the country's largest dagobas. Right: "Nataraja" – Shiva dancing (Anuradhapura Museum).

In the 18th century the reorganization of the *sangha* began in the Kandy kingdom with the help of Thai monks, as well as committed Sinhalese members of the brotherhood, such as Velivita Saranankara. At the end of the 19th century, the American Henry S. Olcott, co-founder of the Theosophical Society, gave new impetus to the doctrine by founding Buddhist schools, trying to counterbalance the country's Catholic institutions. His secretary, Anagarika Dharmapala, succeeded in stirring up nationalistic Buddhist sentiments. Throughout the 20th century, Buddhism has exerted a growing influence on politics. Today, the *sangha* has about 50,000 members.

In Sri Lankan Buddhist temples, the *dagoba*, or reliquary, is usually a conspicuous feature, dome or bell-shaped and often snow-white in color. It contains a casket, usually made of stone, called the *garbhagrha*, which is used to hold relics and other valuable sacred objects. The dagoba itself typically consists entirely of bricks which are covered by a layer of plaster. The house of the gods, or *harmika,* rises up above the apex of the dagoba, crowned by a *chattra*, or symbolic roof. The faithful walk around the dagoba in a clockwise direction and place their offerings on the altars located on the porches of the four cardinal directions (*vahalkadas*), on flower tables, or on *pesavas*, the terraces (usually three in number) which form the base of the dagoba.

Another typically Sri Lankan feature are the so-called moonstones: not gemstones, but carved semicircular stones which, in the classical period, were placed like "doormats" before the entrances of important buildings. The wealth of symbolism depicted upon them underwent a continual process of change up into the Kandy period.

On full moon days, the faithful go to the temples, become absorbed in meditation, read the holy chronicles, and give offerings of flowers or other gifts. No alcoholic drinks are sold or served on these days. The Buddhist month of *Vesak* (May) is a special highlight: it is in this month that the Buddha was born, received enlightenment and died. These important events are celebrated for a period of two days, and people send each other *Vesak* greeting cards with beautiful stamps that are specially designed for the holiday every year.

Hinduism

The Hindu cult and social order developed in India over a period of four millennia, influenced by many different peoples with a mixture of ideas which, often in seeming contradiction, were nevertheless viewed with tolerance and incorporated into the whole. Thus it is hardly surprising that Hinduism appears to be such a confusing multitude of ideas. Like a symbol of its immense religious world, the *gopuram*, the entrance tower, soars up above the *kovil*, the Hindu temple.

This vast and colorful cosmos, with its gods, spirits, animals and significant objects, summons people into the temple to pray and make offerings, but simultaneously exerts so much power that it seems to give benediction from a distance. The god most worshiped in the *kovil* is located on the *gopuram* over the entrance. Here, in brief, is a description of the most important gods.

Shiva (also known as Ishvara) is the main god for the majority of Hindus in Sri Lanka. He has a third eye on his forehead, which not only emits wisdom, but can also produce both creative and destructive thunderbolts. The Shivaists draw three lines of holy ashes on their foreheads to represent these three eyes. The Shiva *lingam* – his phallus – is represented by a stone pillar in the center of the holy of holies in the temple. His *vahana,* or symbolic mount, is the Nandi bull (with hump). Shiva can occur in numerous forms, but the best-known representation is the *Nataraja*, the dancing god (often in a ring of fire).

Parvati (Uma) is Shiva's wife, and is represented bedecked with jewels as a kindly mother.

Their son *Ganesha* (Pillaiyar) is easy to recognize on account of his elephant head and big belly. The god of wisdom, wealth and happy journeys, he is depicted riding on a rat.

His brother *Skanda* (Kandaswamy, Subrahmaniya, Murugan, Karttikeya, Kataragama), who is the mighty god of war, bears a *vel* (spear) or carries a war ensign emblazoned with a cock. He rides on a peacock, which, according to legend, is a conquered demon.

Vishnu is, like Shiva, one of the main gods, and appears in a large variety of forms. His followers mark the sign of a "u" with a vertical line inside in ashes on their foreheads. This mark hearkens back to the time when Vishnu measured the cosmos in three strides and in doing so grew from a dwarf to a giant. His incarnation as Rama is important for Sri Lanka, since this deity, at the request of the other gods, killed the demon prince Ravana who lived on the island of Lanka, and rescued his wife Sita, whom the prince had kidnapped (other of his incarnations include Krishna and Buddha.) Easily recognized by his blue skin, he rides on the sun eagle Garuda.

Above: Catholic procession of the Virgin Mary in Colombo. Right: The Muslim Moors are descendants of Arab traders.

Lakshmi is Vishnu's wife and embodies beauty, luck, wealth and light.

Hindu holidays include *Thai Pongal*, the harvest festival in January; *Maha Shivarathri*, the union of Shiva and Parvati, celebrated with nighttime ceremonies in the *kovils* in February; *Dipavali*, the festival of lights, a happy, ceremonial housecleaning and tidying up in honor of the goddess Lakshmi in November.

The most important destinations for pilgrims include Kataragama (July/August), Chilaw (Munneswaram, August/September, October), and Nallur (July/August). Magnificent processions with enormous decorated floats, but also the daily *poya* ceremonies of the Brahmans in the *kovils*, give an impression of the deeply-rooted devoutness of the Hindus.

Buddhists also worship many Hindu gods, and even add others, such as *Pattini*, the goddess of fertility, *Saman*, the protector of Adam's Peak and the island, *Vibishana* (brother of the demon Ravana) and many other local gods.

Christianity

The Pope's visit to Sri Lanka in 1995 was an overwhelming occasion for the more than one million Catholics on the island. The missionary success of the Portuguese in the 16th century is still evident today in the large concentration of Catholic churches along the central and northern west coast. It is not uncommon for the patron saints of these churches to be martyrs whose dramatic lives and deaths, together with their compassion and steadfastness, made a deep impression upon the impoverished local population, many of whom were fishermen. At road intersections, one often encounters the figure of St. Sebastian, his body pierced by arrows, or that of St. Anthony in a Franciscan habit holding the infant Jesus in his arms, though Mary also occurs frequently.

The persecution of the Catholics during the Dutch colonial period no doubt led to the isolated location of the two most important pilgrimage destinations for Catholics: Talawila on the Kalpitiya Peninsula with the Church of St. Anne (festival July 26), and Madhu in the jungle of the Mannar district with the Church of the Holy Virgin (two-week-long festival around July 2). Reformed churches were established on the island during the Dutch colonial period, while the British and post-colonial periods saw the arrival of the Anglican Church and other Protestant religions, especially in the larger cities.

Islam

Islamic mosques are decorated in a low-key style. Islam, founded in the seventh century by the prophet Mohammed in Arabia, does not allow pictorial representations of god, but prefers instead the use of abstract ornamentation or friezes written in Arabic in the houses of worship. On Fridays around noon, Moors and Malays flock to the latter, but non-Muslims are usually denied entrance. Strict Muslims perform a regime of five prayers every day, regardless of where they happen to be at the time.

In Sri Lanka, three Muslim holidays, also centered around the lunar calendar, are observed: *Id-Ul-Fitr*, the end of the one-month fasting period of *Ramadan* in March; *Milad-Un-Nabi*, the birthday of the Prophet in August; and *Id-Ul-Alha*, the *Hajj* festival at the end of May when many Muslims make the pilgrimage to Mecca. The most popular place of Muslim pilgrimage on the island itself is the shrine of Kuragala (Ratnapura district).

CARGILLS
CARGILLS

Ceylon Carriers
LOT
Iraqi airways
TAROM
EAST WEST AIRLINES
MCJ
ESTD 1855

COLOMBO AND THE CENTRAL WEST COAST

COLOMBO
GALLE ROAD
KOTTE / SITAVAKA
KELANIYA / NEGOMBO
DAMBADENIYA

COLOMBO

To Arabian sailors many centuries ago, the few gray-black cliffs at about the height of present-day **Colombo**, behind which the otherwise regular and sandy shore of Sri Lanka's west coast runs back eastward, must have been a welcome sight: it marked the opening of a small bay that was relatively well sheltered from the southwest winds. However, they preferred to moor at the mouth of the **Kelani Ganga** where it runs into the Indian Ocean, only four kilometers further north, since the wide river also provided access to the regions inland.

The Arabian globetrotter Ibn Battuta came here in the 14th century and spoke of *Calenbou* in his account of his travels. The areas inland from the coast must have appeared green and impenetrable to the new arrivals: a region of small lakes and extensive marshes, divided by hills densely overgrown with lush tropical vegetation.

Present-day visitors to Sri Lanka can encounter the same scenery: the rocks on the coast, the curve of the bay, the winding river and the flat marshland punctuated here and there with an occasional hill. And even though Greater Colombo now extends 60 kilometers from north to south and 15 kilometers from east to west, and has close to three million inhabitants, you could still describe it and its surrounding districts as a "green city."

Preceding pages: Colombo – between the colonial era and the modern. Kelaniya, one of the most important pilgrimage sites in Sri Lanka. Left: Balloon vendor in Colombo.

A Growing City

What made this city so attractive for so many people? It was of little significance during the classical Sinhalese period (up to the 12th century), but a turning point came when the province of *Malayarata*, which also includes this coastal strip, became the most important place of refuge for the island's inhabitants. In the 15th century, the king even built his royal city, Sri Jayewardenepura, only seven kilometers away from the coast. In 1517, the Portuguese set up a trading post on the bay, securing it with a fortress on the rocks and the small promontory south of it, where the downtown city district is even today known as **Fort**.

When the cinnamon trade along the coast flourished, the Dutch became envious and captured the fortress in 1656. In the next few decades the Dutch built canals to link up the lagoons, the marshes

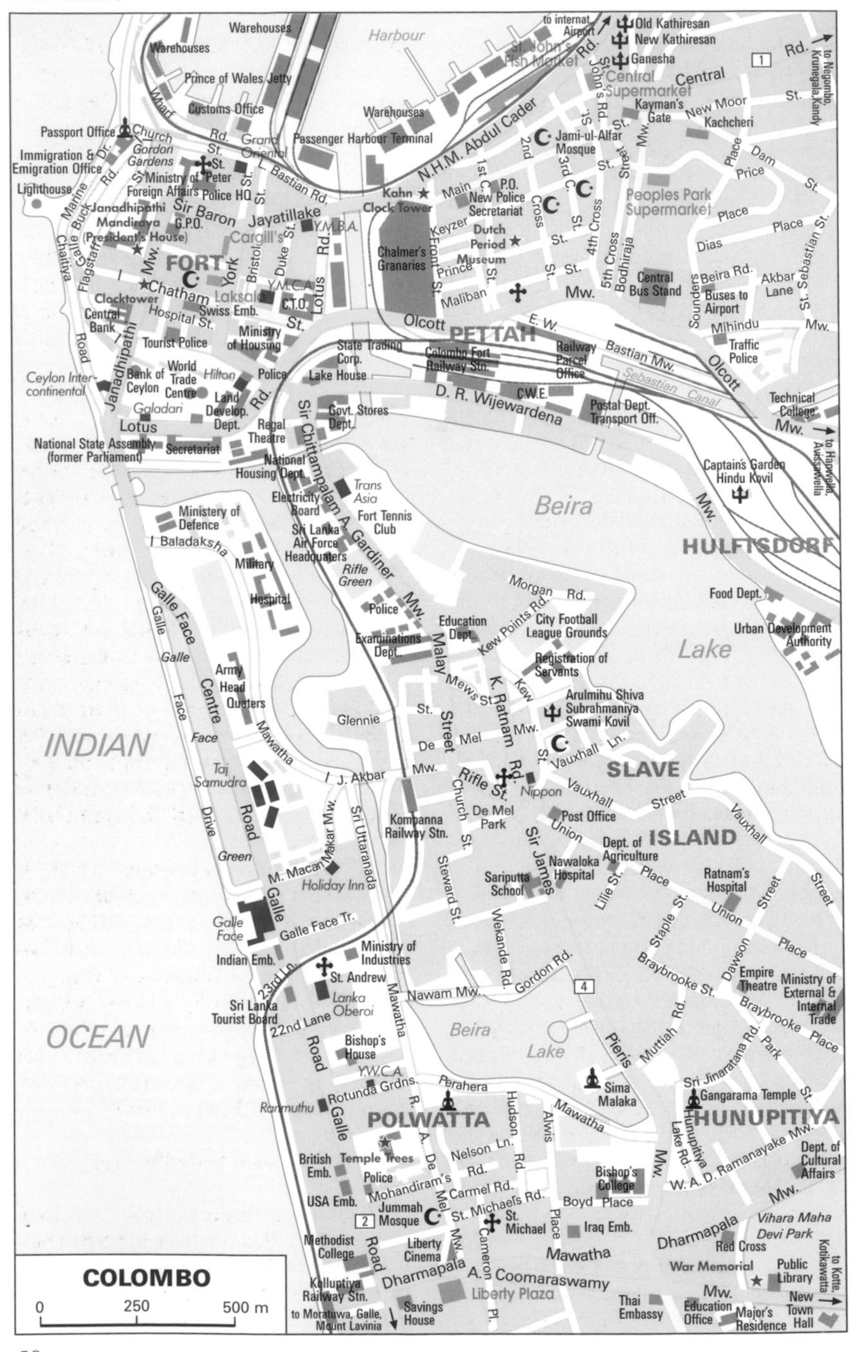
COLOMBO
0 250 500 m
Harbour
INDIAN
OCEAN
FORT
PETTAH
SLAVE
ISLAND
HULFTSDORF
POLWATTA
HUNUPITIYA
Beira
Lake
Warehouses
Prince of Wales Jetty
Customs Office
Passenger Harbour Terminal
Passport Office
Immigration & Emigration Office
Lighthouse
Gordon Gardens
St. Peter
Ministry of Foreign Affairs
Police HQ
Janadhipathi Mandiraya (President's House)
G.P.O.
Cargill's
Y.M.B.A.
Y.M.C.A.
C.T.O.
Laksala
Swiss Emb.
Clocktower
Central Bank
Tourist Police
Ministry of Housing
Bank of Ceylon
World Trade Centre
Hilton
Galadari
Land Develop. Dept.
Police
Ceylon Inter-continental
National State Assembly (former Parliament)
Secretariat
Regal Theatre
National Housing Dept.
Kahn Clock Tower
Chalmer's Granaries
P.O.
New Police Secretariat
Dutch Period Museum
Jami-ul-Alfar Mosque
Old Kathiresan
New Kathiresan
Ganesha
St. John's Fish Market
Central Supermarket
Kayman's Gate
Kachcheri
Peoples Park Supermarket
Central Bus Stand
Buses to Airport
Traffic Police
State Trading Corp.
Lake House
Colombo Fort Railway Stn.
Railway Parcel Office
C.W.E.
Postal Dept. Transport Off.
Govt. Stores Dept.
Technical College
Captain's Garden Hindu Kovil
Trans Asia
Electricity Board
Fort Tennis Club
Sri Lanka Air Force Headquaters
Rifle Green
Ministery of Defence
Military Hospital
Army Head Quaters
Police
Examinations Dept.
Education Dept.
City Football League Grounds
Registration of Servants
Food Dept.
Urban Development Authority
Arulmihu Shiva Subrahmaniya Swami Kovil
Taj Samudra
Nippon
Post Office
Kompanna Railway Stn.
De Mel Park
Dept. of Agriculture
Nawaloka Hospital
Sariputta School
Ratnam's Hospital
Holiday Inn
Galle Face
Indian Emb.
Ministry of Industries
St. Andrew
Lanka Oberoi
Sri Lanka Tourist Board
Empire Theatre
Ministry of External & Internal Trade
Bishop's House
Y.W.C.A.
Sima Malaka
Sri Jinaratana Rd.
Gangarama Temple
Ramuthu
British Emb.
Temple Trees
Police
USA Emb.
Jummah Mosque
St. Michael
Bishop's College
Dept. of Cultural Affairs
Iraq Emb.
Methodist College
Liberty Cinema
Liberty Plaza
Vihara Maha Devi Park
Red Cross
War Memorial
Public Library
Kolluptiya Railway Stn.
Savings House
Thai Embassy
Education Office
Major's Residence
New Town Hall
to internat. Airport
to Negombo, Krunegala, Kandy
to Hanwella, Avissawella
to Kotte, Kotikawatta
to Moratuwa, Galle, Mount Lavinia
Marine Dr.
Church St.
Chaitiya Road
Janadhipathi Mw.
Sir Baron Jayatillake Mw.
York St.
Chatham St.
Hospital St.
Lotus Rd.
Olcott Mw.
D. R. Wijewardena Mw.
N.H.M. Abdul Cader Rd.
Bastian Mw.
Sebastian Canal
Sir Chittampalam A. Gardiner Mw.
Galle Face Centre Road
Galle Face Green
Galle Road
Malay Street
K. Ratnam Rd.
Vauxhall St.
Union Place
Braybrooke Place
Nawam Mw.
Perahera Mawatha
Dharmapala Mw.
A. Coomaraswamy Mawatha
W. A. D. Ramanayake Mw.
Sir James Pieris Mw.

close to the coast and the lakes, thereby connecting and providing easier access to the cinnamon gardens. Apart from the fortress area, they settled mainly in the districts **of Wolfendhal**, **Hulftsdorf** and **Mutwal**. In 1796, the British drove out the Dutch and took over the area; it was they who had the longest-lasting impact on the city. It wasn't only their buildings, although a few colonial-style edifices are still in evidence today: more to the point, the British made decisions which helped make Colombo the island's most important economic center. The construction of the road linking Colombo and Kandy in 1827 provided a direct route to the hill country. As for the country's railway lines, they still don't form a network, but rather radiate out from Colombo. When the Suez Canal was opened in the mid 19th century, a west-facing mole was built to protect the harbor, making it extremely practical for international shipping traffic to and from east Asia to stop off here en route. Finally, when the harbor was extended again at the end of the 19th century, Galle, which had thereto been the leading cxport harbor, lost its importance. Thus Colombo's supremacy was established once and for all.

New and Old Fort

As you approach the present city center of Colombo, known as Fort, the twin towers of the **World Trade Center**, 34 stories high and faced in reflecting glass, are a clear sign that the 20th century has not passed Sri Lanka by. To the left and right of these are the severe, modernistic towers of the **Hilton Hotel** and the **Bank of Ceylon**. These and other new buildings form the southern boundary of the area, measuring roughly one square kilometer, where the fortress used to stand in the colonial era.

Just a stone's throw to the north, however, Fort is by no means as chic and modern as it is to the south. The department stores **Laksala** and **Cargill's** (built in 1906) on **York Street** have an interesting, museum-like flair, and on the parallel street, **Janadhipathi Mawatha**, the majestic late-19th-century **General Post Office** (GPO) is impressive both inside and out. Past this busy street, sheltered by a protective screen of trees and guarded by sentries, stands the **President's Residence** (formerly called the Queen's House), a magnificent villa on the spot where the Dutch and later the British governors once resided.

At the corner of Chatham Street is the **Clock Tower** (1857), topped by a navigational light, a famous city landmark. Almost a century later, when the houses in Fort began to get taller, a new lighthouse was built on the rocks by **Marine Drive** along the coast. A nearby playground, as well as an open-air pool between the rocks, are popular with locals. Not far from here, the **Hotel Intercontinental** commands a view of the entire 11-kilometer coastline to the south, up to the imposing promontory of **Mount Lavinia**, topped by a colonial hotel. The best view northwards out across the harbor (which is not open to the public), is from the famous **Grand Oriental Hotel** on **Church Street**.

Fort offers an intriguing blend of buildings, ranging from venerable to rundown edifices, many of them dating from the colonial period, to ultramodern buildings. Located in the immediate vicinity of the harbor, it is the city's main commercial area, with a concentration of airline offices, travel agencies, insurance and shipping companies, and banks, as well as hotels, both old and modern.

Pettah – Outside the Walls

Though the fortress walls have long since been pulled down, when you enter the district to the east, called **Pettah**, you sense at once that you are entering another world. The Tamil *pettai* and the

Sinhala *pita* both mean "outside," since the local people had their shops outside the European quarter. Today, the shopkeepers in Pettah are predominantly Moors and Tamils. While the neighborhood is crowded and bustling during business hours, there's a visible order provided by the checkerboard layout of its streets. The central east-west axis, **Main Street**, is almost exclusively the domain of textile vendors, while other streets are dominated by spices, ironmongery or jewels, to name but a few. You can buy food, especially fruit and vegetables, in the eastern sector, in and around the district's former town hall.

Catering to the religious needs of Pettah's mainly Muslim inhabitants is the eye-catching red-and-white striped **Jami-ul-Alfar Mosque** on **Second Cross Street**, while on **Sea Street**, home of the gold traders, there are three Hindu *kovils* with colorful *gopurams*: the **Old** and **New Kathiresan** and the **Ganesha Temple**. On **Prince Street**, there's a house dating back to the Dutch period which has been converted into the **Dutch Period Museum**.

Above: Strolling along the promenade in Fort, Colombo. Right: Gate tower of the Skanda Temple on Slave Island.

Diversity up to the Kelani Ganga

The city districts off to the east have retained their Dutch names; here, the reformed **Wolfendhal Church** (1750) offers a glimpse of the Dutch past. The most conspicuous buildings in the south sector of the built-up district of Hulftsdorf are the modern **Law Buildings**, which resemble gigantic pavilions. These are located directly north of the flats which drain the St. Sebastian Canal into the Kelani River. By contrast, the hills which run along the harbor are densely populated. On one of them, the silvery domes of **St. Lucia's Cathedral** (completed in 1906) can be seen from quite a distance. On his 1995 visit, the Pope conferred a special blessing on the cathedral.

Less attention is given to **Christ Church** in Mutwal, Colombo's former diocese church, also known as **Galpalliye**, "Stone Church" due to its dark stone walls. Though this area north of the harbor is densely populated, it is pleasantly green and benefits from a refreshing sea breeze. Two oases of calm on **Temple Road** are two *kovils* on the beach, one dedicated to Shiva, the other to Kali. The marshland beyond accommodates a modern **swimming pool** and a **stadium**. Part of the Kenani flats, it is still known as **Grand Pass** after the *paso grande*, the pontoon bridge with which the Portuguese spanned the wide river. Today, **Victoria Bridge** and **New Bridge** are barely able to cope with the endless flow of traffic over the Kelani Ganga.

Slave Island

South of Fort, on a long, narrow island, was where the slaves had their night quarters; the land was thus called **Slave Island**. Slavery was abolished in 1845.

Today the spot, which is surrounded by what remains of the formerly larger **Beira Lake**, is scarcely recognizable as an island; and it underwent a rapid transformation in the 1990s. Elegant office buildings and stores have sprung up and sprawled out into the adjacent municipal districts. But the island also manages to accommodate various government departments, from the tax authority to the Air Force; a residential area inhabited mainly by Moors; and the **Arulmihu Shiva Subrahmaniya Swami Kovil** (temple dedicated to the god Subrahmaniya/Murugan/ Skanda), of which the entrance tower, consecrated in 1993, is on **Kew Street**. Slums, Christian churches, hotels and the important Buddhist **Gangarama Temple** complete the varied picture. Anyone looking for peace and quiet can visit the **Sima Malaka** meditation island, which belongs to the nearby temple. Designed by contemporary architect Geoffrey Bawa, this simple temple is ornamented with Thai statues of the Buddha.

Cinnamon Gardens

Cinnamon Gardens is the name of the district near the city center where cinnamon trees grew in the colonial period; gradually, these trees were replaced by elegant villas set in extensive, park-like grounds. Also known as Colombo 7, the area still comes across as lushly green, despite the wide, busy streets and an increasing number of offices, government buildings and various other institutions that have gradually encroached on its territory. Its green centerpiece is the **Vihara Maha Devi Park**; opposite the park's northern end is the magnificent **City Hall** with its white cupola (built in 1929). On the park's west side, the modern **Public Library** is almost hidden behind tall trees. South of the park there are public offices, galleries, and also two museums back to back. The **Natural History Museum** has exhibits on Sri Lanka's geology, flora and fauna, and also presents information about modern agricultural methods and irrigation. The **National Museum**, an imposing building from the mid-19th century, offers an overview of Sri Lanka's archeology, history and folklore, and also houses a library.

Above: Colombo's Municipal Park with a view of City Hall.

In addition, Cinnamon Gardens also accommodates the **University**, many public offices, most of the embassies, several private schools and **radio and television stations**.

Furthermore, there's the **Bandaranaike Conference Hall (BMICH)**, which the Chinese built in 1973 opposite their own embassy. Named for Prime Minister Bandaranaike, who was murdered in 1959, it includes a museum display about his life. Finally, there is the quiet, memorable **Hall of Independence**, an attempted copy of the Council Hall of the last king of Kandy which Great Britain gave to Sri Lanka. With this concentration of buildings and facilities, the former cinnamon gardens function as a truly high-class center of the city.

GALLE ROAD

On the southern edge of Fort stands the **Old Parliament**, its majestic çolonnaded entrance, built just after 1929, facing the sea. Guests of honor can look out from the building's flight of steps to the open, sandy expanse of **Galle Face Green**, 1,200 meters long and more than 100 meter wide. Thanks to the pleasantly cool sea breeze it enjoys, the green attracts many people in the evenings, especially families with children. Two large hotels, the **Taj Samudra** and the grand **Galle Face**, form a noble backdrop to this busy scene. This is the starting point of the road of the same name, **Galle Road**, which continues for 115 kilometers to the city of Galle. The seven-kilometer-long stretch through Colombo runs straight as an arrow. Nonetheless, driving along it can be a nerve-racking experience for many: traffic flows slowly and there are few turnoffs.

The **Indian High Commission** stands next to the Galle Face Hotel; the Tudor-style **St. Andrew's Church** (built in 1842) seems strangely out of place when compared with the **Crescat** residential and office tower with supermarket (1996) opposite the **Oberoi Hotel**. The **Tourist Office** is on the opposite side of the street. And the **British High Commission**, right next door to the **American Embassy**, stands opposite a famous address, namely **Temple Trees**, the official residence of the Prime Minister.

Anyone turning off onto **Dharmapala Mawatha** will probably find it easier to get a parking space in the large shopping mall of **Liberty Plaza** than in front of one of the stores on Galle Road. "Newer, classier, higher": facade designs are changing rapidly as we enter the third millenium.

By contrast, further along Galle Road towards the coast, the villa which stands back off the road, **Mumtaz Mahal**, official residence of the speaker of the National Assembly, briefly summons to mind the relaxed and yet dignified atmosphere of the colonial era. The **Sri Lanka Tea Board**, **Sri Lanka Cashew Corporation**, **Sri Lanka Ceramics** and a large number of jewelers are located between here and the intersection at **Bauddhaloka Mawatha**, which forms the border between the districts of **Kollupitiya** (Colombo 3) and **Bambalapitiya** (Colombo 4). Finally, the large shopping center, **Majestic City**, with its generous expanse of glass, is another touch of modernity.

Towns Around Mount Lavinia

With the naked eye you might not notice that Colombo's city limits are located behind **Welawatte** at the **Dehiwela Canal**. The road is just as built-up after you've passed this boundary; and the next town, **Dehiwela-Mount Lavinia,** has more than 200,000 inhabitants. It becomes a little hillier in Mount Lavinia, where **Hotel Road** continues towards the coast to the historic **Mt. Lavinia Hotel**, as well as to the train station and to other hotels.

In **Ratmalana**, the grounds of the **Domestic Airport** border on Galle Road. Then comes **Moratuwa**, an important industrial center with 170,000 inhabitants. Traffic moves smoothly along the seven-kilometer highway which runs parallel to the coast, railway line and the shabby shanty towns occupied by fishermen and carpenters. Anyone opting instead for the old main road east of **Bolgoda Lake** cannot fail to notice the numerous timber stores and sawmills.

Avoiding the Big City

Leaving **Panadura** at its southern edge, however, you clearly sense an end of the conurbation around Colombo, and you won't come to the next town, **Kalutara North**, for another 14 kilometers. The coast, railway line and road run al-

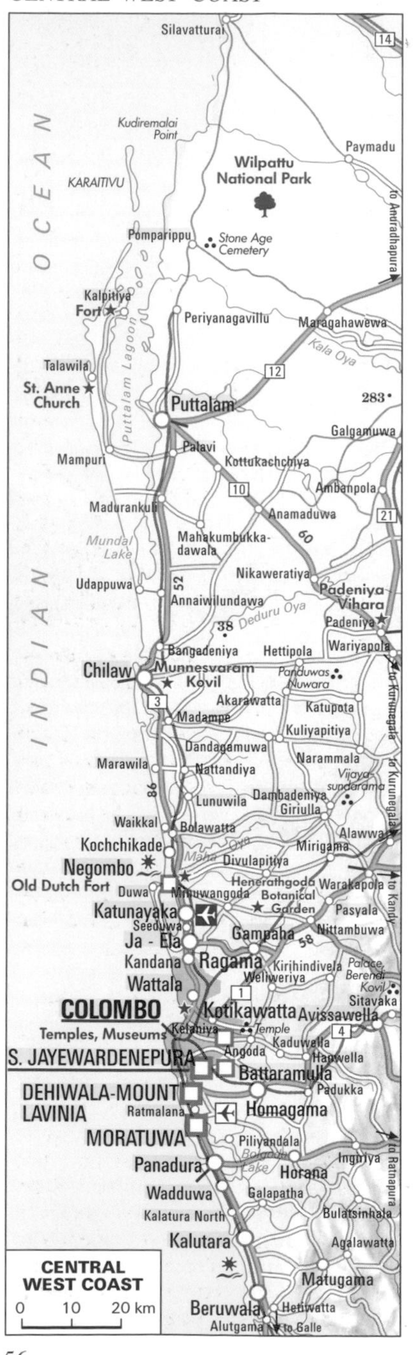

most parallel to each other, separated by just a few hundred meters. However, the presence of coconut groves, private gardens and fishermen's huts interspersed by pandanus bush creates an appropriately dense backdrop along the beaches between **Wadduwa** and Kalutara North, against which hotels, all the way up to five-star establishments, are nestled.

Inland, the scenery fascinates by its variety: rice paddies, coconut groves, rubber plantations and many private gardens. Anyone wishing to avoid the usual traffic chaos in Colombo and who wants to take the quickest, most direct route from the west coast to Kandy, should choose the route from Kalutara North via **Horana**, **Padukka** (Mipe Junction) and **Hanwella** to **Pasyala** on the A1. Here you have the opportunity to stop off at one of the brickworks in the damp clay flats, to watch latex milk being tapped and processed in the rubber plantations, or to go shopping at one of the inexpensive and well-stocked markets in the towns along the way.

The temple at **Galapatha**, situated 12 kilometers south of Horana on a bend in the road, atop a hill, presents an interesting collection of lovingly-tended devalas of Natha, Skanda, Saman, Pattini and numerous local gods.

KOTTE

Luckily, even locals sometimes substitute the name **Kotte**, pronounced with a long "o," for the name of their state capital **Sri Jayewardenepura**, which is so difficult for foreigners to pronounce. The name describes the fortified capital which Bhuvanekabahu VI (1411-1466), the last Sinhalese king who managed to unite the empire, had built here in 1415. Up until the death of King Don Juan Dharmapala (1551-1597), who was completely subservient to the Portuguese, Kotte was the island's capital, though in 1565 his opponents from Sitawaka al-

most managed to raze it to the ground. The Portuguese were far more interested in the fort at Colombo, due to its position near the coast, and left Kotte and its king to their own fates. This explains why nothing very spectacular remains of the old capital today. Anyone willing to take a little extra time to explore the site of the old city of Kotte is first rewarded by the view of the modern **Parliament Building**, built in 1973 (designed by architect Geoffrey Bawa) seen from an unusual perspective. And if you are tired of the constant traffic problems in the city center, you will appreciate the wisdom of the authorities in locating important state institutions here, well out of town.

If you take the broad boulevard of **Sri Jayewardenepura Mawatha**, which runs between Colombo and the new Parliament Building, and take the southern exit leading to either Kotte or Pita Kotte, you come to a hilly area between **Rampart Road** and **Beddegana Road**. Today, this is a pleasant green residential area which extends eastwards up to **Diyawanna Lake**. The old city lay in these hills, protected by the marshland around it. If you walk along the lake shore, you come closer to the modern parliament complex than if you approach from the main street, where the entrance to the parliament grounds is strictly guarded and only authorized persons, but not tourists, are allowed to enter.

Above: Collecting latex sap and processing rubber.

Gothama Thapovanaya Monastery

Though the flat hills and marshes in Colombo's hinterland are being increasingly built up with small houses, the area has remained green, since residents grow not only useful plants but also attractive ornamental plants in their gardens. North of Kotte and the expensive residential area of **Battaramulla** off **Koswatta Road**, in an area of new green districts and in a secluded setting, is a monastery complex in a large park-like area, **Go-**

thama Thapowanaya. The monastery, which accommodates 38 monks and a large number of novices, with all the facilities for their accommodation and education, is also glad to accommodate any foreign guests who want to immerse themselves in monastic life, whether for a long or short period of time, following the monks' rules and meditating in the calm of the luxuriant park. Outside the monastery grounds is an orphanage, which is also run by the monks.

SITAVAKA

About three kilometers further north you pass through **Angoda** and come to the old road to **Avissawella**, which runs along the left bank of the Kelani Ganga and leads to some of the former river crossings, such as **Kaduwella** and **Hanwella**. **Avissawella** is a busy center for the industry generated by the rubber plantations which surround it; it's also a traffic hub, since the well-built A4, which connects Colombo with Ratnapura. From here, the A7 leads to the hill country (Hatton/Adam's Peak, Nuwara Eliya), and crosses the rapidly-flowing Kelani river about one kilometer east of the city center. The small suburb of **Sitavaka** (or Seetewaka), contains the name of Sita, wife of the hero Rama; according to the old Indian epic *Ramayana*, Sita was carried away to Lanka by the monster Ravana and held captive. There is nothing in Sitavaka to prove this, but by following signs a little way from the A7 you can see remains of the **defensive walls** and **palace** which King Rajasinha I (1581-1593) had built near the river, thereby entering into competition with the king of Kotte, who had effectively become a puppet of the Portuguese. Rajasinha was one of the most vehement opponents of the European colonial rulers, and had proved a considerable thorn in their side with his repeated

Above: A wide selection of tempting tropical fruit. Right: The elephant is still valued as a work animal.

sieges of their fort in Colombo. The **Berendi Kovil** built on the other side of the Kelani River (follow signs east of the bridge on the A7, 1 km) – although the kovil may never have been completed – attests to his great love for Hinduism. Today, dense jungle surrounds the solid foundations of this Shiva temple, which are sparsely but elegantly adorned with animal motifs, and support a platform accessible from all four sides.

A few kilometers further east along the Sitavaka River you can take canoeing trips of varying levels of difficulty.

KELANIYA

Some 145 kilometers long, the Kelani Ganga is the fourth-longest river in the country. The reservoirs in the hill country are not always able to contain its masses of water. Dikes protect the hinterland near the coast in places; other areas are regularly flooded after heavy rain, especially when the southwest monsoon slows the run-off of water into the sea.

About 10 kilometers inland from the river estuary is one of Sri Lanka's 16 most important destinations for pilgrims, the **Kelaniya Raja Maha Vihara**. According to the "Great Chronicle," Buddha arrived here with 500 followers eight years after his enlightenment, on the second day of *Vesak* (May). He had been invited by the local prince, Maniakkhika, who had learned to revere the Buddha during one of his two previous visits. The Enlightened One preached from a magnificent throne, exactly on the spot where the white **dagoba** stands today.

2,500 Years of Tradition?

Kelaniya, which the Portuguese colonial rulers destroyed and the Dutch did not allow to be rebuilt, seems to have been a focal point of Buddhist adoration in the Middle Ages. Only the restoration of Buddhism in the era of Kirti Sri Rajasinha (1747-1782) along with the liberal position of the British toward religious belief made it possible to rees-

tablish the monastery as a place of pilgrimage. The dagoba is almost overshadowed by the **image house**, decorated at the beginning of the 20th century, in keeping with historical tradition, with a frieze of geese, dwarves and elephants.

You enter the building from the east, stepping over a moonstone "doormat." The entrance hall and the adjacent room to the north are the 18th-century image rooms. In the middle of the north wall in the entrance hall is a depiction of the man who hosted Buddha and his followers: the Naga king Maniakkhika. Archways decorated with *makara* (mythical creatures) rise up above him and above both entrances to the adjoining room, which contains a statue of the reclining Buddha. By the feet of the Enlightened One there's still room for a Vishnu devala, hung with Buddhist flags. On the upper section of the walls are frescoes of Buddha's 500 followers, while on the lower portion are images of important Hindu gods, which are also worshiped by Sri Lankan Buddhists.

Above: Frieze with geese and dwarves on the image house of Kelaniya. Right: Making offerings at the mighty bo tree in Kelaniya.

The other parts of the image house date from the early 20th century. In the reliquary room on the south side, the impressive large-scale pictures by Soliyas Mendis portray Buddha's three visits to Sri Lanka. The artist was obviously equally keen to show the terrible destruction of the temple during the Portuguese period and the expulsion of the monks, who were able to escape with their lives and their valuable relics by crossing a pontoon bridge to the other side of the Kelani River. There's not an inch of empty wall here; around the large paintings are smaller pictures illustrating historical events and legends.

In the rear section of the image house, in front of a panorama of the snow-covered Himalayas, there is a seated figure of the meditating Buddha. Here, too, pictures on the walls record important events from Buddha's life and the history of Buddhism in Sri Lanka: such as the transport of a cutting from the sacred bo tree on a (European-looking) ship from India to Sri Lanka, accompanied by Sanghamitta, or the smuggling of the Sacred Tooth relic hidden in the piled-up hairdo of the princess Hemamale.

One special feature of the monastery complex is the **bo tree** standing next to the image house. On a slight elevation, the tree is surrounded by a shining gilt fence, as well as a low altar on which believers place offerings of artistically-arranged flowers. Colorful votive flags flutter from the railing and branches.

On Sundays or *poya* days (full moon holidays), mingling with the many devotees and observing their lively yet respectful ceremonial activities can be quite an experience. White-clad children and pilgrims collect in groups around a reader or prayer leader, listening attentively and devotedly from their seats on the ground in one of the monastery complex's many shady spots, or within the large open preaching hall. Hundreds of oil lamps flicker in the long rows of iron stands placed there for this purpose. People kneeling on the ground, absorbed in prayer, are distracted neither by wandering dogs, people hurrying past, nor screaming children.

Even more impressive are the marvelous processions of the *Duruthu Perahera*, which for two days in January thrill hordes of spectators with decorated elephants, music, acrobats and ornate floats. But even on quiet days, this holy place is not without a special atmosphere. When you come from the high dike of the Kelani River, you face, at the bottom of a flight of steps, the whitewashed ornamental archways over the southern entrance; these so delighted German zoo founder Hagenbeck that he copied them for the entrance to his zoo in Hamburg.

Eager students at the *pirivena* – a college which is part of the monastery – hasten across the grounds toward their

classrooms. The snow-white dagoba, unusually shaped like a pile of rice, glistens mysteriously in the sun, hiding from view like an untold secret the treasure which is supposed to be walled up within it, the jewel-encrusted throne from which Buddha allegedly preached two and a half thousand years ago.

Historical Smuggling Act – Gampaha

Tourists seldom venture to **Gampaha**, the district capital, which lies a mere 30 kilometers northeast of Colombo on the railway line to Kandy. The A1 bypasses the place by five kilometers, but it can be reached easily via the A33 from **Ja-Ela** (on the A3 about halfway between Colombo and Katunayake).

It is not so much the town itself as it is the **Henerathgoda Botanical Gardens** which are the attraction here. Just two kilometers outside the town center, the gardens are popular amongst the locals, but in the 19th century they fulfilled another purpose. It was here that around

2,000 seedlings of rubber trees (*hevea brasiliensis*) were brought in 1876. These seeds had been smuggled in from Brazil and had germinated in the botanical garden at Kew Gardens, London. They proved to flourish fully in this tropical environment as well as in their own country of origin, and they provided the basis for the rubber plantations which now thrive throughout south and southeast Asia. The park of Henerathgoda still houses a few veterans of this original planting of the first rubber trees grown outside Brazil, which the gardeners like to show off with great pride.

NEGOMBO

The quickest way to the beach: From **Katunayake**, which is the only international airport on the island, it is about 10 kilometers to **Negombo**. The town's location at the northern entrance to the 15-kilometer-long **Negombo Lagoon** in the south predestined it to serve as a shipping port, while the eight kilometers of unbroken sand beach stretching to the north have made it a very popular and busy vacation spot. The town's 65,000 inhabitants live largely from fishing and tourism. Others have chosen to make their living in the city of Colombo, and do so by means of a 40-kilometer commute every day.

Above and right: The harbor city of Negombo lives from fishing – and tourism.

To protect the harbor entrance, the Portuguese and Dutch built a small **fort** at the northern end of the lagoon; you can visit its gate buildings (1678), behind which the prison is located. On its eastern side is the downtown area, which extends one kilometer to the railway station. To the north begins the beach, its first two kilometers dominated by fishermen (**fish market** one kilometer from the fort), the next three kilometers the province of the tourists, with rows of hotels (none, however, in the top price class). The beach's final extremity, however, is again in the hands of the fishermen.

A Canal at the Coast

For the Portuguese and Dutch colonial rulers, Negombo was an ideal collection point and export harbor for cinnamon. Inland, and parallel to the coast, they built a canal from Kelani Ganga to the lagoon in Negombo (called the **Hamilton Canal**, or **Dutch Canal**) and then continued it northwards to the lagoon at **Puttalam**. This 100-kilometer waterway not only provided access to the cinnamon gardens, but also meant that shipping was not affected by the weather during the southwest monsoon, which jeopardized coastal shipping. Today, the canals are hardly used any longer for inland shipping; it's mainly tourist boats which from time to time venture into their calm waters to drift by the coconut groves, lush private gardens, marshlands and small towns.

Anyone who has spare time and wants to avoid the heavy traffic on the main road between Negombo and Colombo should opt for the coastal road which, while it is not free of potholes, is certainly less traveled. Another option is to follow the canal. Taking this route, you'll glean a clear impression of how much is being undertaken to drain the marshlands between the coastal road and the main road and turn them into residential areas.

Churches on the Coast

In Negombo, but also in many other coastal towns north of the Kelani Ganga, there is a conspicuously large number of churches, most of them Catholic. Large numbers of fishermen from the *karava* caste converted to Catholicism during the Portuguese period and were thus able to escape their lowly caste status. Church festivals are very popular, such as those in honor of a church's patron saint. The first festival in the year, on January 20, is dedicated to St. Sebastian. On this day every community with a church of St. Sebastian puts up a decorated flagpole (not unlike the procedure observed at Hindu festivals) and organizes colorful processions, as well as distributing free

meals to the needy (a concept borrowed from Buddhist holidays).

Famous, too, are the passion plays at **Duwa**, the small fishing community at the tip of the spit of land opposite the fort in Negombo. These last almost the whole day on Good Friday. Organized each year by the locals, these plays are held at the church near the sea and in Negombo, and are attended by thousands of visitors.

Chilaw

The A3 leads north across the **Maha Oya River** and to **Waikkal**, where white sand beaches and hotels sit alongside beautiful villas from the colonial period. 15 kilometers north of here, a small holiday resort has developed along the beach and lagoon of **Marawila**. Just before **Madampe**, the rows of coconut plantations and private gardens are interrupted abruptly by a small plain of rice paddies. The necessary tank for these fields was built by a local prince, who also bequeathed his name to the **Tanniya Vallabahu Devala**. In front of the temple is a statue of a snow-white horse, a warning to passing travelers: anyone who carelessly passes by will meet with a similar fate to that of the rider: his horse threw him when he tried to ride past without making a temple donation.

Above: Coconut milk is a standard refreshment. Right: Sometimes even a scheduled bus needs help getting started.

The road continues north through a sea of coconut palms to **Chilaw**, the northern tip of the "Coconut Triangle" – the other two points are Colombo in the south and Matale, 85 kilometers inland – where almost half of the island's coconut production is located. *The Coconut Research Institute* has been in **Lunuwila** since 1929.

Like Negombo, Chilaw is situated at the end of a lagoon (**Chilaw Lake**) and has a small fishing port. A bridge leads to the broad sand beach of the spit, where, on the site of the former Dutch fort, the renovated **Rest House** has space for dining or simply relaxing in view of the sea.

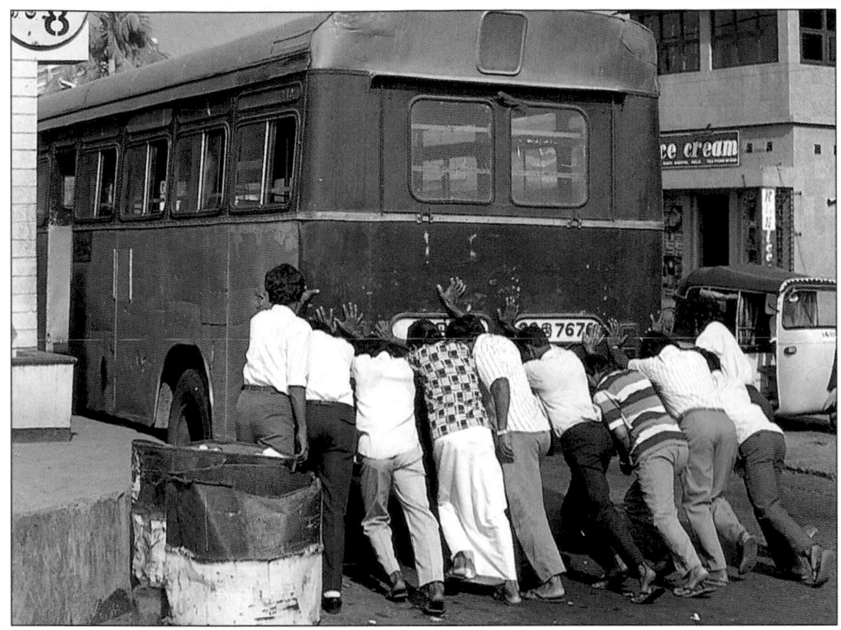

Several festivals between August and October attract Hindu pilgrims to the **Munnesvaram Kovil** (three kilometers on the B33 towards Kurunegala). It is thought to be on the site of the oldest Shiva temple in Sri Lanka. Devotees believe this to be the place where Rama, the hero of the *Ramayana* epic, made a sacrifice before returning to India with his wife Sita after freeing her from captivity. In 1578, the Portuguese completely destroyed the temple, and rebuilding did not start until 1753; additional alterations continued up into the 20th century.

Into the Dry North

Just three kilometers north of town you cross the **Deduru Oya**, the historical border between the old Sinhalese regions of Malayarata (the wet region and the western hill country) and Rajarata (the irrigated northern dry zone). Leading north, the A3 runs almost dead straight and parallel to the railway alongside the flat **Mundal Lake**. If you turn off at **Palavi** and continue west on the B730, across the marshland which runs into the **Puttalam Lagoon** further north, the large rectangular basins at the southern end of the lagoon indicate how dry the region is: because of the evaporation, this is a salt-producing area.

This quiet minor road leads to the spit of land more than 50 kilometers long, whose main town, **Kalpitiya,** has a sheltered harbor on the lagoon (40 kilometers from Palavi). Having driven out the Portuguese Jesuits, who had done a lot of work toward colonializing the area, in 1644, the Dutch built a small town with a checkerboard street layout and constructed a fort to defend it, an edifice which today houses the Navy. This military presence is a reminder of the proximity of the island of Mannar, a Tamil-influenced region, which can be reached in just five hours on a small ferry. A boatman has to be skilled and experienced indeed in order to navigate the area around the lagoon and **Karaitivu**, the narrow island extending northwards,

through the islands and shallows of **Dutch Bay** and **Portugal Bay**. Fishing and pearl-diving have been the main occupations of the inhabitants on the west coast for as long as anyone can remember. The Sinhalese-Tamil conflict has also brought newcomers – mainly Muslim fishermen from the Mannar district, who have created temporary housing for themselves in the form of palm-leaf huts and have resumed their customary work in the lagoon.

While the lagoon side of the spit is characterized by the green of private gardens and coconut groves, the side facing the sea is made up entirely of sand dunes with little vegetation and the occasional *villu* (seasonal lakelet). In **Talaivillu** (or Talawila), 17 kilometers south of Kalpitiya, the magnificent **St. Anne's Church** towers up in this bare landscape. The church stands in a spacious park with stations of the cross and plentiful accommodation for pilgrims. Legend has it that on this spot St. Anne appeared to a Portuguese man who had fallen asleep on the beach, having looked in vain for work. On July 26, thousands of Catholics, as well as Muslims, flock here to enliven the usually so quiet and barren landscape.

Above: Leopard in Wilpattu National Park. Right: In the Maha Oya Valley.

Like Chilaw, the district capital **Puttalam** has just under 30,000 inhabitants. The main road north ends here, and somewhat further north the railway comes to an end at the country's most important cement factories. Just a few miles outside the town the jungle begins, interrupted by historic old tanks which have been brought into use again, and new rice paddies on the former site of the old Sinhalese irrigation civilization.

But in fact, the culture of this region, now so sparsely populated, goes back even further. **Pomparippu**, 35 kilometers north of Puttalam and accessible on generally poor roads, is home to a Stone Age burial ground. Some 25 kilometers further north, where the coast forms a prominent cape and then dips back eastwards, the harbor of **Kudiremalai** must have been located; this may well have been used by sailors from India and Arabia. Both these locations lie within the dry section of **Wilpattu National Park**, home to a wealth of wildlife, notably large numbers of leopards; but which has been closed due to military blockades.

DAMBADENIYA

One of the blackest chapters in Sri Lanka's history was the regime of Magha from Kalinga in eastern India. He seized power in 1215, ending with his death in 1236. While the Sinhalese withdrew from the Rajarata and sought refuge in the mountains and the wet impenetrable southwest of the island, monks kept the relic of the Sacred Tooth, the symbol of the rightful king, hidden in Kotmale in the hill country. In 1232, even before

Magha's death, Vijayabahu III acceded to the throne. After a big festival in Kotmale, he took the relic to the new capital, **Dambadeniya**, 35 kilometers from the west coast and five kilometers north of the **Maha Oya River** (on the B27, about halfway between Negombo and Kurunegala). As he was not allowed to enter the old capital of Polonnaruwa and was afraid to hide the Sacred Tooth relic anywhere near his new palace, he had a special tooth palace built some 25 kilometers further southeast in the midst of the wilderness, on the towering cliff of **Beligala** (see page 215).

For the site of his own new palace he had also chosen a mighty rocky mountain which allowed him a good view of the surrounding area. It was his son and successor Parakramabahu II (1236-1270) who first brought the tooth to Dambadeniya and built the **Vijayasundarama Temple** for it at the foot of the hill; today there is still a fairly large monastery on this site. The paintings within the two-story **Tooth Temple** date from a later era. The **defensive walls** here have been partly restored. Nestled in a picturesque landscape, the fortress hill is reached by a flight of three hundred steps; you can still see the foundations of the **palace complex**. There is an unforgettable view from the top of the hill, which is deservedly a favorite meditation spot for monks from the present-day monastery.

Panduwas Nuwara – Residence of a King and Hero

Before Parakramabahu I became one of the most important Sinhalese kings (1153-1186), his uncle made over to him Dakkhinadesa, the province southwest of Rajarata. Though no conclusive evidence exists, it is assumed that he made **Panduwas Nuwara** a capital (on the B33 halfway – 35 kilometers – between Kurunegala and Chilaw). This 12th-century complex has yet to be thoroughly excavated and researched. Surrounded by a moat, and itself several feet wide, the wall of the **Citadel** surrounds an area

measuring 300 by 285 meters, with only one entrance, which faces east.

Located within this wall, the **Palace** consists of a central building (30 by 27 meters) made of solid brick walls – which may have supported further stories of wood – and a surrounding gallery. It is very reminiscent of the palace built by Parakramabahu in Polonnaruwa. Here, too, only theories exist about which of the rooms was used for what purpose. Because of an inscription in the first room on the south side, we know that King Nissanka Malla visited this spot to watch dancing displays. Ponds and fountains in other areas of the Citadel were presumably also used for recreational or aesthetic purposes.

Outside the walls, countless dagobas, image houses and other buildings which appear to have been temples and monasteries are scattered around the grounds. There is also a modern monastery which was built atop older ruins; this is a popular goal for pilgrim tourists, who gaze in awe at the remains of the tower in which king Panduwasudewa (fifth century B.C.) kept his daughter Ummani Chitra a prisoner on account of her disastrous prophecies. He himself is said to be buried here, as well. At the entrance to the ruined complex there's a small and somewhat modest **museum**. Directly on the main road a little further east is the **Kotavehera**, a temple whose foundations have been restored and which has an unusually low-lying central room.

Anyone traveling from Kurunegala to Anuradhapura who wants to visit a quiet temple should stop off at **Padeniya Vihara** (A28, 25 kilometers from Kurunegala). It has an image house set atop carved pillars which dates from the Kandy period. You look down from the high location onto a pretty pond dotted with lotus blossoms. The scattered ruins of sentry posts and stone pillars are a reminder that this area was part of the classical Sinhalese empire.

Above: A spunky flower vendor offers his wares.

AVISSAWELLA

Accommodation

MODERATE: **The Plantation Hotel**, 250, Kalukohutenna, Kitulgala, tel. 036-87575.
BUDGET: **Avissawella Rest House**, 250 meters from the bus station, tel. 036-2299. **Kitulgala Rest House**, Ginigatena Road (35 km from Avissawella toward Nuwara Eliya on the A7), tel. 036-87528.

Transportation

BUS: Frequent service to Colombo, Ratnapura, Nuwara Eliya.

COLOMBO

Accommodation

LUXURY: **Ceylon Intercontinental Colombo**, 48 Janadhipathi Mw., Colombo 1, tel. 01-421221. **Colombo Hilton**, Echelon Square, Colombo 1, tel. 01-544644. **Galadari Hotel**, 64 Lotus Road, Colombo 1, tel. 01-544544. **Taj Samudra Hotel**, 25 Galle Face Centre Road, Colombo 3, tel. 01-446622. **The Lanka Oberoi**, 77 Steuart Place, Colombo 3, tel. 01-437437. **Holiday Inn**, 30 Sir Mohamed Macan Markar Mw. Colombo 3, tel. 01-42 2001-9. **Pegasus Reef Hotel**, St. Maria Mw., Wattala (12 km from Colombo Fort, 20 km from Katunayake airport, on the coast), tel. 01-930205-9. **Trans Asia Hotel**, 115 Sir Chittampalam A. Gardiner Mw., Colombo 2, tel. 01-544200.
MODERATE: **Ceylon Inns**, 501 Galle Road, Colombo 6, tel. 01-58 0475. **Galle Face Hotel**, 2 Kollupitya Road, Colombo 3, tel. 01-541010-16. **Grand Oriental Hotel**, 2 York Street, Colombo 1, tel. 01-448734-5. **Hotel Empress**, 383 R.A. De Mel Mw. (Duplication Road), Colombo 3, tel. 01-574930. **Hotel Galaxy**, 388 Union Place, Colombo 2, tel. 01-69 9320. **Hotel Janaki**, 43 Fife Rd., Colombo 5, tel. 01-502169. **Hotel Nippon**, 123 Kumaran Ratnam Road, Colombo 2, tel. 01-431887. **Hotel Ranmuthu**, 112 Galle Road, Colombo 3, tel. 01-43 3986-8. **Hotel Renuka**, 328 Galle Road, Colombo 3, tel. 01-573598. **Hotel Sapphire**, 371 Galle Road, Colombo 6, tel. 01-583306. **Palm Village Hotel**, 262 Colombo Road, Uswetakeiyawa (between airport and Colombo Fort, on the coast), tel. 074-795114.
BUDGET: **Chanuka Guest House**, 29 Frances Road, Colombo 6, tel. 01-585883. **Lake Lodge**, 20 Alwis Terrace, Colombo 3, tel. 01-326443. **Orchid Inn**, 571/6 Galle Rd., Colombo 6, tel. 01-583916. **Ottery Tourist Inn**, 29 Melbourne Ave., Colombo 4, tel. 01-583727. **Tropii Coast**, 18 Sellamuttu Avenue, colombo 3, with internet café, tel. 01-301349. **Villa Palma Holiday Resort**, Beach Road, Pamunugama (on the coast between Colombo and Katunayake), tel. 01-236619. **Wayfarer's Inn**, 77 Rosmead Place, Colombo 7, tel. 01-693936. **Y.W.C.A. Guest Accommodation**, 7 Rotunda Gardens, Colombo 3, tel. 01-323498.

Restaurants

All **luxury-class hotels** have restaurants offering international food as well as a limited selection of local fare. Restaurants with particularly good views over the city include the **Palms** in the **Colombo Intercontinental Hotel**, as well as, to a lesser degree, the **California Grill** in the **Galadari Hotel**.
Don Stanley's, 15th floor, 42 Navam Mw., Colombo 2, tel. 074-719191. **Beach Wadiya**, 2 Station Avenue, Colombo 6 (outstanding fish dishes in very modest surroundings, or under the palm trees directly on the beach of Wellawatte; reservations recommended on weekends and holidays), tel. 01-588568/575367. **Chinese Dragon Cafe**, 232 Galle Road, Colombo 4 (Chinese cuisine, inexpensive), tel. 01-502733. **Chinese Lotus Hotel** (Chinese), 265 Galle Road, Colombo 3, tel. 01-575367. **Chinese Park View Lodge**, 70 Park Street, Colombo 2 (Chinese and Sri Lankan cuisine), tel. 01-326255. **Don Stanley's Café**, 69 Dr. C.W.W. Kannangata Mw., Colombo 7 (high-class international restaurant with several rooms in the upscale district of Cinnamon Gardens), tel. 01-686486. **Gourmet Palace**, 399A De Mel Mw. (Duplication Road), Colombo 3, tel. 01-576400. **Green Cabin**, 453 Galle Road, Colombo 3 (good food, in the shopping district), tel. 01-588811. **Jade Gardens**, 126 Havelock Road, Colombo 5, tel. 01-580678. **Miyako Restaurant**, 45 5th Lane, Duplication Road, Colombo 3 (Japanese and international cuisine), tel. 01-576400. For anyone fed up with rice and curry, try: **Pizza Hut**, 321A Union Place, Colombo 2, tel. 01-333763, take-out service: 01-333760, or **McDonald's**, 498 Galle Rd., Colombo 3. **Paradise Road**, 213 Dharmapala Mw., Colombo 7 (tiny cafeteria with upscale snacks), tel. 01-686043. **Seafish Restaurant**, 15 Sir Chittampalam A. Gardiner Mw., Colombo 2 (very popular seafood restaurant), tel. 01-326915. **Sea Spray Restaurant**, 2 Galle Road, Colombo 3 (in the Galle Face Hotel, fish and all kinds of seafood).

Transportation

AIR: **International Airport Katunayake**, 35 km north of Colombo Fort; information tel. 073-2366 and 073-2377. Domestic flights: **National Airport Ratmalana**, 12 km south of Colombo Fort; flights may be temporarily cancelled for security reasons, see also p. 241. Currently only flights between Colombo and Jaffna.
TRAIN: **Colombo Fort**: The country's most important train station, all towns on the rail network can be accessed by trains from here, information: tel. 01-440048 / 435838. *BUS*: The state bus station (*Central Bus Stand*) is east of the train station of Colombo Fort on Olcott Mw., information: tel. 01-32 8081. A bit to the north, buses run by private firms depart from the Private Bus Stand and the side streets in the area. *TAXI:* The price per kilometer is fixed, but you should still negotiate fares before setting out.

THREE-WHEELER TAXI: These are cheap and quick for traveling short distances; always negotiate the price beforehand.

Tourist Information

Sri Lanka (Ceylon) Tourist Board, 80 Galle Rd., Colombo 3, open Mon-Fri 9 am to 4:30 pm, tel. 01-4370-59/60. Katunayake Airport branch, tel. 01-452411; at the Colombo Fort train station, tel. 01-435838.

Post Office / Telephones

General Post Office (GPO), Janadhipathi Mw., Colombo 1, Poste Restante, tel. 01-326203; counter for standard mail (letters) open 24 hours. **Central Telegraph Office**, Duke Street, Colombo 1, tel. 01-326267. **Internet cafés** see page 246.

Hotel Chain Reservation Offices

Aitken Spence Hotel Managements, 315 Vauxhall St., Colombo 2, tel. 01-447161. **Ceylon Hotels Corporation**, 411 Galle Road, Bambalapitiya, Colombo 4, tel. 01-503497. **Connaissance de Ceylan**, 58 Dudley Senanayake Mw., Colombo 8, tel. 01-685601. **Confifi Group of Hotels**, 33 St. Michael's Rd., Colombo 3, tel. 01-333320. **Jetwing Hotels**, 46/26 Navam Mawatha (Jetwing House), Colombo 2, tel. 01-345700. **Keels Hotel Management Services**, 130 Glennie Street, Colombo 2, tel. 01-421101. **Tangerine Tours**, 236 Galle Rd., Colombo 3, tel. 01-343720-7.

Travel Agencies / Taxi Hire

Aitken Spence Travels, Vauxhall Tower, 305 Vauxhall Street, Colombo 2, tel. 01-345112-24. **Hemtours**, 75 Baybrooke Place (Hemas House), Colombo 2, tel. 01-300001/2. **Jetwing Travels**, 46/26 Navam Mw. (Jetwing House), Colombo 2, tel. 01-345700. **Walkers Tours**, 130 Glennie Street, Colombo 2, tel. 01-421101-15.

Shopping

SHOPPING CENTERS: **Liberty Plaza**, De Mel Mw. / corner Dharmapala Mw., Colombo 3. **Majestic City**, Galle Road, Colombo 4. **Crescat**, 89 Galle Road, beside the Lanka Oberoi Hotel.

BOOKS: **Lakehouse Bookshop**, 100 Sir Chittampalam A. Gardiner Mw., Colombo 2 (very large selection). **Buddhist Cultural Centre**, 125 Anderson Road, Nedimala, Dehiwala (Buddhist books), tel. 01-714256. **International Buddhist Library**, Sri Sambuddhaloka Viharaya, Lotus Road, Colombo 1, tel. 01-435532.

FABRIC, CLOTHING, ARTS AND CRAFTS, ANTIQUES: **Barefoot**, 704 Galle Road, Colombo 3, tel. 01-589305. **Boutique Ranmal**, 646 Galle Road, Colombo 3. **Leather Collections**, 26 Flower Road, Colombo 7. **Odel**, 5 Alexandra Place, Colombo 7; tel. 01-682712. **Folklorica**, 104 Bullers Road, Colombo 7. **Mira Hamsa**, 3 Galle Face Court, Colombo 3. **Kandyan Antiques**, 36 Flower Road, Colombo 7, tel. 01-723287. **Paradise Road**, 213 Dharmapala Mw., Colombo 7, tel. 071-686043.

TEA: **Sri Lanka Tea Board**, 574/1 Galle Road, Colombo 3, tel. 01-582121.

Hospital

General Hospital, 10 Regent Street, Colombo 8, tel. 01-691111.

CHILAW / MARAWILA

Accommodation / Restaurants

MODERATE: **Club Palm Bay**, Marawila, all-inclusive range of sports, tel. 032-54956-9. **Aquarius Beach Hotel**, Beach Road, tel. 032-54888. *BUDGET:* **Mario Beach Hotel**, Beach Road, Marawila, tel. 032-54552/3. **Rest House**, 500 meters west of Puttalam Road, on the beach, Chilaw, tel. 032-22969. **Sanmali Beach Hotel**, Marawila, tel. 032- 54766/7.

Transportation

TRAIN: Colombo and Puttalam several times daily.
BUS: Frequent service to Colombo, several times a day to Puttalam, Anuradhapura, Kurunegala.

Excursions

Munneswaram Kovil and **Panduwas Nuwara** are on the Chilaw-Kurunegala road. The **Panduwas Nuwara Museum** is open daily (except Tue) 8 am to 5 pm.

DEHIWELA-MOUNT LAVINIA

Accommodation

MODERATE: **Mount Lavinia Hotel**, 102 Hotel Road, Mount Lavinia (colonial-style, lovely terrace by the swimming pool), tel. 01-715221-7. **Berjaya Mount Royal Beach Hotel**, 36 College Avenue, Mount Lavinia, tel. 01-739610-5.

BUDGET: **Cottage Gardens**, 42-48 College Avenue, Mt. Lavinia, tel. 01-719692 (pension). **Haus Chandra Hotel**, 37 Beach Road, Mt. Lavinia, tel. 01-732755. **Hotel Riviras**, 50/2 De Saram Road, Mt. Lavinia, tel. 01-717786. **Ocean View Tour Inn**, 34/4 De Saram Road, Mt. Lavinia, tel. 01-738400. **Ranveli Beach Resort**, 56/9 De Saram Road, Mt. Lavinia, tel. 01-717385. **Hotel Sea Breeze**, 22/5A De Saram Road, Mt. Lavinia, tel. 01-714017. **Sea Spray Beach Resort**, 45 Vihara Road, Mt. Lavinia, tel. 01-730532. There are a number of guest houses along Hotel Road, De Saram Road and Station Road.

Restaurants

Frankfurt Lavinia Beer Garden, 38/8 De Saram Rd., Mt. Lavinia, tel. 01-716034. **La Langousterie**, 50/2 De Saram Road, Mount Lavinia (fish specialties) tel. 01-717731. **Mount Grill**, 221 Galle Road, Mount Lavinia, tel. 01-722558. **New Golden Bridge**, 17 Hotel Road, Mount Lavinia, tel. 01-717981.

Transportation

TRAIN: Frequent train service to Colombo and several trains a day to Galle/Matara; not all trains stop at Dehiwela and Mount Lavinia.
BUS: Buses leave for Colombo every few minutes, but if Galle Road is jammed, these are usually slower than the train. There are frequent bus services to Galle.

GAMPAHA

Accommodation

BUDGET: **Rest House**, by the train station, tel. 033-2299.

Transportation

TRAIN: Frequent service to Colombo; most trains to Kandy, Batticaloa, Trincomalee and Anuradhapura stop here.
BUS: Frequent buses to Colombo, as well as service to Kandy and Kurunegala.

Sights

Henerathgoda Botanical Garden, open daily 7:30 am to 5 pm, cars allowed on a few of the park's roads.

HANWELLA / HORANA

Accommodation / Restaurants

BUDGET: **Hanwella Rest House**, on the high banks of the Kelani Ganga, Hanwella, tel. 036-5042. **Horana Rest House**, Rest House Road, Horana, tel. 034-61299.

KALPITIYA

Accommodation

BUDGET: **Rest House**, Main Road, tel. 022-3242.

Transportation

BUS: Several buses a day to Puttalam and Colombo.

Excursions

Boat excursions to **Puttalam** and **Dutch Bay**, as well as to coral reefs and pearl banks; these aren't organized for tourists, so you can simply ask boat-owners in the harbor yourself; **St. Anne's Church**, **Talaivillu**.

KATUNAYAKE

Accommodation

MODERATE: **Airport Garden Hotel**, 234-236 Colombo-Negombo Road, Seeduwa (quiet, on the lagoon, five minutes from the Katunayake Airport), tel. 01-252950. **Hotel Goodwood Plaza**, Canada Friendship Road, Katunayake (on the access road to the airport), tel. 01-252561. **The Tamarind Tree**, Katunayake, tel. 01-253802.
BUDGET: **Sirimedura Hotel**, 842/2 Negombo Road, Seeduwa, tel. 01-253646.

Transportation

BUS: Regular bus service between Katunayake and Colombo, as well as direct buses to and from Kandy.
TAXI: Taxis are always available. To figure out a realistic price frame within which to negotiate, ask the hotel representatives at the airport about the current going rate.

MORATUWA / PANADURA

Accommodation

BUDGET: **Hotel Blue Horizon**, 6 Lady De Soysa Drive, Moratuwa, tel. 01-647120. **Ranmal Holiday Resort**, 346/5 Galle Road, Moratuwa (quiet, on Lake Bolgoda, with a fitness center), tel. 038-98921-2.

Transportation

TRAIN: Suburban trains and passenger trains on the Colombo-Galle/Matara line stop in Moratuwa and Panadura.
BUS: Frequent service toward Colombo and Galle; buses also run from Panadura to Ratnapura.

Excursions

Ratmalana Airport (for domestic and sightseeing flights) see p. 241; headquarters of the **Sarvodaya Organization**: 98 Rawatawatte Road, Moratuwa, tel. 01-647159.

NEGOMBO, WAIKKAL

Accommodation

MODERATE: **Blue Oceanic Beach Hotel** and **Royal Oceanic Hotel**, Ethukala (squash, tennis, Ayurvedic therapy), tel. 031-79000-3. **Browns Beach Hotel**, 175 Lewis Place (squash, tennis, water sports, weight-training room), tel. 031-22031-2. **Camelot Beach Hotel**, 345-347 Lewis Place, tel. 031-22318. **Club Hotel Dolphin** and **Dolphin Cottages**, Kammala, South Waikkal (7 km north of Negombo), tel. 031-33129. **Ranweli Holiday Village**, Waikkal, tel. 031-22136.
BUDGET: **Catamaran Beach Hotel**, 209 Lewis Pl., tel. 031-22206. **Golden Star Beach Hotel**, 163 Lewis Pl., tel. 031-33564-5. **Goldi Sands Hotel**, Ethukala, tel. 031-79021. **Hotel Windmill Beach**, Ethukala, tel. 031-79572. **New Rest House**, Circular Road, tel. 031-79299. **Old Rest House**, "Lagoon View," tel. 031-79199. **Hotel Sea Garden**, Ethukala, tel. 031-79000-3. **Seashells Hotel**, Palangathurai, Kochchikade (north of Negombo), tel. 031-78715. **Sea Spray**, Kochchikade, good value all-inclusive hotel, tel. 031-77549. **Sunflower Beach Hotel**, 289 Lewis Pl., Kudapaduruwa, tel. 031-38154. **Topaz Beach Hotel**, Ethukala, tel. 031-79265.

Restaurants

Several restaurants/bars close to all the beach hotels.

Transportation

TRAIN: Trains to Colombo every two hours or so.
BUS: Buses to Colombo leave every 10 minutes.
TAXI, THREE-WHEELER TAXI: When going to the airport, negotiate the price first!

WADDUWA

Accommodation

MODERATE: **Siddhalepa Ayurvedic Resort**, Samanthara Rd., tel. 034-96967-70. **The Blue Water**, top-class all-inclusive hotel, tel. 034-35067/8. **Villa Ocean View**, Molligodawatte, Wadduwa, all-inclusive, tel. 034-32463.
BUDGET: **Wadduwa Holiday Resort**, 286/3 Galle Road, Wadduwa, tel. 034-32815.

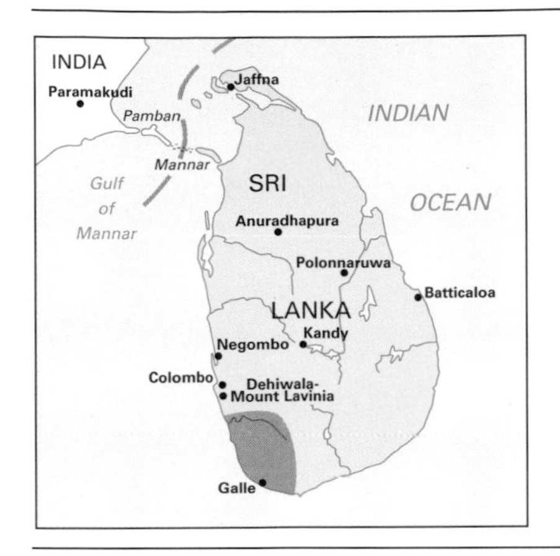

THE SOUTHWEST COAST
A Tropical Paradise

KALUTARA
BERUWALA
BENTOTA / AMBALANGODA
HIKKADUWA
GALLE

KALUTARA

Though the **Kalu Ganga** ("Black River") is only 129 kilometers long, it gives the impression of being a powerful river at the spot where most visitors to Sri Lanka experience it: in the district capital of **Kalutara**, shortly before it flows into the Indian Ocean. Both the A2 road and the railway line cross it at this point. Its navigability from Ratnapura, made possible by several tributaries in the Adam's Peak and Sinharaja Forest regions where rainfall is plentiful, was taken advantage of well into the 20th century by inland shipping traffic. The so-called "coffee boats" transported highland products to the coast, taking anywhere from 20 hours to four days. Today, canoe and inflatable boat tours are available to tourists on the river.

The town's accessible location contributed to its importance. Kalutara, with 35,000 inhabitants, comes across as a big city, with a wide road through its downtown area and a bridge which is extremely long by Sri Lankan standards.

Located directly on the south bank of the river, the temple of **Gangatilaka Vihara**, built near the former ferry dock, lends the town a distinctive appearance. This small old temple, where passing believers pray for a good journey as they drive by, lies on the west side of the main street; on the east side, by contrast, is an enormous white dagoba, which you can see from a considerable distance. An indication of its modern design is a series of windows running around the base of the cupola: this dagoba can be entered. Inside, you discover that this construction is in fact the roof of a circular hall, at the center of which stands a small, white dagoba, which is the actual reliquary. A painted frieze above the windows depicts stories from Buddha's life. Looking out to the northeast, you see the impenetrable vegetation of the river flats and the rubber plantations of the western **Sabaragamuwa Mountains** as far as the dark highland massif, topped, on clear days, by the triangular summit of Adam's Peak. The extensive temple and monastery complex on both sides of the road are connected by an underpass near the river bank. The road has been widened to allow drivers on both sides to stop, say prayers and make offerings without holding up traffic. Small collection boxes are set up at short distances along the road.

During the colonial period, the town's main business activity was the cinnamon

Preceding pages: The beaches of the southwest coast draw tourists from around the world. Left: Fish market of Beruwala.

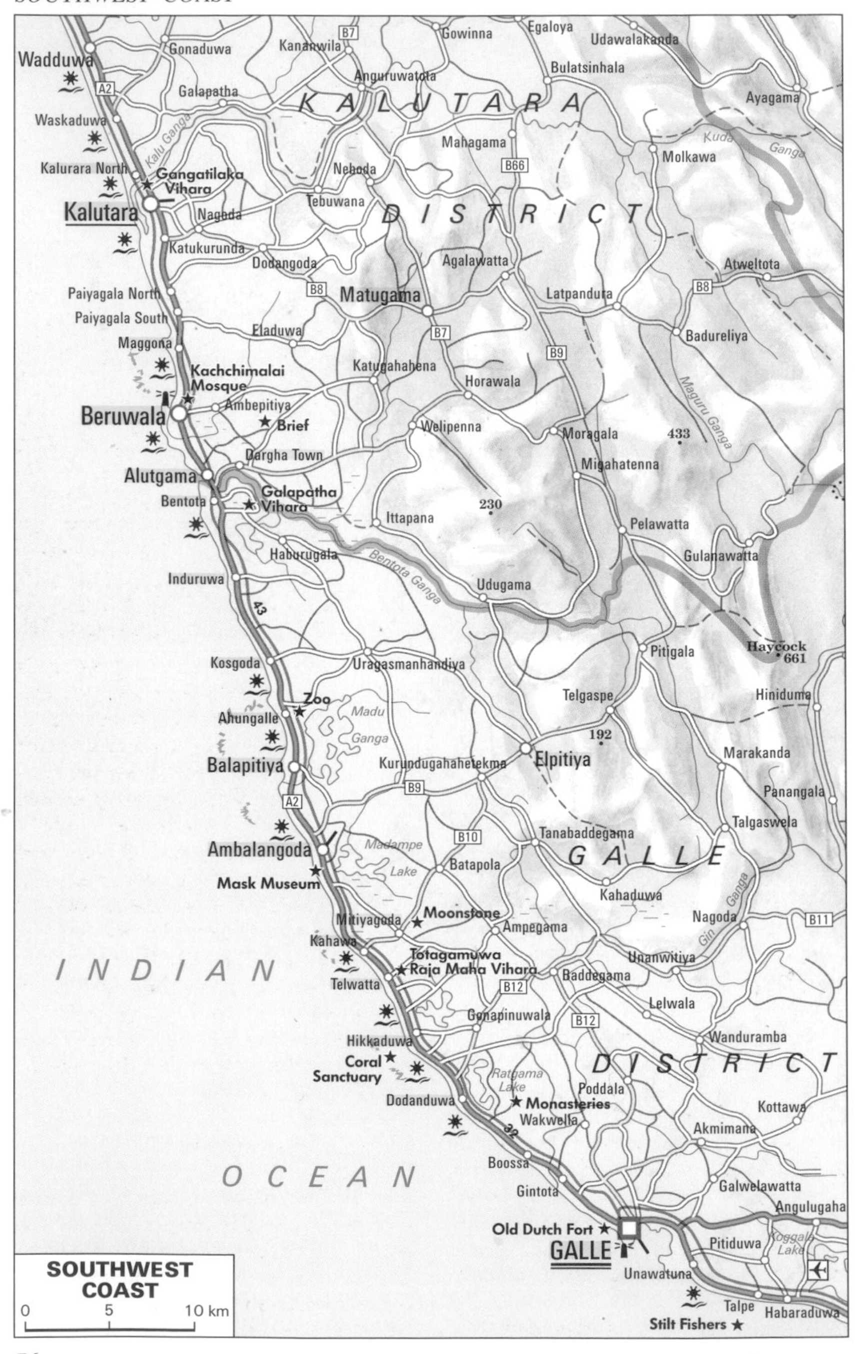

Wadduwa
Gonaduwa
Kananwila
Gowinna
Egaloya
Udawalakanda
Bulatsinhala
Anguruwatota
Galapatha
KALUTARA
Ayagama
Waskaduwa
Kalu Ganga
Mahagama
Kuda Ganga
Molkawa
Kalurara North
Gangatilaka Vihara
Neboda
Kalutara
Tebuwana
Nagoda
DISTRICT
Katukurunda
Dodangoda
Agalawatta
Atweltota
Paiyagala North
Paiyagala South
Matugama
Latpandura
Badureliya
Maggona
Eladuwa
Katugahahena
Horawala
Kachchimalai Mosque
Maguru Ganga
Beruwala
Ambepitiya
Brief
Welipenna
Moragala
433
Dargha Town
Migahatenna
Alutgama
Bentota
Galapatha Vihara
230
Ittapana
Pelawatta
Haburugala
Bentota Ganga
Gulanawatta
Induruwa
Udugama
43
Pitigala
Haycock 661
Kosgoda
Uragasmanhandiya
Telgaspe
Hiniduma
Zoo
Ahungalle
Madu Ganga
192
Balapitiya
Kurundugahahetekma
Elpitiya
Marakanda
Panangala
Talgaswela
Ambalangoda
Madampe Lake
Tanabaddegama
Batapola
GALLE
Mask Museum
Kahaduwa
Gin Ganga
Mitiyagoda
Moonstone
Ampegama
Nagoda
Kahawa
INDIAN
Totagamuwa Raja Maha Vihara
Uranwitiya
Telwatta
Baddegama
Lelwala
Gonapinuwala
Hikkaduwa
Wanduramba
Coral Sanctuary
DISTRICT
Ratgama Lake
Poddala
Dodanduwa
Monasteries
Wakwella
Kottawa
32
Akmimana
Boossa
OCEAN
Gintota
Galwelawatta
Angulugaha
Old Dutch Fort
GALLE
Pitiduwa
Koggala Lake
Unawatuna
Talpe
Habaraduwa
Stilt Fishers
A2
B7
B66
B8
B9
B10
B11
B12
SOUTHWEST COAST
0 5 10 km

trade. Today, though there are still large numbers of cinnamon trees in the hinterland, the area is dominated by coconut groves, rubber plantations and rice paddies. Between May and July, local markets also sell the delicious mangosteen fruits, a specialty of this region. The three-kilometer spit of Kalutara South provides a pleasantly secluded location for a number of hotels. But beyond this area space is in short supply: the road and railway line move ever closer to the coast and finally meet in **Paiyagala**, not far from the church and the **memorial** to Father Joseph Vaz, the Portuguese missionary canonized in 1995 on the occasion of the Pope's visit. Those traveling by car are rewarded by views of the picturesque, palm-lined beach between **Maggona** and **Beruwala**. Any available space on the narrow coastal strip is occupied by fishermen's huts squashed up against the bushy pandanus trees.

BERUWALA

Well-tarred and well-tended, the main road passes through Beruwala. Anyone who prefers to stay near the coast, on the other hand, will have to put up with the potholes when traveling west. The unexpectedly broad curve of the bay ends with a small raised spit of land: the sea swirls powerfully against the rocky projection from the west, but the attractively decorated, snow-white **Kechchimalai Mosque** stands firm on the hill (*malai*), defying the strong winds. Though it does not date back to the first Moors (the Islamic section of the population) in Sri Lanka, it is one of the island's oldest mosques. It is a reminder of the fact that this sheltered bay was the first place that Arabs landed on the island, probably some time in the eighth century, after which they settled down and stayed. Many of their fellow-Muslims were to follow them. Beruwala's population is still predominantly Moorish, mainly employed either in fishing or the gem trade.

Above: Batik – a time-consuming craft.

In a memorial room on the east side of the mosque is the tomb of Sheikh Ashraff. Around the beginning of November, at the end of a 30-day religious service of recitations known as a *bohari mulu*, he is commemorated in a big way. The community prepares a sumptuous celebratory meal, the streets near the mosque are lined with colorful stands, and whole families turn out in their best clothes. As in Muslim communities throughout Sri Lanka, the end of *Ramadan*, the month of fasting (February/March) is also an occasion for celebration.

Malu – Fish!

A long stone wall east of the mosque provides a secure anchorage for hundreds of colorful fishing boats. The larger boats are suitable for deep-sea fishing and go out on tours of about one week, generally with a four-man crew, to fish the grounds

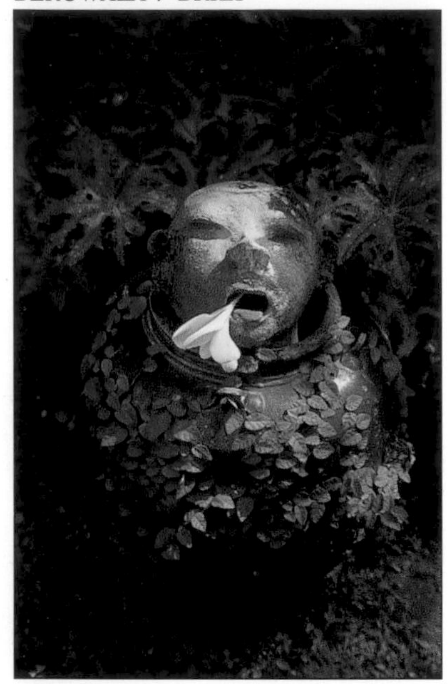

of the Maldive Islands some 400 nautical miles – 740 kilometers – away. The smaller boats, dugout canoes equipped with outriggers, tend to fish at night close to the coast. The fish are auctioned off every morning on the beach opposite the Rest House. Traveling hawkers come on bikes, get some crushed ice from one of the ice factory's waiting trucks, pack their fish into a wooden crate, and fasten it onto their carriers.

Natural Breakwaters

Several small rocky islands, crowned with palms, lie off the coast of Beruwala, acting as natural breakwaters protecting the beach. One of these islands supports an operational lighthouse; its beams circle around the sea every night.

On the southern section of the beach, where coral reefs, rather than islands, provide protection, the fishermen are no longer on their own: in this area, the lush growth of trees and abundant blossoms conceal and separate from one another a number of large hotels and a few smaller ones, all surrounded by forbidding-looking fences, and the larger ones monitored by uniformed security personnel.

Brief – An Artist's Paradise

On the six kilometers of the A2 between Beruwala and **Aluthgama**, large signs reveal the location of most of the hotels which are hidden among the palm groves on the coast. However, souvenir and jewelry stores are also clear indicators of where you'll find the crowds of potential buyers in the sun-chairs around the glistening blue swimming pools. This makes it all the more surprising that the hustle and bustle in the streets of Aluthgama is so typically Sri Lankan. Likewise, there are no signs of tourism on the way to **Dharga Town** (from the center of Aluthgama east on the B7 toward **Matugama**). This by-road is lined with several well-preserved villas in the colonial style. If you're looking for **Brief**, locals will be happy to point out the way from Dharga Town (from the town center, go north and continue for five kilometers). The secluded villa and garden, once home to sculptor Bevis Bawa (1909-1992), brother of famous Sri Lankan architect Geoffrey Bawa, stand in a quiet location between coconut plantations and rice paddies. The villa is the result of more than six decades of loving planning, both by the artist and his friends and helpers. If you're interested in a closer look, you can gain admission to this paradisiacal garden and the elegant, tasteful house.

BENTOTA

The **Bentota Ganga** makes a large curve to the south before turning to flow northward into the Indian Ocean. At this

Above: In the bewitching gardens of the Villa Brief, home to sculptor Bevis Bawa. Right: Mangrove landscape near Bentota.

point, river and sea form a narrow spit of land almost three kilometers long which is a dream location for hotels. Some of these are are accessible only by boat. North of **Bentota**, where there is only a hundred-meter-wide strip of sand between river and sea in places, there is no room for a road. This is why some houses have no land access. What could be more romantic for a newly-arrived visitor than, after hours in an airplane and a bus journey of several more hours, to chug along on a small, comfortable ferry through luxuriant tropical scenery to his holiday destination?

The wide Bentota River and its lagoon-like hinterland are ideal for further boat trips. One destination might be the monastery of **Galapatha Vihara**, although the only relic of the past here is a stone door-frame dating from the 12th century; however, it does allow visitors to survey a modern, brightly-painted temple. The **Bentota Art Center** (south of Bentota on the A2), which is supposed to introduce tourists to the intricacies of local handicrafts, is only open during the tourist season (December to April).

Alcohol Record

Between Induruwa and Kosgoda the road runs along the beach once again, offering attractive views of the sea between the coconut palms. If you look up into the crowns of the coconut trees, you will see many of them joined by two parallel coconut-fiber ropes. The *toddy tappers*, local argot for the palm wine collectors, balance on these in the morning and evening to collect the slightly sour, milky, opaque palm sap from the round buckets placed under the blossoms, and to cut into the stem of the blossom once again to encourage the flow of sap.

This slightly intoxicating beverage is sold to local men from the early morning onwards, but a considerable proportion is transported by ox-cart to the distillery to be made into *arrack* (a spirit form of toddy). Alcoholic drinks are sold throughout the country in licensed stores. In fact,

Sri Lanka is unfortunate enough to hold the somewhat dubious position of the country with the highest alcohol consumption in the world.

One Rupee for a Giant Turtle

In **Kosgoda**, where the road curves back into the hinterland, there are some hotels in wonderful locations, not too crowded together. On some sections of the beach here, there's a special tourist attraction: several organizations are at work trying to save the endangered giant sea turtles. The enormous creatures – their shells can exceed one meter in diameter – lay their eggs, the size of ping-pong balls, in the sand; the main reason their numbers are dwindling is that the poorer segments of the population simply help themselves to the eggs, which are a welcome source of extra protein in an otherwise meager diet. In an attempt to stop eggs being stolen, the "Save the Turtles" organizations pay one rupee for every egg handed over to them. Not a bad source of income, if you are lucky enough to find 100!

Above: Toddy tappers. Right: A giant sea turtle lays its eggs, guarded by conservationists (Kosgoda).

These eggs are then buried in the sand in special fenced-off areas, where the heat causes them to incubate. Once they have hatched, the young turtles are kept in a tank of water for three days to prevent them from being eaten by other sea animals or birds, since their shells are still quite soft. Then, they are released into the sea. Tourists are welcome to take a look, find out about turtles and even release one of the them into the sea themselves. Naturally, donations are also welcome.

Shifting Sands

For visitors, **Ahungalla** has a long sand beach and a renowned five-star hotel to offer. The unblemished light sand along the entire west coast is moved by both sea currents and southwest winds

toward the north. Sand walls come into being, and sand bars stretching northwards form along the coast and on the west side of the wide mouth of the river. The mouths of smaller rivers are protected by breakwaters. If a sand bar blocks the flow of a river, the hinterland is threatened with flooding; when the west wind is strong and the sea is rough, sea water can also pour into the flat hinterland and likewise cause flooding.

AMBALANGODA

South of the important fishing center of **Balapitiya**, the road touches the coast in several places, which meant that the railway line could only be accommodated on the other side of the lagoon marshes. The sand beach here is interrupted in several places by charming smaller bays. **Ambalangoda** is widely known as a fishing and market center. In the town itself there are only a few small hotels, although they do give you a sense of typical Sri Lankan accommodation.

The town is a center for a still-thriving form of southwest-coast folk art: **mask carving** and **dancing**. The two are inextricably linked. A visit to the **Mask Museum**, built with German assistance, or the **Mask Workshop** give a fascinating view of how these masks are created and used. The mask and dance experts of the Wijesooriya family realized that not enough was being done to maintain the traditional mask dances and that they were in danger of being forgotten altogether. With a **Dance School** (diagonally across from the museum; rehearsals in the afternoons) and a workshop, they have succeeded in keeping the old traditions alive.

There are two totally different types of dance-dramas in the area: *kolam*, uplifting and instructional, and *sanni yakuma*, a form of ritual healing through exorcism. *Kolam* plays always require the figures of the king and queen, since they are said to have invented the mask dances. The royal couple wear very elaborate, high masks, and move accordingly

with slow dignity. They form a framework for various funny, serious or didactic Buddhist dance-dramas, usually set in a village environment.

The *sanni yakuma* actually belongs to the area of traditional medicine. If a sick person does not get better after either Ayurvedic (traditional treatment using herbal medicines) or taking Western medicines, this is thought to be due to demons who interfere with the relationship between the sick person and his social environment, thus causing illness. The ritual, in which not only the performance of various dances but also cleansing ceremonies play an important role, consists of luring the demons, appeasing them (paying!), and finally driving them away. The leader of the 18 *sanniyas*, or illness demons, is called *Maha Kola*. His mask face is frightening; it also bears the 18 *sanniyas*, nine on the left and nine on the right, each of them representing a different illness. In addition, each individual *sanniya* has its own characteristic mask. You can buy an informative booklet about masks and dances at the museum. Their sales room stocks a good supply of souvenirs, as do other local stores.

Above: Wood-carvers in Ambalangoda keep an old tradition alive. Right: At the dance school of Ambalangoda.

Around the bus stop in the town center, on the other hand, Sri Lankan commercial life pulsates, and the few small guest houses here are particularly geared to individual travelers who are looking for a bit of local color. The town has a bustling fishing harbor, and is an important center for trade with the densely-populated hinterland. Very few strangers to this part of the world seem to show much interest in the villages along the B9 secondary road heading east towards **Elpitiya**. This town, some 15 kilometers away, is situated at the edge of the southwestern foothills of the Sabaragamuwa region.

Lake Madampe, surrounded by swampy lands, remains invisible to those who choose to remain on the well-paved main road, the A2, which follows the

coast. The lush green shore areas, surrounded by mangroves, can for the most part only be reached by boat. A small river running south of Ambalangoda feeds into the lake. Heading further south, the main road gets closer to the coast, which hereabouts is lined in places by dark towering cliffs.

Moonstones in Mitiyagoda

For the nest 12 kilometers, you can enjoy wonderful views of the Indian Ocean. However, there are also a number of other sights worth seeing off the main road. In **Kahawa**, a by-road branches off into the hinterland and runs the three kilometers to **Mitiyagoda**. A sign indicates the mining here of moonstone. Moonstone is feldspar, a fairly soft mineral and thus not a precious stone in the true sense; by polishing it, however, you can transformed it into gently shimmering moon-colored pieces of jewelry. Mining moonstone is no easy task; should you wish to see the work in progress, have someone take you during working hours to the marshy lowland area where the mines are located.

Following the A2 another two kilometers southwards, and turning off in **Telwatta** onto the road which passes the railway station, you'll come, after a couple of hundred meters, to an intersection and the monastery complex of **Totagamuva Raja Maha Vihara**. The history of this monastery is typical of the fate of legion Buddhist temples throughout the southwestern area of Sri Lanka. It is not clear exactly when the monastery was founded, but four columns on the site are believed to have been built between the 8th and 10th centuries. What is certain is that the temple had already been long in existence by the reign of King Vijayabahu (1055-1110). Until well into the 16th century, it was known as a monastery school or center of academic learning (*pirivena*), going by the name of *Totagamuva Vijayabahu Pirivena* after the place where it was located and its king, who had freed the country from the

southern Indian Cholas. It was an important institution at the time of Totagamuva Sri Rahula, who was the abbot here around the middle of the 15th century and the most outstanding scholar of his time. He was an expert in the Buddhist writings, spoke six languages, and wrote poems which are still praised today. He is also believed to have been the teacher of King Parakramabahu VI (1411-1466). After this period, little mention is made of the monastery, but it must have continued to exist, as it is supposed to have been destroyed in 1580 during the marauding missionary campaign by the Portuguese commander De Souza, during which the famous Devundara shrine (Cape Dondra) was also destroyed. The area was reclaimed by jungle, but around 1765 the site of the famous temple was rediscovered by an abbot from Tangalla. This was a period of revival for the Buddhist faith under King Kirti Sri Rajasinha (1747-1782). Since then, a new monastery has been built on the site (including two statue houses, a dagoba, a capital house, a prayer hall, monks' quarters, a bell tower and two devalas), with many stylistic touches characteristic of the time: most of the buildings date from the late 18th and 19th centuries. This applies to the **wall paintings** as well; these were executed by *sittaras* – local, deeply religious artists. Their depictions of the exemplary life of the Enlightened One (*charithas*) and the admirable deeds of his earlier lives (*jatakas*) were intended to motivate people to follow his example.

Above: Snake-charmer with cobra. Right: Vacation paradise of Hikkaduwa.

Anyone who is familiar with these stories will recognize them on the walls of the image houses, perhaps with the help of a monk, and will appreciate the loving and sensitive style of painting used by these simple but talented artists.

HIKKADUWA

The resort of **Hikkaduwa** extends for several miles along the coast. Some people see it as the incarnation of a tropical paradise; for others, it is the embodiment of a tourist nightmare. Both views are equally justified. The coast, especially the southern section, is wonderful and the quiet hinterland has an exceptional charm; at the same time, no other resort in Sri Lanka has such a large concentration of hotels, guest houses, restaurants and souvenir shops.

The coral reefs for which Hikkaduwa was once so famous have lost their beauty on account of this very fame. The large numbers of foreign visitors have prompted clever locals and foreign residents to try and make the tourists feel as much at home as possible. You can be served here in any language and do not have to go without spaghetti carbonara, German cheesecake, or English breakfasts. Many tourists who come back to Hikkaduwa time and again and feel very much at home here are attracted by the

wide range of tourist facilities at moderate prices and the professional way special tourist needs are dealt with.

Meditation Islands on Ratgama Lake

Not far away from the bustling, loud main road you can find peace and tranquility amid palm groves and flowering private gardens, which absorb the noise. For complete silence, try a boat trip on **Ratgama Lake**, about six kilometers south of Hikkaduwa. To reach it from the busy town of **Dodanduwa**, you can either turn off onto the by-road at the **Kumara Raja Maha Vihara Temple** (a showy building near the station), or take the next minor road further south which leads to the interior (signpost: *Parappaduwa Nuns*). A path leads to the lake shore, where you can generally find a few outrigger canoes for hire. Sitting on the central support beam, relax and let yourself be rowed for an hour or two past shores lined with mangroves and around the lake's islands, watching the native kingfishers, cormorants, crocodiles and monitor lizards, or simply enjoying the tranquility. You can only visit the two islands, **Parappaduwa** and **Polgasduwa**, if you've been invited beforehand. They accommodate a meditation convent and monastery; there are a number of foreigners among the monks and nuns. Guests are welcome to look around the **Gangarama Temple** on the lake's western shore. A monastery student will unlock the image house so that visitors can admire the very realistic groups of statues which illustrate dramatic situations from some extremely gruesome legends.

GALLE

From here, the main road keeps to the coast all the way to **Galle**. A peninsula extending about one kilometer to the south shelters the large bay at Galle on the side affected by the southwest monsoon, making this location unique on the entire west coast. However, large rocks, shallows and coral reefs make it difficult

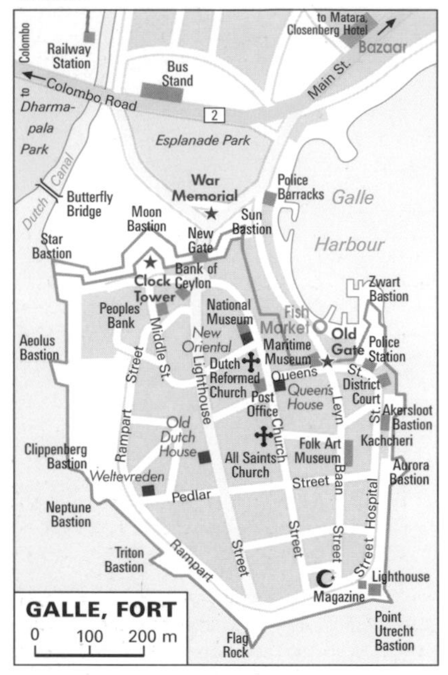

to enter the bay. When the harbor in Colombo was expanded at the end of the 19th century, Galle had to relinquish its position as the island's most important port city. Today it is the province and district capital, an industrial center, and headquarters for a large number of businesses, particularly those owned by Moors. With 90,000 inhabitants, Galle has the largest population concentration in the southwest of Sri Lanka.

Many visitors to the town make directly for the **Fort**. Forbidding, and discouragingly high (for any would-be intruder), the gray defensive walls, with their three bastions, tower up on the far side of the firing range. The Dutch built these walls after they had taken the previous small fort from the Portuguese in 1640. After building a fortification around the peninsula, they erected, within it, a settlement with streets laid out on a checkerboard grid. The only access was east of the three main bastions at the harbor, where there is still a small gate (**Old Gate**). In 1796, the English took over from the Dutch and built the **New Gate** in the wall on the land side, which is the point of entry for most traffic today.

A short distance away, the narrow **Clock Tower**, dating from 1883, rises up, marking the spot from where you can enjoy a view from the wall over the esplanade and the big city spread out behind it. You have fine views of the sea from the southernmost of the three bastions, from **Flag Rock**, or from the **Lighthouse**. Below the Lighthouse is a crumbling old building which the Dutch erected as a powder magazine in 1782. Opposite it stands a gleaming white **mosque** with two towers, a reminder of the large Moorish population of the Fort today. Many of the houses date from the colonial period, and some are open to the public: **Old Dutch House**, a small guest house on Lighthouse Street; a magnificently-restored **private museum** with sales rooms on Leyn Baan Street; the **Dutch Reformed Church** (1754) on Church Street; or, right next to it, the **New Oriental Hotel** with its colonial charm, built in 1684 to house Dutch and, later, British offices, which has been a hotel since 1863. The adjacent **National Museum** also recreates the world of the colonial era. Along Queen's Street, past **Queen's House** (the former British governor's residence, now offices), the traffic is heavier than it is anywhere else in this generally quiet city: this is the route to the law courts and several administrative buildings. The gatehouse from the Dutch period, emblazoned with the coat-of-arms of the Dutch East India Company, now houses an interesting **marine museum** and leads to the **harbor**.

The east side of the harbor bay is also flanked by a peninsula. Captain Bailey built his villa here, with a view of the sea, towards the end of the 19th century; it has since been converted into the elegant **Closenberg Hotel**, surrounded by landscaped gardens.

AHUNGALLA

Accommodation

LUXURY: **Triton Hotel**, Galle Road, tel. 09-6404. *MODERATE:* **Lotus Villa**, No. 162/19 Waturegama, Ayurveda hotel. Minimum stay of 14 days. An introductory day can be arranged, tel. 09-64082.

Transportation

TRAIN and *BUS* along the Colombo-Galle route.

Excursions / Activities

Elephant Rides on the grounds of the Triton Hotel; **Boat Tours** on the Madu Ganga River and the adjoining lagoon: **Sarasi Boat Service**, 206 Galle Road, Bridge View (sea side), Balapitiya (ca. 4 km south of Ahungalla); **Day Trips** see Aluthgama, Ambalangoda, Bentota, Beruwala, Dodanduwa, Galle, Hikkaduwa, Kosgoda.

ALUTHGAMA
(see also BENTOTA, BERUWALA)

Accommodation

LUXURY: **Eden Hotel**, Kaluwamodara, tel. 034-76075. **Lanka Princess**, Kaluwamodara; Ayurveda; tel. 034-76711. *BUDGET:* **Blue Lagoon Guest House**, 3rd Lane, Rantembligahawatta, Kaluwamodara, tel. 034-76062. **Dilmini Tourist Guest House**, 304 Welipanna Rd., tel. 034-75052. **Hemadan**, 25A Hotel Sea Sands Road (on Bentota River), tel. 034-75320. **Nilwala**, Galle Rd., Kaluwamodara (with a watersports center, Bentota River), tel. 034-75017. **Mutumuni Lagoon Resort**, 16 Galle Rd., Moragalla (Ayurveda center, small hotel and restaurant, pool, lagoon view), tel. 034-76766. **Queen River Inn**, 28 Galle Rd., Kaluwamodara, tel. 034-75460. **Terrena Lodge**, River Ave. (Bentota River), tel. 074-289015.

Transportation

TRAIN: Express trains on the Colombo-Galle route stop at Aluthgama. *BUS:* There is a major bus station at the halfway point between Colombo and Galle, also countless connections to destinations inland.

Excursions / Activities

As the Bentota River is less than ideal for swimming, the small hotels along the river generally offer their guests free boat transfers to the nearby sea coast. But you can windsurf, waterski etc. on the river itself under professional supervision: **Water Sports Center Rani**, Hotel Nilwala, Galle Road, Kaluwamodara, tel. 034-75228. There are additional activities in the beach hotels of Bentota or Beruwala, north of Aluthgama. In the hinterland, 4 km north of Dharga Town: **Brief**, villa and park-like gardens of sculptor Bevis Bawa, who died in 1992; open daily 8 am-5 pm, admission 125 Rs.

AKURALA / AMBALANGODA

Accommodation

There are no large hotels either in the centrally located town of Ambalangoda or Akurala, 4 km further south. Groups of rocks or cliffs often divide the beaches here into attractive bays. *MODERATE:* **Dream Beach Resort**, 509 Galle Rd., Ambalangoda, tel. 09-58873. **Sun Oriental Resorts**, 786 Galle Rd., Randombe, Ambalangoda, ayurvedic treatments. *BUDGET:* **Blue Horizon Tour Inn**, 129 Main Street, Ambalangoda, tel. 09-58475. **Hotel Beauty Coral**, Akurala (on the beach). **Ocean Reef Hotel**, Akurala (on the beach). **Orchid Lodge**, Randombe, Ambalangoda. **Rest House**, Ambalangoda (on the sea), tel. 09-58299. **Shangrela Beach Resort**, 38 Sea Beach Road, Ambalangoda, tel. 09-58342. **Sumudu Tourist Guest House**, 418 Main Street, Patabendimulla, Ambalangoda (large private house, informal atmosphere, good food, near the Mask Museum).

Restaurant

Sea Food Restaurant, Parrot Junction, Madampagama (on the sea).

Transportation

TRAIN: Ambalangoda is a stop on the express train line from Colombo-Galle. *BUS:* Frequent connections to Galle and Colombo, as well as inland destinations.

Excursions / Activities / Sights

Mask Museum, 426 Patabendimulla (on the sharp bend in the A2 at the north entrance to town), Ambalangoda, open daily 8 am to 6 pm – there's an adjacent workshop where masks are made, and a shop; **Traditional Dance School**, diagonally opposite the Mask Museum, rehearsal times Mon to Fri 2 to 5 pm; **Batik**, M. Dudley Silva, 53 Elpitiya Road, Ambalangoda.

BENTOTA
(see also ALUTHGAMA, INDURUWA)

Accommodation

LUXURY: **Bentotal Beach Hotel** (on the peninsula between the Bentota River and the sea), tel. 034-74176. **Tai Exotica**, Natl. Holiday Resort, tel. 034-75650. *MODERATE:* **Hotel Ceysands** (between river and sea, access by ferry only), tel. 034-75073. **Hotel Serendib**, tel. 034-75248. **Lihiniya Surf Hotel**, National Holiday Resort, tel. 034-75126. **Hotel Club Paradise** (on the peninsula), Sri Budhasa Ayurveda Center, tel. 034-75354. **Ayurveda Walauwa**, Galle Road (colonial-style villa in well maintained gardens, away from the beach and road, Ayurveda, yoga), tel. 034-75372-3. **Club Villa Benota**, 138/15 Galle Road (colonial-style villa), tel. 034-75312. **Villa Taprobana**, 146/4 Galle Road, Rabolgoda (nine rooms, restaurant, large garden), tel. 034-75618. **The Villa (Mohotti Walauwa)**, 138/18 and 138/22 Galle Road (15 rooms in colonial-style villa), tel. 034-75311. *BUDGET:* **Hotel Susantha**, Resort Road, Pitaramba, tel. 034-55554.

Restaurants

There are restaurants in all the larger hotels and in **Susantha**; countless smaller restaurants are located to the south of Bentota.

Transportation

TRAIN: Many of the trains between Colombo and Galle stop here, but not all of the express trains.
BUS: Regular service to Colombo and Galle.

Excursions / Activities

Most hotels offer their guests boat trips on the Bentota River, but the noisy motor boats scare off the animals. On outrigger boats, which are paddled, you'll get a better impression of the tranquil mangrove lagoons. Accessible both on the river and by land is the **Galapatha Vihara** monastery, 4 km east of the A2. **Sports:** *Club Intersports* (CIS) between the Ceysands and Bentota Beach hotels offer jet-skiing, water-skiing, surfing, as well as tennis and squash.

BERUWALA
(see also ALUTHGAMA)

Accommodation

LUXURY: See ALUTHGAMA.
MODERATE: **Barberyn Reef Ayurvedic Resort**, Moragalla (long bathing beach, protected by a coral reef which often shelters it from the southwest monsoon, Ayurvedic treatments), tel. 034-76036. **Beach Hotel Bayroo**, Moragalla (variety of sports, plus a coral reef protecting the beach), tel. 034-76297. **Confifi Beach Hotel**, Kaluwamodara, tel. 034-76217. **Club Palm Garden**, Kaluwamodara, tel. 034-76115. **Hotel Swanee**, Moragalla (pleasantly small, good value all-inclusive deals), tel. 034-76006. **Neptune Hotel**, Moragalla, extensive all-inclusive complex, tel. 034-76031/2. **Riverina Hotel**, Kaluwamodara, Ayurvedic treatments, tel. 034-76044. **The Villa Riviera**, Moragalla, tel. 034-76245. **Tropical Villas Hotel**, Moragalla, 400 meters from the beach, tel. 034-76157. **Wornels Reef Hotel**, Moragalla, tel. 034-76043.
BUDGET: **Hotel Berlin Bear**, Maradana Road (on the beach, in the Muslim quarter), tel. 034-76525. **Nanda Tourist Inn**, Galle Rd., Moragalla (five rooms with shower/toilet, small restaurant), tel. 034-76066. **Sagarika Holiday Bungalow**, Beach Side, Moragalla (10 rooms with shower/toilet, restaurant, bar, sea view), tel. 034-76074. **Hotel Sumadai**, Bandarawatte (near fishing harbor, 16 rooms, restaurant, bar, music, boat tours to the lighthouse island), tel. 034-76404. **Rest House**, opposite the harbor. **Ypsylon Guest House**, Moragalla (with diving school), tel. 034-76132.

Restaurants

Restaurants in every hotel, and countless small restaurants near the hotels, generally with Western food; near the town you'll find local restaurants.

Transportation

TRAIN: The Bentota train station is several miles from any of the hotels; the Aluthgama train station tends to be more convenient, and express trains on the Colombo-Galle route also stop there.
BUS: Bus station at the center of town; private buses and mini-buses will stop on request by the access roads to the hotels.

Sights

A **fish market** takes place every morning after sunrise at the harbor shore opposite the Rest House. The **Kechchimalai Mosque** at the end of the harbor can only be viewed from the outside.

DODANDUWA

Accommodation / Restaurant

BUDGET: **Dream Village**, 414 Galle Road (*cabanas* on a lonely bay). **Lake Rest**, "Santhohini". **Ocean Beach Club**, Pathuwata. **Sea Side Inn**, Pathuwata (12 rooms, without AC, inexpensive), tel. 09-77413. **Summer Inn**, Galle Road. **Sun Lagoon Inn**, Sri Saranajothi Mw. There are countless Guest Houses on the beach and east of the road.

Transportation

TRAIN: Passenger trains on the Colombo-Galle route stop here. *BUS:* Countless stops along the A2.

Excursions / Activities

Outrigger canoe rides can be arranged on quiet **Ratgama Lake**; the best time to see the animal life is early morning or late afternoon.
For a visit to the **Gangarama Temple**, access is from the lake as well as from town.
A visit to the international **Buddhist Monastery** on Polgasduwa island or the **Convent** on Parappaduwa is possible by prior arrangement only.
The **Kumarakanda Temple** is near the train station; access to all.

GALLE

Accommodation

LUXURY: **Light House Hotel**, Dadella, tel. 09-23744.
MODERATE: **Lady Hill Hotel**, 29 Upper Dickson Rd., colonial-style villa with a view of the fort, 15 rooms, tel. 09-44322. *BUDGET:* **Closenberg Hotel**, Magalle (colonial-style building east of the harbor bay, in landscaped gardens), tel. 09-24313. **New Oriental Hotel**, 10 Church Street (in the fort, oldest hotel on the island), tel. 09-34591. **Old Dutch House**, 46 Light House Street (in the historic fort, quiet guest house), tel. 09-22370. **Hotel Weltevreden**, 104 Pedlar St., Fort (seven rooms), tel. 09-22650.
PRIVATE ROOMS (PAYING GUEST ACCOMMODATION): **Mrs. Shakira Khalid**, 106 Pedlar St., Fort (3 rooms), tel. 09-34907. **Dr. Stanley P. Ladduwahetty**, 3 Rampart St., Fort.

Restaurants

In the Closenberg Hotel and the New Oriental Hotel, both have colonial atmosphere.

Transportation

TRAIN: The train station is situated less than 1 km from the Fort, all express trains from Colombo-Matara stop here; direct train to Anuradhapura once a day.

BUS: The bus station is located near the Fort; regular departures for Colombo; frequent services eastwards to destinations along the south coast. Local buses toward Ratnapura.

Sights / Museums

Tours of the historic **Fort** last approximately one hour; **National Museum**, Church Street, next to the New Oriental Hotel, open daily except Mondays and Tuesdays, 9 am to 4:30 pm; **Maritime Museum**, Old Gate, open daily 9 am to 5 pm; **Historical Mansion**, museum, art gallery and sales room, 31, 39 Leyn Baan Street, Fort, open 8 am to 6 pm, tel. 09-34114; **Natural Silk Factory**, 691 Colombo Road, Gintota (4 km west of Galle, with sales room for silk fabric and clothing), tel. 09-23379.

HIKKADUWA

Accommodation

MODERATE: **Blue Corals Hotel**, 332 Galle Road, tel. 09-77679. **Coral Gardens Hotel**, Galle Road (largest hotel in town, diving school, glass-bottomed boat, the dock is a good place for ocean swimming), tel. 09-77180-9. **Hikkaduwa Beach Hotel**, 298 Galle Road, tel. 09-77327. **Hotel Lanka Supercorals**, 390 Galle Road, tel. 09-77387/8/9. **Hotel Reefcomber**, 57 Galle Road, tel. 09-77374. *BUDGET:* **Coral Front Inn**, 279 Mian Rd. (500 meters from train station, beer garden, Internet, inexpensive). **Coral Reef Beach Hotel**, 336 Galle Rd., tel. 09-77197. **Hotel Pardiso**, 406 Galle Rd. (15 rooms, seafood restaurant), tel. 09-77654. **Pearl Island Beach Hotel**, Thiranagama Junction (at the southern edge of Hikkaduwa, lovely beach, few tourists). **Sea View Hotel**, 295 Galle Rd. (six rooms with balcony, sea view), tel. 09-77677. **Sunils Beach Hotel**, Narigama (southern district of Hikkaduwa with a lovely beach), tel. 09-77187. *In the hinterland (not on the beach):* **Bird Lake**, Baddegama Rd., Pathana (situated on a lake in a large park, 2 kilometers from Hikkaduwa), tel. 09-77018. **Lawrence Hill Paradise**, 47 Waulagoda (20 rooms in bungalow style set in extensive gardens, only a five-minute walk to the beach, swimming pool, diving school), tel. 09-77544. **Plantation Hotel**, Baddegama Road (10-minute drive to Hikkaduwa; in plantation area, bird watching, Sri Lankan food), tel. 09-52405.

Restaurants

Restaurants in all hotels, along Galle Road and the beach; especially popular is the relaxed atmosphere of Narigama with the **Black Rock Cafe**, **Blue Moon Restaurant**, **Brother's Spot**, **Hemingway**, **Ranjith's Restaurant** (popular, noisy), **Rita's Restaurant**, **Sunrise Restaurant**, and others. Farther north, toward town center: **Blue Fox**, **Curry Bowl Restaurant**.

Transportation

TRAIN: Almost all the trains on the Colombo-Galle route stop here. Hikkaduwa extends several kilometers along the coast, so most hotels are not very close to the station.

BUS: Regular bus service to Colombo and Galle, several buses a day run directly to Katunayake airport.

Vehicle Rental

Cars, motorcycles and bikes can be rented at a large number of vehicle rental firms in Hikkaduwa. Make sure to test your vehicle before signing for it!

Water Sports

Poseidon Diving Station, Galle Road, tel. 09-57294. Many hotels offer water sports and rent out equipment.

Excursions / Activities

There is a very wide range of vehicle rental companies and excursion organizers.

INDURUWA / KOSGODA

Accommodation

INDURUWA: *LUXURY:* **Saman Villas**, Aturuwella (small luxury hotel amongst the rocks, surrounded by beach on both sides), tel. 034-75433. *MODERATE:* **Induruwa Beach Resort**, Galle Road, modern complex with all-inclusive program, tel. 034-75445. *BUDGET:* **Emerald Bay Hotel**, Galle Rd. (lovely beach), tel. 034-75363. **Long Beach Cottage**, Galle Road (on beach, all rooms with sea view, free transfer from Aluthgama station), tel. 034-75773. **Venus Tourist Beach Resort**, Kaikawala. **Whispering Palms**, Galle Road, tel. 034-70203.

KOSGODA: *MODERATE:* **Kosgoda Beach Resort**, Nape (well maintained, on the beach), tel. 09-64017. *BUDGET:* **Miriama Beach**, Galle Road.

Transportation

TRAIN: Passenger trains on the Colombo-Galle route stop at Induruwa, Maha Induruwa and Kosgoda.

BUS: Frequent services to Colombo and Galle.

Excursions / Activities

Both Kosgoda and Induruwa each have a **turtle hatchery**, where you can visit the breeding places as well as the pools with both baby and adult turtles. Money donations welcome!

KALUTARA

(see also WADDUWA, page 71)

Accommodation

LUXURY: **Royal Palms Beach Hotel**, De Abrew Road, Waskaduwa, tel. 034-28113-7. *MODERATE:* **Golden Sun Resort**, Kudawaskaduwa, Kalutara North, new beach hotel with both superior and standard rooms, tel. 034-28484. **Hibiscus Beach Hotel**, Mahawaskaduwa, tel. 034-22704. **Hotel Mermaid**, Kalutara N., tel. 034-22613. **Tangerine Beach Hotel**, De Abrew Road, Waskaduwa, tel. 034-22295. **The Sindbad**, St. Sebastian's Rd., Katukurunda, tel. 034-22537. *BUDGET:* **Garden Beach Hotel**, 62/9 Sri Sumangala Mw., Kalutara North, tel. 034-22380.

THE SOUTH
Pilgrims' Routes, Dream Coasts

UNAWATUNA
WELIGAMA
MATARA
DONDRA
TANGALLA

UNAWATUNA

Sri Lanka's tranquil south begins east of Galle's generous harbor bay. The roads get rougher, the towns smaller, and the bays, surrounded by rocks, quieter and more isolated. **Unawatuna**, a small bathing resort, is a paradise for insiders – for the time being, at least. From here, the main road (A2) continues for a number of kilometers along the coast. Large, modern hotels have sprung up in **Talpe** and **Koggala** in response to the great need for accommodation. This is an ideal location for anyone who is seeking nothing more than sand, sea, palm trees and comfort. Koggala is no longer dependent on tourism alone, however. In 1992, a free-trade zone was set up east of the airport and close to the road and railway line, creating more than a thousand jobs. Author Martin Wickramasinghe (1890-1976) lived in Koggala, and the **Folk Art Museum** named after him is worth visiting.

In **Ahangama**, paintings in the **Kataluwa** temple complex provide excellent examples of the talent of local 19th-century artists. The fishermen in Ahangama have developed a special method of catching fish without boats and without any threat from the massive breakers crashing along this shore: they perch on stilts fixed firmly in the sand of the shallow coastal area, and cast out their lines.

Preceding pages: Buddhist monks still enjoy high popular esteem. Left: On the beach of Unawatuna.

WELIGAMA

Weligama is also known for its stilt fishermen. Near the ceramics stores as you enter the town, an asphalt road branches off to the north. It crosses the railway line, passes through rice and garden country, and meets the winding railway line a second time. Just before it does so, you come to a carefully fenced-off and well-tended lawn area with two boulders. These are part of a **Natha Devala**. A richly-decorated statue some four meters high has been carved from the larger boulder. Medallions bearing *Samadhi* (meditating) Buddhas adorn the piled-up coiffure.

The figure, dressed like a rich prince, has both hands raised, the right hand in a *vitarka mudra* (instructional gesture); the gesture made by the left hand is not clear. Such *Bodhisattvas* were created in Sri Lanka under the temporary influence of *Mahayana Buddhism* between the 8th and 10th centuries. Though it remains unclear whom the figure represents, it is popularly called **Kustaraja** ("Leper

King"), which would indicate its being a protector against skin ailments; it is therefore plausible that the figure represents the *Bodhisattva* Avalokiteshvara, the compassionate ruler of the worlds.

Weligama, population 20,000, is a busy center for the surrounding rural area. Anyone looking for a tranquil spot on the beach will find it on the west side of this almost four-kilometer-long bay, where the A2 (the through road) does not run near the beach. Another spot that's guaranteed to be quiet is **Mirissa** on the east side of the bay, beyond the bridge over the Polwatta Ganga.

MATARA

The varied route through palm forests, past settlements hidden in dense greenery and attractive sections of coast, leads to the district capital, **Matara**, an important traffic hub. The railway line, which more or less follows the A2 from Colombo, ends here, at least until construction is completed on the extension of the line eastwards to Kataragama. The journey to Colombo takes four hours by train.

As a port on the mouth of the **Nilwala Ganga**, Matara has been overtaken in importance by Galle. However, the river determines the course the road takes into the northern hinterland. The main road (A23), which joins up with the A17 south of Akuressa, accompanies the river to the area where it has its source, namely the Sabaragamuwa Mountains, then continues on to Ratnapura. At the edge of the mountains, a few miles north of Matara, you encounter the first tea and rubber plantations on the rolling hills.

Matara has a good 40,000 inhabitants, several modern, air-conditioned stores in its center, and the Broadway Cinema. Heavy traffic rushes over the wide bridge across the Nilwala River, and on the eastern outskirts the campus of **Ruhuna University** is a town highlight; even so, there's still room in the downtown area for a little-used horse racetrack. The old **Dutch Fort** appears very solid; the central bus station adjacent to it seems oversized; and the **clock tower** behind the fort walls, which rises up higher than all of them, has something of a solitary air. The Portuguese also used the old harbor at the mouth of the Nilwala, and the Dutch secured it by building typical 18th-century fortifications. Walls and a narrow gate barricade the promontory dividing the Nilwala River from the sea. Today, this fort accommodates apartments, schools, administrative offices, the old **Dutch Church**, and, on the side facing the sea, several hotels and the Rest House.

On the north side of the river next to the racetrack, the Dutch built another defense in 1765: the **Star Fort**, a small but imposing star-shaped fortification. The fort was further protected by a moat and was entered through a gateway decorated with a coat-of-arms. Inside there is

Above: Stilt fishermen are the attraction at Weligama. Right: A modern dagoba in Weligama.

a low pentagonal building with a courtyard. Today, it houses the **Museum of Ancient Paintings**, a small but excellent museum which leads one to forget altogether that the building was originally put to military use. Here, you can observe copies of wall paintings from throughout the country, from pre-Sinhalese animal drawings through paintings from the classical Sinhalese period and the Kandy era up to the modern period. One particular emphasis is on the colorful decoration of the temples in the southern provinces. Don't be put off by the Sinhalese writing in the descriptions of the works; it's worth taking the time to engage the help of one of the obliging museum assistants. Anyone with a genuine interest can learn a wealth of fascinating facts and see some of Sri Lanka's lesser-known treasures.

Two Giant Buddhas

Less valuable, but making up for this in terms of size and therefore ideal for the many busloads of pilgrims who flock here, is the Purvarama Maha Raja Vihara monastery in **Vehera-hena**, three kilometers east of Matara (signposted from the main road). The seated, brightly-painted outdoor figure of the Samadhi Buddha is 39 meters high. Sheltering his back and sides is a five-story image house, which continues underground in a basement level extending under the lotus pond at the front of the complex. About 20,000 pictures adorn this labyrinth of rooms, stairways and corridors. As usual, the life of the Buddha and *jatakas*, or stories from his earlier lives, are depicted in great detail. In addition, some of the walls are decorated with portraits of contemporary citizens who donated large sums of money to the temple; their names, as well as the sums they donated, are clearly written under their pictures. From the upper floor of the complex there is a view of the rice-growing lands of the Nilwala flats and the surrounding region of palm trees and gardens.

The Buduraja Temple in **Wewurukannala**, 20 kilometers further east,

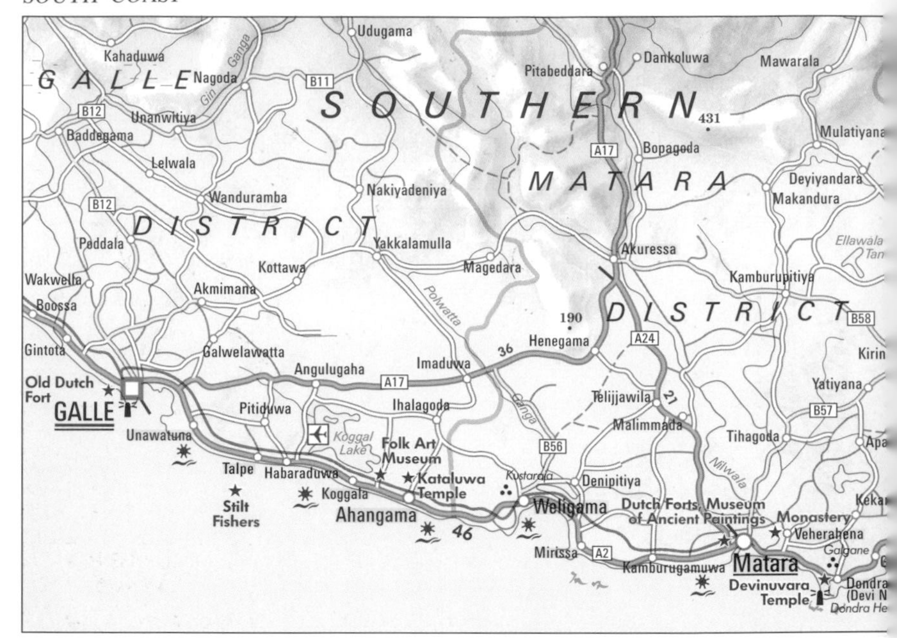

seems like an attempt to go the temple in Veherahena one better. Here, the Samadhi Buddha (1975) is 50 meters high and, rather than a coat of paint which can easily fade, it was given a lower-maintenance surface of mosaic stones. Here, too, a building supports the sitting Buddha, but most of it, up to the observation platform, is hidden behind the coconut palms. The temple and monastery complex form a unit which has been developing for centuries: the dagoba and bo tree standing on a raised terrace; a small 350-year-old image house and a large one adorned with baroque decorations dating from the mid-19th century; as well as an assembly house and accommodation for the monks, all grouped around a large square.

DONDRA

The two temples with the gigantic Buddha statues are just a few miles away from the main road, which in July/August is crowded with pilgrims making for Kataragama to the east. The Buddhist **Devinuvara Temple** in **Dondra** (the southernmost point of Sri Lanka) lies directly on their route. An imposing two-story Vishnu *devala* and a standing gigantic Buddha almost dominate the site, but Shiva and other Hindu and Buddhist gods can also be worshiped here. Consequently, whether the pilgrims journeying to Kataragama are Hindu or Buddhist, both religious groups are equally accommodated. Many pilgrims even have Dondra as their final destination in July/August, when there is a 10-day *perahera*, a magnificent procession.

In the Middle Ages there must have been a rich and famous Upulvan, or Vishnu temple, at the southern tip of the island. However, the Portuguese destroyed it completely in the 16th century, and its exact location remains unknown. Whether the small, simple building of hewn stone, said to date from the seventh century and just a short distance north of the temple in **Galgane**, belongs to this Upulvan complex or not remains uncer-

tain (follow the short road north of the clock tower in Dondra; one kilometer).

The A2 goes through **Gandara**, three kilometers east of Dondra. The community's temple here has been renovated thanks to the enthusiasm of the local monks, a lot of *shramadana*, or unpaid teamwork by local community members, and the know-how of the archeological service. The Purana Maha Vihara is on a small elevation directly south of the road in a section of thin forest. It has an image house with paintings from the Kandy period, and is a generally attractive complex, decorated with colorful flowers. The town's welfare office is also here.

Dramatic Coast

On its way to **Dikwella**, the A2 keeps winding its way along picturesque sections of coastline; by the time you get to the town center, you've already passed a number of hotels and the broad road branching off to Beliatta. Groups of rocks thrusting their way into the sea repeatedly force the road to detour inland until just before Tangalla. Despite this, there are small access roads to the fishing villages located on the secluded bays.

To reach **Kudawella**, with its trim fishing boats, turn south between the milestones 185 and 186 (signpost: People's Bank). At the extreme tip of the bay, which can only be reached on foot, you can observe an amazing natural phenomenon when there are strong breakers during the southwest monsoon: masses of water are forced into cracks in the rocks at great pressure, and spray out high into the air like a fountain, accompanied by an incredible roaring sound. Locals are quick to spot visitors wandering lost through the confusing tangle of village paths and, sensing that they're looking for the **blow hole**, point them in the right direction.

TANGALLA

Even before you get to **Tangalla**, you notice the Tangalla Bay Hotel. The Sri

Lankan architect Valentin Gunasekera set it like a stylized ship upon the coastal spit with its many cliffs. It offers a panoramic view of the sea.

Government institutions, such as the post office, police station, naval base, hospital and the Rest House are all located on the hill facing the sea just before you enter Tangalla. Around the harbor area with its fleet of colorful fishing boats visitors can also find accommodation and restaurants. The marketplace is the center of activity; from here, a by-road leads to the rural center of **Beliatta**.

Mulkirigala

There is an attractive road through coconut groves and valleys with rice paddies to the 211-meter rock temple of **Mulkirigala** (signposted from Beliatta). From the present-day monks' accommodation at the foot of the immense rock, you ascend via numerous steps to a series of natural caves which were inhabited by monks as early as the first century B.C. It is possible to see the hand-made drip ledges on the overhanging rocks. Special structures, recently built, now protect seven caves located at different levels. All have wall paintings and contain numerous sculptures of the Buddha. The works of art are not as old as the monastery, but were continually changed and updated to reflect the fashions of the day. Most of the paintings date from the 19th century and depict legends from Buddha's life. In 1827, George Turnour found an important commentary on the *Mahavamsa* ("Great Chronicle") in the monastery library.

There is a gleaming white dagoba on the very top of the rock, and the view from here is incomparable. To the south the sea is visible some 15 kilometers away; to the north the jagged peaks of the hill country; while to the east you can get some idea of the jungle, which becomes sparser from here onwards.

Above: The beach of Tangalla in the mist of the breakers.

DIKWELLA

Accommodation

MODERATE: **Dickwella Village Resort**, Batheegama (variety of sports facilities, including tennis and a diving school), tel. 041-55271/2. *BUDGET:* **Dickwella Beach Hotel**, 112 Mahawela Road, tel. 041-55326. There are also several small guest houses.

Transportation

BUS: Service several times a day to Galle/Colombo and Hambantota/Tissamaharama.

Excursions

Wewurukannala Buddha, 2 km north of the A2; you can reach **Mulkirigala** through Beliatta.

KOGGALA / TALPE

Accommodation

MODERATE: **Hotel Paragon**, Matara Road, Talpe (specializes in Ayurvedic treatments), tel. 09-83460/1. **Club Horizon**, Habaraduwa, tel. 09-83297. **Hotel Kabalana**, Galle Road, Ahangama, Koggala, tel. 09-53294. **Koggala Beach Hotel**, Habaraduwa, tel. 09-83243. *BUDGET:* **Adere Guest House**, 430 Thalathuduwa Road, Koggala, tel. 09-83865. **Hotel Beach Haven**, Matara Road, Talpe, tel. 09-53362. **Hotel Club Lanka**, Galle Road, Ahangama, tel. 09-53296. **Sagara Guest House**, Kataluwa, Ahangama.

Transportation

TRAIN: These towns are on the Galle-Matara train line, but not all trains stop in Talpe and Ahangama.
BUS: Several buses a day to Galle/Colombo and Matara/Hambantota.

Museum

Martin Wickramasinghe Folk Art Museum, opposite the Koggala Beach Hotel, admission 15 Rs.

MATARA

Accommodation

BUDGET: **Mayura Beach**, Seabeach Road, Matara. **Paradise Beach Club**, 140 Gunasiri Mahimi Mw., Mirissa, tel. 041-50380. **Polhena Reef Gardens Hotel**, 30 Beach Road, Polhena, tel. 041-22478. **Rest House**, Matara (on the beach, near the bus station), tel. 041-22299. Several quiet guest houses in the Fort.

Restaurants

Mayura Beach, Seabeach Road (with a bakery); **Matara Rest House**, tel. 041-22299.

Transportation

TRAIN: Matara is the last stop on the railway line. Several trains a day to Colombo-Fort and Maradana; one a day to Vavuniya/Anuradhapura, Trincomalee, Kandy.
BUS: Bus station at Fort/Clock Tower, 1 km from the train station; frequent service to Galle/Colombo; other routes include Ratnapura, Hambantota.

Museum

Museum of Ancient Paintings, Star Fort, open daily except Tuesdays, 8 am to 5 pm. **Veherahena Buddha**.

Hospital

Tel. 041-22261.

TANGALLA

Accommodation

MODERATE: **Tangalla Bay Hotel**, Pallikudawa, tel. 047-40346. **Nature Resort**, Medilla, tel. 047-40844. *BUDGET:* **Hotel Harbourdocks Inn**, 145 Beach Road, tel. 047-40567. **Manahara Beach Cottage & Cabanas**, Moraketiyara, Mahawela Road, Nakulugamuwa, tel. 047-40585. Numerous guest houses along Beach Road and in Medaketiya.

Restaurants

There are a nummer of restaurants along Beach Road and around the marketplace.

Transportation

BUS: Frequent services to Galle/Colombo and along the south coast; local connections to inland destinations, toward Beliatta and Wiraketiya (for Mulkirigala).

Hospital

Base Hospital: Tel. 047-40261.

Excursions

Bird watching on the **Kalametiya Lagoon**, 20 km east of Tangalle; cliff temple of **Mulkirigala** (15 km, past Beliatta); temples of **Naigala** and **Kasagala** on the Wiraketiya-Ranna road.

UNAWATUNA

Accommodation

MODERATE: **Unawatuna Beach Resort**, Parangiriyawatte (hotel rooms and simple cabanas), tel. 09-32247. *BUDGET:* **Point de Galle**, Mihiripenna, tel. 09-83206. **Sea View Guest House**, Devala Road, tel. 09-24376. **The Strand**, Devala Road (colonial villa). **Villa Cormoran**, 8-roomed hotel with sea view, tel. 09-53201. **Sri Gemunu Guest House**, Dalawella, in gardens, rooms with sea view, tel. 09-83202. There are countless small hotels and private accommodations.

Transportation

TRAIN: The train station is 2 km from the beach; only passenger trains on the Colomo/Galle-Matara line stop here. *BUS*: Frequent bus service to Galle/Colombo and along the south coast.

WELIGAMA

Accommodation

MODERATE: **Bay Beach Hotel**, Kapparatota, tel. 041-50201 (with the water sports school: **Bay Beach Aqua Sports**, tel. 041-50201 and 071-32464);
BUDGET: **Jaqa Bay Resort**, Pelena, on the beach, 3 km from Weligama, tel. 041-50033. **Weligama Bay Inn**, originally the Rest House, in a flowering garden on the coast road, tel. 041-50299. Many small hotels and private accommodations.

Transportation

TRAIN: Passenger and express trains on the Colombo/Galle-Matara line stop here.
BUS: Frequent connections to Galle/Colombo and along the south coast.

THE SOUTHEAST
Pilgrim Sites And Safari Parks

HAMBANTOTA
BUNDALA AND KIRINDA
YALA
TISSAMAHARAMA
KATARAGAMA

HAMBANTOTA

Anyone traveling along the south coast on the A2 from the west toward the district capital of **Hambantota** will pass through the small town of **Ambalantota** without a second glance. How could a visitor know that the river **Walawe Ganga**, today traversed by a bridge, used to be a considerable obstacle to pilgrims, and that an *ambalama*, or shelter for pilgrims and travelers, was therefore set up here, forming the origins of the present-day town as well as providing it with its name? The most attractive friezes in the **Girihandu Vihara**, the old monastery near the bridge, show scenes from Buddha's life in the Amaravati style dating from the second to fourth centuries A.D.

Something of the history of the bustling administrative town of Hambantota is also reflected in its name. *Hamban* is a derivative of *sampan*, the name of the boats used by the Malay immigrants who arrived during the Dutch colonial period and have formed a part of the town's Muslim population ever since. Indeed, dugout fishing boats with outriggers line the edge of the elegant curve of the harbor, of which you have a fine view from the Rest House. The remaining government buildings are located nearby, not far from the small fort which the English constructed at the beginning of the 19th century. About a hundred years later, the young Leonard Woolf took up his post here; from 1908 to 1911, he served as a government assistant, riding or cycling around his district on tours of inspection. He collected and documented his deep insights into the lives of the people in the backwoods of Ceylon in his novel *The Village in the Jungle*.

Preceding pages: Yellow-billed storks in search of food in Yala National Park. Left: Dust – part of an elephant's personal hygiene.

A major industry in Hambantota is the production of salt. The salt water evaporates so thoroughly from the *lewayas*, the flat lagoons immediately behind the coastal dune barriers, that all one has to do is scrape up the thick layer of salt left behind. Like the north of the island, this area of Sri Lanka is also largely without rain for several months of the year. As you leave Hambantota traveling eastwards on the A2, you'll go past the extensive man-made **salterns**. At the beginning of the dry season, the salt workers pray to the god Kataragama that it won't rain in January/February or from June to September. Every time it does rain, the salt solution in the pans is diluted, which threatens the jobs of the 1,200 seasonal workers – many of them women.

The Old Province of Ruhuna

Were it possible for one of the old Sinhalese kings from the classical period to return today to see his province of Ruhuna (also spelled *Rohana*, one of several alternate spellings), he would rub his eyes in surprise at the broad expanses of new rice-growing land. Today, the large reservoirs intended to compensate for the disadvantages of the annual dry periods, which do so with greater or lesser success, such as the **Lunugamvehera Reservoir** or the **Badagiriya Tank**, are larger than they were in the period before the 13th century. More than a thousand years ago, Ruhuna and the other classical region of irrigated land in the north of the island, Rajarata, were supplied with water from tanks. But here in the south, everything seems to have taken place on a smaller scale. The reservoirs couldn't compare in size to the huge tanks in the north, the canals were shorter, and the rice paddies were accordingly smaller. Settlements here also tended to be more modest in size. The provincial capitals of the south, Mahanagahula – a ruined city approximately on the site of the present-day **Ramba Vihara** monastery, some 25 kilometers northwest of Hambantota – and **Tissamaharama**, could not compete with the greatness of Anuradhapura or Polonnaruwa.

Above: A woman at work in the salterns of Hambantota.

And yet in spite of this, Ruhuna played an important role. Not infrequently, kings from Rajarata sought refuge here from invaders from southern India, marshalling strength and allies before returning to drive the intruders back to the mainland. However, in the 12th century, when the southern Indians destroyed the irrigation systems and drove the Sinhalese people back into the hill country and the southwestern part of the island, Ruhuna was also deserted. This has created another element that would astonish an old Sinhalese king returning today: in the extreme southeast corner of his empire,

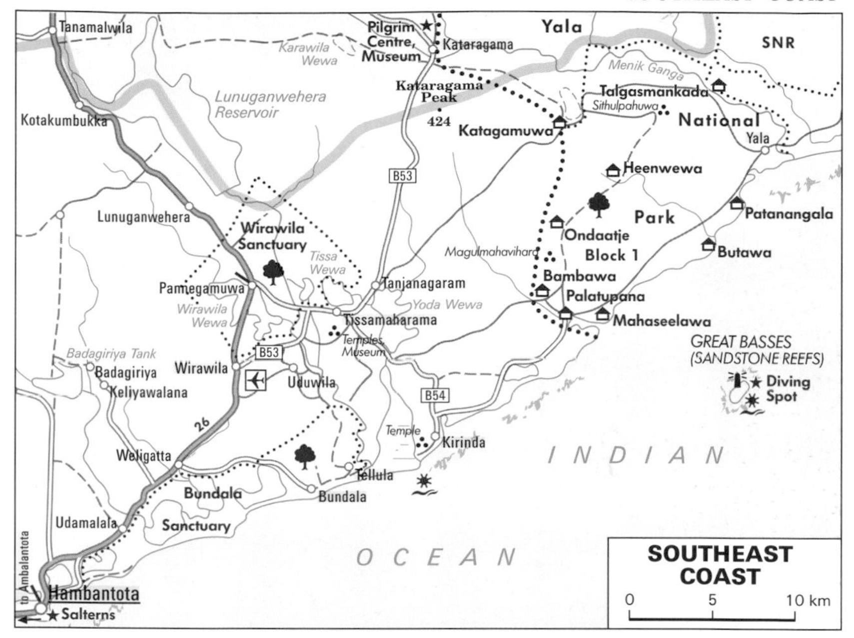

where in his day rice was cultivated around small tanks and a number of monasteries were scattered throughout the countryside, natural flora and fauna have now taken possession of the land. Indeed, this process of letting nature take over is actively supported by people today.

BUNDALA AND KIRINDA

East of the salterns in Hambantota the *lewayas* continue. In this region, however, they no longer benefit people, but rather serve as a playground for countless waterfowl, especially during the winter when the migratory birds from the Asian mainland stop over here. In addition, the savanna land in the **Bundala Sanctuary** affords a suitable biosphere for herds of elephants. Water buffalo and cattle also feel at home close to settlements. At the entrance to the sanctuary (roughly one kilometer south of the A2; signposted), you pay your entrance fee and are assigned an attendant from the conservation authorities. For anyone who wants to stay overnight, there's a campground near the sea. The *lewayas* at Bundala are just a small section of a long chain of lagoons frequented by migratory birds; other lagoons noted for their bird life include the **Kalametiya Lagoon**, about 20 kilometers east of Tangalla, and the swamps in Kumana (Yala East).

Further inland, the great tanks of **Wirawila** and the surrounding area also form a nature reserve. East of here, the **Kirindi Oya River** winds its way south towards the sea, having fed several reservoirs en route. Close to its lower reaches stand the ruins of **Tellula** and **Nediganvila**, evidence of the fact that the river was an important lifeline for the province of Ruhuna at a very early date.

A few miles east of the river mouth, directly on the coast, are the towering rocks of **Kirinda**. This small port, with a sweeping view of the solitary coastline, could have been designed to lend credibility to the legend of Viharamahadevi. It was the site of the miraculous landing and rescue of the lovely prince's

daughter, whose father had sacrificed her to the ocean god by putting her to sea in a boat with no oars. Kavantissa, the ruler of Ruhuna in the second century B.C., found her and took her as his wife, and she gave birth to the national hero Dutthagamani, the first man to unite the Sinhalese empire, and his brother and successor Sadhatissa. The temple rocks on the sea, with a statue of Viharamahadevi and a small white dagoba, are popular with pilgrims.

YALA NATIONAL PARK

Just a few kilometers inland from Kirinda, a much-used road riddled with potholes leads off to the entrance of the largest nature reserve in Sri Lanka: **Yala (Ruhunu) National Park**. It covers a total of 1,572 square kilometers, though only a limited section is open to the public; principally the 139 square kilometers comprising **Yala Block I**. Those interested in spending the night in the park in one of the houses owned by the Department of Wildlife Conservation should be aware that, at present, only the "Ondaatje" bungalow can be rented (accommodates around 10 people; must be booked in advance in Colombo, tel. 01-694241). In addition, there are two campgrounds; and two hotels on the coast, located near the park entrance but outside the conservation area.

Above: Wild water buffalo in Yala National Park. Right: A busy insect world provides a feast for chameleons.

Large numbers of people visit the park, which is open from 6 a.m. to 6 p.m.; you pay the entrance fee for yourself and your vehicle at the **Palatupana** entrance, where you're also allocated a guide, since no one is allowed to tour the park on his own. At this entrance, there's also an informative exhibition about the park's flora and fauna, which can be seen during the park's opening hours. Rules governing visits to the park are quite strict, which both protects the park and ensures the safety of those touring it. With a few

exceptions, visitors are not allowed to leave their vehicles, and open vehicles are not permitted; furthermore, photographers may not use their flashes.

The Animals of Yala Park

The guide from the Department of Wildlife Conservation knows which of the park's animals frequent which areas. Still, on a safari of only a few hours and conducted from a jeep, you naturally cannot expect to encounter every last one of the many animals which live here.

Large numbers of the following animals reside in the park: **elephants** (*Elephas maximus*), which form the main attraction, followed by **wild water buffalo** (*Bubalus bubalis*); **sambhur** (*Cervus unicolor*); **spotted deer** (*Axis axis ceylonensis*), easily recognizable on account of their distinctive markings; **leopards** (*Panthera pardus*), which tend to be more active at night but are also sighted during the day in Yala; **sloth bears** (*Melursus ursinus*), whose favorite food is termites; **toque monkeys** (*Macaca sinica*) with their wig-like "hair style"; **grey langurs** (*Presbytis entellus*) with a black face, grey coat and unusually long tail; **wild boar** (*Sus scrofa*); **gold jackals** (*Canis aureus*); **stripe-necked mongoose** (*Herpestes vitticollis*); **monitor lizards** (*Varanus bengalensis*); **pythons** (*Python molurus*); and **marsh crocodiles** (*Crocodylus palustris*).

Some of the more notable birds include: **peacocks** (*Pavo cristatus*); **Malabar pied hornbills** (*Anthracoceros coronatus*); **jungle fowl** (*Gallus lafayetti*); **black-necked storks** (*Xenorhynchus asiaticus*); and **blue-faced malkohas** (*Rhopodytes viridirostri*). Between September and May, thousands of birds from Asia spend the winter here, and you can even see birds from Europe. Nocturnal creatures, which are rarely sighted, include the **slender loris** (*Loris tardigradus*), **pangolin** (*Manis crassicaudata*) and **porcupine** (*Hystrix cristata*).

Two figures may give you an idea of how varied the fauna in Yala is: there are

32 different species of mammal and 142 types of bird, five of which are endemic.

Land Types in the Park

Yala National Park extends over an area about the size of Greater London; within this area are a wealth of different landscapes. The coastal strip, with its dune barriers and lagoons surrounded by mangroves, is a paradise for water animals, especially birds. Adjoining this area, an expanse of open, park-like grassland stretches inland, dotted with scrub and a few isolated trees. This is the habitat of the animals of the savanna, such as elephants.

The best time to observe the animals here is during the dry period; not only are the roads easier to drive on then, but, as the waterholes gradually start to dry out, the animals are forced to stay closer to them. A fair number of these waterholes are tanks built long ago by the people of *Ruhuna* – the area was once used for rice cultivation – and left open for many centuries. Though the houses of the farmers from this period have long since disappeared, there is other evidence of the presence of early settlers. Here, as in the central northern province, there are natural groups of rocks rising up out of the landscape; millennia ago, hermit monks made their homes here, founding monasteries and leaving their mark in the early Buddhist *Brahmi* inscriptions which you can still see on drip ledges of cliff caves. Such testimony to earlier civilizations occurs throughout the park.

Above: Sloth bears feed on termites (Yala National Park). Right: Ancient water tanks can still be seen in Ruhuna.

Sithulpahuwa is one of the most important monasteries in the country, with 61 Brahmi inscriptions, two restored dagobas, and a statue of the reclining Buddha six meters long. It is located in the north of Yala Block I and is a popular destination for pilgrims; thousands of whom flock here in the month of *Poson*, in June. Evidence of the heavy pilgrim traffic is present in the large numbers of primitive pilgrim hostels, as well as numerous signs in Sinhala reminding visitors not to consume alcohol in this holy area. From the B54 (Tissamaharama-Kirinda), there's a direct access road to Sithulpahuwa; you reach the border of the park at **Bambawa**, where, close to the entrance, are the ruins of a dagoba and the remains of a bathing pond. Five kilometers further on, the pilgrims' route passes **Magulmahavihara**, another monastery from the second century B.C., which has a restored dagoba, statue caves and bathing ponds. When the pilgrim traffic is light, this road is ideal for observing nature, as it passes through alternating stretches of open parkland and dense jungle. Adjacent to the whole wooded area is the drier savanna region.

Several riverbeds cross the national park, but even the largest of them, the **Menik Ganga**, carries little or no water

during the dry periods. Forests have grown up along the rivers. During periods when the rivers are flowing with water, they are also great places at which to observe animal and bird life. With the exception of the SNR (Strict Natural Reserve) in the center of the national park, which, as its name implies, is strictly protected, all sections of the park are open to nature lovers – in theory. In fact, however, most of them, apart from Block I, are not sufficiently developed for the public or are – in the eastern part – deserted because of political difficulties.

From Hunting to Nature Conservation

In the 19th century, Sri Lanka's wealth of wildlife was decimated as a result of the enthusiasm for hunting and trophy-collecting shared by European settlers and visitors. Toward the end of the 19th century, the idea of nature conservation began to receive worldwide attention; accordingly, around 1900, plantation owners created a conservation area for wild animals in the thinly-populated southeastern part of the island, on what is today Yala Block I, around the turn of the century. West of this reserve, an area was set aside where hunting was permitted. In 1908, H.H. Engelbrecht, a South African who had once been an English prisoner of war, became the country's first gamekeeper; his vast experience of African wildlife more than qualified him for the job. The nature reserve was extended in 1938; that same year, Sri Lanka's second-largest park, Wilpattu, was created. In 1969, Yala East, with an area of 181 square kilometers, was added. It was enlarged in 1973 with an area adjacent to the east, the 44 square kilometers of Kudimbigala.

TISSAMAHARAMA

The famous King Devanampiya Tissa, who was responsible for spreading Buddhism in Sri Lanka, had a brother in the southern part of the country called Maha-

naga. The latter is said to have made **Mahagama**, later known as **Tissamaharama**, the capital of his empire Ruhuna in the third century B.C. The **Tissa Wewa**, a tank enlarged in the second century A.D. which provides such a picturesque backdrop for the Rest House, may also date from about this time. In the second century B.C., Kavantissa, father of Dutthagamani, the uniter of the empire, is thought to have donated the nearby **Great Dagoba**. For Buddhists, this is one of the 16 most sacred pilgrimage sites in the country. Not far away from here, together with the remains of a monastery complex, stands the restored **Sandagiri Dagoba**, believed to have been built around two thousand years ago.

Rice paddies and private gardens may well be covering up a wealth of other ruins which could reveal more about the old Tissamaharama. Visible for all to see,

Above: Procession around the July full moon to honor the god Skanda (Kataragama). Right: Shivaitic Sadhu.

on the other hand, are two dagobas located close together and near the main road. The **Yatala Dagoba** sports a frieze of elephants around its rectangular platform, and is surrounded by a moat. Near this historic site, a small, modern **museum** contains a collection of some of the most important finds from Ruhuna. A nearby copse contains a large number of columns of roughly equal height, collectively referred to as a "palace." However, the true function of this building, which would appear to have originally consisted of several stories, is unknown.

The nearby **Menik Dagoba**, which has been extensively restored, belongs to the monastery of Menik Raja Maha Vihara.

KATARAGAMA

Kataragama, the name of this sacred place, is also used to refer to the god who is worshiped here: Skanda, the god of war. This son of the Hindu gods Shiva and Parvati is highly respected by Sri Lankan Hindus and Buddhists alike. The

legends which surround him help to explain why this is so.

Most of the Hindu gods, as the initiated know, are native to the Indian mainland. This applies to Skanda, too, who is also known as Karttikeya in northern India, and Subrahmaniya or Murugan in southern India. He is a powerful, belligerent god. His standard of war is emblazoned with a fighting cock; his mount is a peacock, said to be able to kill poisonous snakes, and thus one's worst enemies; and in one of his 12 hands he carries the *vel,* or spear, which is a reminder of his victory over the demon Taraka. His six heads stem from the *Krittikas*, the six Pleiades, his foster mothers who reared him in the Ganges. Before Skanda had ever heard a thing about the island of Lanka, he was married to Devayani; but one day Narada, the messenger of the gods, told him that an extraordinarily beautiful woman named Valli Amma lived there. Thought to be the daughter of a sacred hermit and a deer, she grew up in the southeastern part of the island, raised by a chief of the *Veddah*s, the resident population of Lanka before the arrival of the Sinhalese. Skanda approached the girl in the guise of a beggar and, with the help of a trick by his clever brother Ganesha, was able to persuade Valli Amma to marry him. Devayani tried in vain to get her husband to return to India. Finally, she accepted her lot and likewise moved to Sri Lanka. There, in Kataragama, all three live today in their shrines on the sacred ground.

For Hindus and Buddhists, Kataragama is one of the most important sites of pilgrimage on the island. The Buddhists see it as one of the 16 most sacred places because Buddha visited it and Devanampiya Tissa planted a cutting of the bo tree of Anuradhapura here. Dutthagamani is said to have donated the Kataragama shrine after his victory over the ruler Elara (in 161 B.C.), who had invaded Lanka from southern India. Hindu legend, on the other hand, has it that Skanda has lived here since before the arrival of the Sinhalese.

True believers, however, are not concerned with such inconsistencies. Even the Muslims have a small mosque within the holy grounds and make a pilgrimage to the ten-day *Esala Perahera* festival in July/August. Apart from the shrines for Skanda, Valli Amma and Devayani, there are further shrines for Hindu deities, including Vishnu and Ganesha, as well as a Buddhist monastery and memorial shrines for Hindu and Muslim holy men. Any visitor who is unfamiliar with the complicated assortment of gods and divinities populating the cosmos of southern Asia can brush up on his knowledge in the **museum** near the **Kataragama Devala**, the main temple for Skanda/Kataragama; this display is a good way to get to know the most important gods and the ways they are traditionally depicted.

Kataragama, which is just 20 kilometers away from Tissamaharama, really comes to life in the days preceding the festival of the July full moon. In the 10 nights prior to the *poya* (full-moon) day, the Sinhalese *kapurala*, the priest of the Kataragama devala, removes a cloth from the holy of holies, which bears an abstract symbol of the god Skanda known as a *yantra*. The cloth is borne by an elephant, accompanied by the sounds of drums and conch-shell horns and the enthusiasm of the hordes of pilgrims, to the southern end of the holy precinct, to the temple of Valli Amma. It remains there for almost an hour, symbolizing the union of the god with her, and is then carried back to its original place.

Above: A Kavadi dancer endures pain for a better future (Kataragama).

Just before the night of the full moon, the procession also goes to the **Kiri Dagoba** ("Milk Dagoba") at the northern end of the holy precinct in order to honor Buddha. The next morning, the ceremony of the water cutting is held in the Menik Ganga, which flows past the south of the holy area. The *kapurala*, or priest, makes the sign of a *mandala* (a holy sign) in the river with a sword and immerses the cloth with the *yantra* in the water: the god is being bathed. After this ceremony, thousands of pilgrims also bathe in the holy water to cleanse themselves of their sins and to share in the divine power.

During the festival, you can watch the pilgrims' frenetic efforts to atone for their sins: they walk barefoot over red-hot coals, have metal hooks inserted into their backs so that they can be hung up and swung back and forth, torment themselves by having metal arrows inserted into their tongues, and subject themselves to other unpleasant castigations.

For many Sri Lankans, the pilgrimage to Kataragama is an annual duty. Former president Premadasa ensured that the pilgrims had easy access to the holy place by having the excellent B53 built from Buttala through the northwest section of the Yala park. The triangular peaks of the Kataragama rocks seem to hail pilgrims from a distance as they make their way to the shrines from north, east and west.

HAMBANTOTA

Accommodation

MODERATE: **The Oasis**, Sisilasagama, tel. 047-20650/1/2. **Peacock Beach Hotel**, Galwala Tissa Road (on a long sand beach), tel. 047-20365.
BUDGET: **Rest House**, above the harbor, tel. 047-20299. **Sea Spray**, Galwala Tissa Road, tel. 047-20352. other simple guest houses.

Restaurants

Jade Green Restaurant, Galwala Tissa Road (opposite the Peacock Beach Hotel), tel. 047-20387. **Rest House**, tel. 047-20299.

Transportation

BUS: There are several connections a day toward Galle/Colombo, Tissamaharama, and into the highlands.

Excursions / Sights

The hotels organize tours to the nature reserves and parks of **Bundala**, **Wirawila**, **Yala** and **Uda Walawe**. To visit the **salterns** east of the city, it's best to register in advance at the administrative office of **Mahalewaya**, tel. 047-20208. Bird watching at the **Kalametiya Lagoon**, 20 km west of Hambantota.

Hospital

Base Hospital: Tel. 047-20261.

TISSAMAHARAMA / KATARAGAMA

Accommodation

TISSAMAHARAMA: *MODERATE:* **Tissamaharama Resort**, at the Tissawewa Tank (boat tours on the lake, jeep safaris through the nature reserve), tel. 047-37299. *BUDGET:* **Chandrika Guest House**, Kataragama Road, tel. 047-37143. **Hotel Tissa**, Kachcheriyagama. **Lake Side Tourist Inn**, Akurugoda, at the lake, tel. 047-37216. **Priyankara Tourist Inn**, Kataragama Road, tel. 047-37206. **Queen's Rest House**, 169, Kachcheriyagama, tel. 047-37264. **Singha Tourist Inn**, Tissawewa Mw., tel. 047-37090.
KATARAGAMA: *BUDGET:* **Jayasinghe Holiday Resort**, 32A Detagamuwa Road, tel. 047-35146. **New Hotel Lakshitha**, New Town, tel. 047-35213. **Visaka Rest**, 34 Sella Kataragama Road, tel. 047-35263. **Chamila Rest**, 85 Tissa Road, tel. 047-35217. Accommodations are generally booked solid during the festival in July/August.

Transportation

BUS: Daily direct buses from Tissamaharama toward the southern coast/Colombo, as well as Wellawaya/highlands/eastern coast/Ratnapura.

Excursions / Sights

All the hotels and accommodations in Tissamaharama can organize **jeep safaris** to the nearby nature reserve and parks: Wirawila, Bundala, Yala. From Tissamaharama to Palatupana (entrance to Yala National Park) it's 18 km.

Museums

Yatala Archeological Museum (next to the Yatala Dagoba), open every day except Tuesdays, 8 am to 5pm; **Kataragama Museum**, open daily from 8:30 am to 4:30 pm.

YALA / BUNDALA

Accommodation

YALA: *MODERATE:* **Yala Safari Beach Hotel**, Palatupana (2 km from the park entrance, on the coast), tel. 047-20471.
BUDGET: **Brown's Safari Beach Hotel**, Amaduwa, tel. 047-35175. 2 km from the park entrance, on a sheltered bay, with excellent diving through the shipwrecks and around the Great Basses Islands in April; information about diving excursions from **Bay Beach Aqua Sports**, Kapparatota, Weligama, tel. 041-50201 and 071-32464.
BUNGALOWS, CAMPING: In Yala National Park, the Department of Wildlife Conservation owns two campgrounds and nine bungalows which sleep a maximum of 10 people each (at present only the "Ondaatje" bungalow is available). Advance reservations required: Director, Wildlife Conservation Department, Wildlife Reservation Center, 18 Gregory Road, Colombo 7, tel. 01-694241. Bungalows on the sea: **Mahaseelawa**, **Buttuwa**, **Patanangala**; Bungalows in the jungle: **Ondaatje** (at the Bandu Wewa tank), **Heenwewa**, **Talgasmankada** (on the Menik Ganga), **Yala** (on the Menik Ganga shortly before the river flows into the sea), **Katagamuwa** (at the Katagamuwa Wewa Tank); there is no electricity in the park; bring fuel for camping stoves and lamps.
BUNDALA: Depending on the weather, there are two campgrounds available to visitors.

Transportation

No public transportation is available; four-wheel-drive vehicles recommended.

Park Rules

YALA: Admission fee for foreign tourists is US $10 a day, with additional charges for vehicles (according to size) and the obligatory guide. Vehicles must be closed, and you can only leave them at selected marked points. You may not use a flash when taking pictures, or your headlights; you can only drive on the specially marked roads, and leaving these can mean that the driver is banned from entering the park in future. Speed limit is 25 kmh; you may not drive nearer to an elephant than 30 meters; noise is prohibited, as is littering. Only bungalow residents may swim in the sea here. Visitors must leave the park by 6:30 pm, at which time bungalow residents must also return to their bungalows.
BUNDALA: Admission fee for foreign tourists is US $5 per day, with additional charges for vehicles and the obligatory guide. The parks are open from 5:30 am to 6:30 pm.

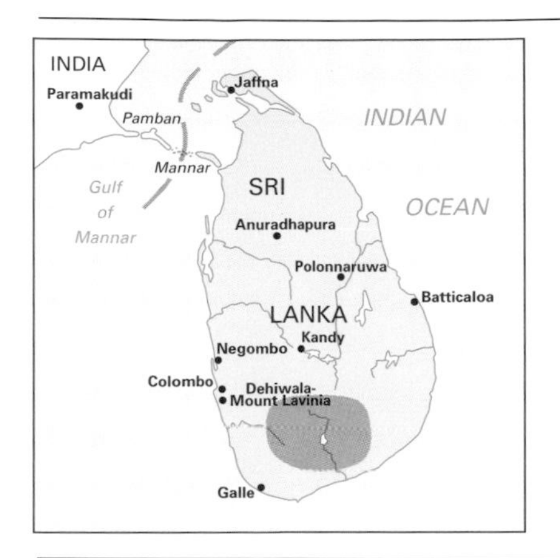

LAND OF PRECIOUS STONES

RATNAPURA
SINHARAJA FOREST
UDA WALAWE
SAMANALAWEWA

RATNAPURA

Ratnapura ("City of Jewels") is the capital of the mountainous province of Sabaragamuwa, which means "land of the wild." For millions of years, the valleys between the highland mountain ranges and the foothills have been filling up with crushed debris and rubble eroded from the mountains, which used to be much higher. In the layers of sediment and residue remaining from alluvial deposits, man has been finding an amazing variety of precious stones for the last thousand years. Gem-extraction methods have basically remained the same down to the present day. On the valley floors, among the rice paddies, gem miners dig vertical shafts, which they line with supports of wood and fronds of fern, down to the *illam*, the layer of deposits which contains the precious stones. The mud of the illam is then dug out, bucket by bucket; when it comes above ground, it's washed and sifted in large wicker "pans" in a river or pond until only the coarser gravel remains. Experts then go through the thousands of stones to sort out the few valuable gems from the many worthless stones. Gems found in this way include rubies, sapphires, emeralds, tourmaline, topaz, garnets, a number of variously colored quartz stones, and many others. The difficult tasks of digging out and sorting the gems are carried out almost exclusively by the Sinhalese, while most of the gem dealers tend to be Moors.

Preceding pages: Typical gem mine near Ratnapura. Left: Perhaps there are rubies in the gravel.

Center of Gem Country

In Ratnapura, as well as in other larger towns and tourist areas, some dealers have created extremely informative **gem museums** alongside their businesses. The **Ratnapura National Museum** also provides insight into the extraction and polishing of gems; on top of this, it exhibits pre-Sinhalese bones, tools and ceramic finds from Sabaragamuwa province, notably from the Paleolithic and Neolithic Ages. Some of the finds here stem from gem pits, while others were unearthed at excavation sites such as the one at **Batadombalena**, a set of prehistoric cave dwellings near **Kuruwita** (12 kilometers north of Ratnapura, off the A4). They all indicate that this part of the island was settled very early on.

A water-level mark on the museum building, which dates from the colonial era, is a visible reminder of the devastating floods of the **Kalu Ganga**. In some years Ratnapura receives more than 4,000 mm of rain, which makes prospecting for gems impossible.

Adam's Peak, the sacred mountain just 20 kilometers away as the crow flies, is often enshrouded in clouds; its conical peak is most likely to be visible between January and April. At this time, pilgrims head for **Palabaddale**, embarking on an hour-long bus trip through **Gilimale**, a settlement which received the royal order to provide for the pilgrims as early as the 12th century. From Palabaddale, they then make the ascent on foot to the top of Adam's Peak in five to seven hours. The local god *Saman*, who lives at the top of the mountain, protects the whole island. He has been identified as *Yama*, the god of death, but also as *Lakshman*, the brother of *Rama* in the Indian epic *Ramayana*.

In the 16th century, the **Maha Saman Devala** (on the A8 toward Panadura, three kilometers from Ratnapura) fell victim to the missionary zeal of the Portuguese. Under the Kandy king Rajasinha II (1635-1687), the Buddhist temple was rebuilt; today, it's an important destination for pilgrims during the temple festival in August. The tyranny of the Portuguese is depicted in a relief embedded in the wall to the right of the steps up to the temple, which shows a Portuguese horseman killing a Sinhalese warrior.

The monastery complex of **Potgul Vihara**, six kilometers south of Ratnapura, afforded the Portuguese an unsurpassed view of the western hill country, and they therefore used it temporarily as a military camp. The monastery temple was rebuilt in the 18th century. A landslide and rock fall in 1991 caused a fair amount of damage, but the complex, which is located against a rocky face at the end of a long stairway, still affords visitors who don't have the time or physical stamina to climb Adam's Peak a good opportunity to enjoy the lush green landscapes and the sweeping view.

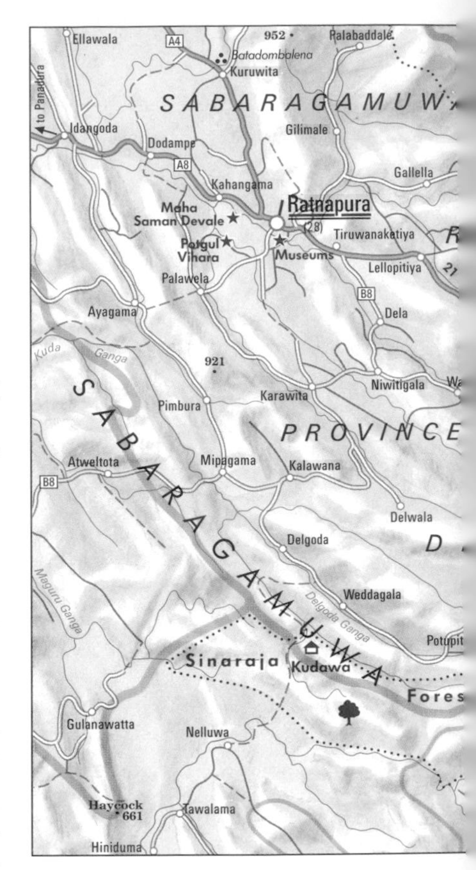

The downtown section of Ratnapura is similar to many other Sri Lankan towns, both in appearance and in its hustle and bustle; it's distinguished, however, by the gem auctions along the Senanayake Mawatha Road. Most of the hotels and guest houses, including the Rest House, are concentrated on the outskirts of town, and are set in very attractive, green, flowering surroundings. The **Kalawathie Hotel** offers courses in Sri Lankan arts as well as Ayurvedic healing.

SINHARAJA FOREST

It's only about 50 kilometers from Ratnapura to the nature reserve of **Sinharaja Forest** (four kilometers towards Pelma-

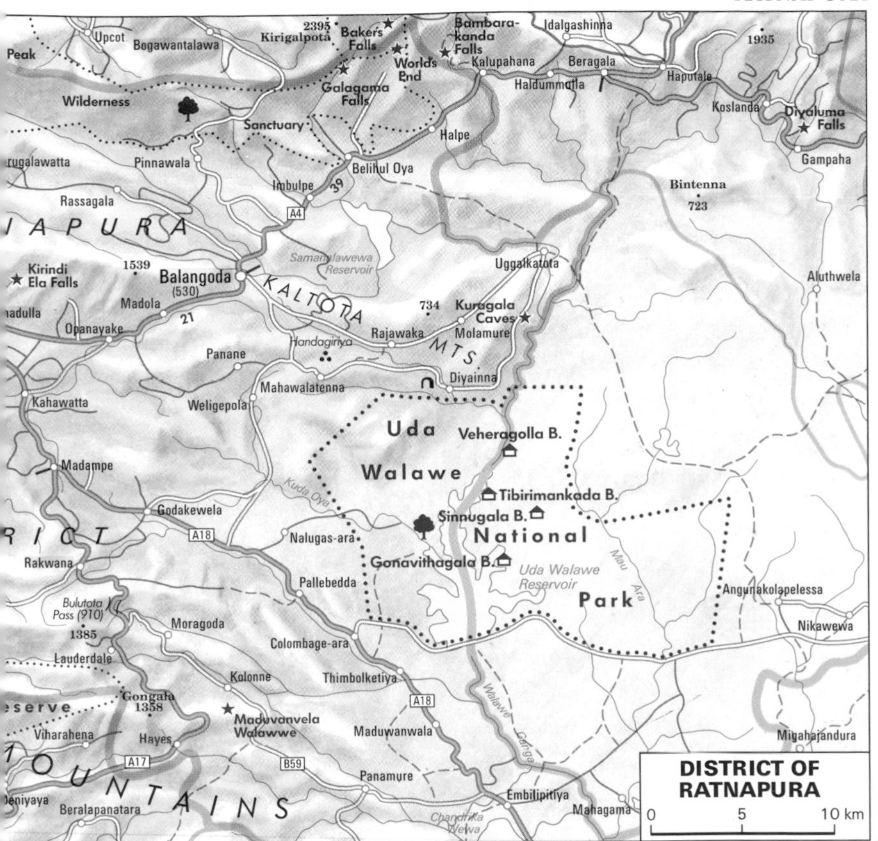

dulla on the A4, then take the B8 through Niwitigala and Karawita to Weddagala, from where signs direct you to the Sinharaja Forest Reserve). Given the bad roads and magnificent scenery, you should allow a good hour and a half to reach the park entrance. According to legend, the forest belonged to the old Sinhalese kings (*raja*), who were said to be descended directly from a lion (*sinha*).

Declared a biosphere reserve by UNESCO in 1988, the reserve, 89 square kilometers in area, was added to the sites on the World Heritage List a year later. Its evergreen tropical rain forests boast some incredible statistics. Of the many types of trees and lianas, 66 percent are endemic. In addition, over half of Sri Lanka's endemic mammals and butterflies, and nearly all 21 of the island's endemic bird species, live here.

The reserve is open between 6 a.m. and 6 p.m., and can only be toured on foot. Having paid the entrance fee, visitors are accompanied by a forest official who is well acquainted with the numerous pathways and the reserve's unique wildlife. You can choose from among a wide variety of routes, ranging from short walks to strenuous day hikes. Overnight accommodation is available at the entrances of **Kudawa** (accessed from Ratnapura-Weddagala), or **Pitadeniyaya** (access from the south via the A17 and **Deniyaya**). It consists of very simple dormitories which must be booked in advance

(Forest Department Battaramulla or District Forest Department Galle). Camping is not permitted.

UDA WALAWE

In 1972, Sri Lanka opened the **Uda Walawe National Park**. Extending over 34 square kilometers, the reservoir named after the Walawe River was created as part of the national Mahaweli Program and irrigates some 25,000 hectares of land south of the dam (which is 4,000 meters long). The park, 308 square kilometers in area, is located to the north of the reservoir and the road which crosses it. It is flanked to the north by the foothills of the hill country and to the west by the foothills of the Sabaragamuwa Mountains. This magnificent backdrop shadows its lowland areas from the rain, but the grass, scrub and forest vegetation receives moisture the whole year round from the rivers coming down from the mountains. Once the last farmers living in the national park were finally allocated new land and moved out in 1978, the animals could roam around unhindered.

Above: Safari in Uda Walawe National Park.
Right: Sapphire from Sri Lanka.

Uda Walawe is known for its large herds of elephants, but also for three types of deer. Wild boar and buffalo are common, but bears and leopards are only seen occasionally. The park has a wealth of avian life and is especially known for its numerous birds of prey. Following the example set by the Yala and Wilpattu parks, visitors can only tour this national park in four-wheel-drive vehicles and must abide by park regulations.

The park is a welcome alternative to the relatively crowded Yala park. As for accommodation, there are four bungalows and three campgrounds (book through the Department of Wildlife Conservation). Between the town of **Embilipitiya**, 30 kilometers away on the A18, and the park entrance, there are a number of hotels, as well as people offering jeep safaris.

Less-Traveled Roads in the South of Sabaragamuwa Province

The journey from Ratnapura to Galle along the south coast involves crossing the 910-meter **Bulutota Pass**. The A17 winds its way past the peaks of the eastern Sabaragamuwa Mountains, more than 1,300 meters high, first traversing rubber and tea plantations, and then, in the higher altitudes, passing through numerous pine forests. The local center of **Rakwana** makes a good stopping-off point and, thanks to its small Rest House, is a convenient base for excursions to the Sinharaja Forest and the surrounding area. Allow plenty of time, as the roads are often winding and full of potholes. However, even though you may need to calculate well over an hour for the 40-kilometer journey to the park entrance, the diverse views of the mountain forests and the tea, cinnamon and rubber plantations are adequate compensation (from Rakwana, take the road to Kalawana).

South of the Bulutota Pass, the minor B59 road to Embilipitiya branches off into the lowlands, thus joining up the two main roads, the A17 and A18. Few tourists venture to the old villages on the edge of the plain. In **Maduvanvela** the *walawwe* (manor house) of the chief of the **Kolonne** *korale* (district) has remained standing to the present day. The extensive building has 34 rooms, with the chief's "law court" located in a side wing. Ornately decorated, this wooden building from 1905 has features borrowed from the colonial style of architecture. It lies south of the road, situated in attractive parkland.

SAMANALAWEWA

The A4 runs east of Ratnapura in a large curve tracing the southern edge of the hill country. Before reaching the important intersection at **Pelmadulla**, the road passes through lush green valleys

which are rich in gems. Subsequently, however, it rises to a height of more than 500 meters, the altitude of the most important local center along this stretch, **Balangoda**. This settlement is characterized by temples, churches, mosques, numerous stores, schools and administrative offices, as well as a lively flow of activity. Balangoda provides access to the small villages of the adjoining hill country to the north, a cross-country link to Bogawantalawa via the ridge of the Peak Wilderness Sanctuary, and to the south the villages of the hill country around Kaltota.

The A4 rises another several hundred meters and, as it approaches the rugged southern slopes of the hill country, there are numerous bridges crossing its cold streams and stoney river beds. Primeval forests cling to steep, barely accessible slopes; farmers have managed to create extremely narrow terraced rice fields in the tiny valleys. The landscape itself is a lush, brilliant green because of the vast amounts of available water. To prevent

this precious water running away to the south unused, a plan was created as early as 1960 to dam off the two larger river courses of the Walawe Ganga and Belihul Oya, directly behind their confluence. In 1991, the work was finished with the help of the Japanese. The idea was that in the ensuing years the **Samanalawewa** ("Butterfly Tank") reservoir would fill up in the deeply cut river valleys. It is not visible from the main road and disappears behind the round hills covered with *patana* (grassland).

The landscape is drier than at the mountain edge, as the land is sheltered from the rain during the southwest monsoon and is subject, especially from May to July, to strong, hot winds from the southwest. The Sinhalese made use of these hot winds hundreds of years ago, setting up thousands of small smelting ovens to produce iron; thanks to the wind conditions, the iron had some of the qualities of steel. South of this area, which wasn't really accessible until modern roads were built towards the end of the 20th century, the Kaltota Mountains form a border to the lowlands of Ruhuna, the southeastern section of the classical Sinhalese empire.

Above: Rice paddies near Balangoda on the southern slopes of the central highlands.

The ancient ruins at **Handagiriya** and the drip ledges at the caves in **Kuragala** are evidence of settlements more than two thousand years old. However, Kuragala (Kaltota Road from Balangoda; 25 kilometers) became a sacred Muslim place after the hermit Muhaddi Abdul Kadir Assiz from Jelani lived here for many years. In one of the steep cliffs people claim to see the ship on which the holy man is said to have traveled from Baghdad. Muslim pilgrims congregate here in August for a big festival. However, the place is worth visiting at any time of the year on account of the incomparable views it commands of the southeast of Sri Lanka, which make it worth your while to brave the bad roads and the difficult ascent to the top of the rocks.

BALANGODA

Accommodation

BUDGET: **Rest House**, tel. 045-7299. **Balangoda Rest Inn**, 110 Old Road, tel. 045-87207. **Chamara Rest House**, 7/5 Karawaketiva Road, tel. 045-87244. **I.G. Tourist Rest**, 339/10 Samagi Mw., Akkatra18, Balagahamulla.

Transportation

BUS: Daily service to Colombo via Ratnapura, to the highlands via Haputale, to the south and east coasts via Wellawaya; several buses a day toward Kaltota (for Kuragala), a few local buses in the mountain valleys toward Rassagala and into the highlands toward Bogawantalawa.

Hospital

District Hospital, tel. 045-7261.

Excursions

Mountain hikes into the foothills of the highlands and the Kaltota region. Point of departure for trips to the Muslim shrine of Kuragala (25 km from Balangoda).

RATNAPURA

Accommodation

BUDGET: **Dharshana Inn**, 68/5 Rest House Road, tel. 045-22674. **Kalavathie Holiday and Health Resort**, Polhengoda Village (Ayurvedic therapy, cultural events), tel. 045-22465. **Nilani Lodge**, 21 Dharmapala Mw., tel. 045-22170. **Ratnaloka Tour Inn**, Kosgala, Kahangama (near the gem mines, 5 km west of Ratnapura), tel. 045-22455. **Rest House**, Rest House Road (old colonial-era building in a lovely hilly setting), tel. 045-22299. **Hotel Gemland**, 12 Mudduwa Road, tel. 045-22153.

Restaurants

Chamber Restaurant, 6 Ehelepola Mw. Batugedara (on the A 4 to Pelmadulla, 1 km outside Ratnapura), tel. 045-22398. **Pathaya Garden Palace**, 14 Senanayake Mw., tel. 045-23029. **Rest House**, Rest House Road, tel. 045-22299.

Transportation

BUS: State buses depart from the old train station, no longer operative, northwest of the city center. Private buses leave southeast of the city center. There's service to Colombo at least every half-hour, and daily service to the south coast as well as into the highlands via Haputale.

Excursions / Sights

Kalavathie, Polhengoda, tel. 045-22565, offers tours throughout the Ratnapura district; **Ratnaloka Tour Inn**, Kosgala, Kahangama, tel. 045-22455, organizes trips to Sinharaja Forest.

To make the ascent of **Adam's Peak** at night, take the State bus to the last stop, Palabaddale (it runs several times a day); the last bus departs at around 5:30 pm, the trip takes an hour. The hike to the summit (12 km) takes about five hours; take a flashlight, as the electric lighting along this route is not consistent during the pilgrimage season, January to April. Food is available in Palabaddale (see page 130).

Museums

Ratnapura National Museum, west of town center, signposted, tel. 045-22451, mainly prehistoric finds, especially of objects turned up in gem mines, open daily except Fri 9 am to 5 pm; **Gemmological Museum of Gem Bank**, 6 Ehelepola Mw, Batugedara, tel. 045-22398; **Gem Museum of Nilani**, 12 Bandaranayake Mw., tel. 045-22407; **Gem Museum of Ranjith Pathirana**, 26 Bandaranayake Mw., tel. 071-28069.

SINHARAJA FOREST

Accommodation

DENIYAYA: *BUDGET:* **Rest House**, tel. 041-7299; **Pitadeniyaya Camp** at the southeastern entrance to the reserve, reservations at the Divisional Forest Office Galle, tel. 09-23106.

RAKWANA: *BUDGET:* **Rest House**, Deniyaya Road.

WEDDAGALA: *BUDGET:* **Kudawa Camp** (communal rooms) at the northwestern entrance.

Excursions

You walk from the park entrance, with an obligatory guide. Entrance 50 Rs., guide 100 Rs. Excellent maps and brochures available for the nature trails of **Waturawa** (5 km from Kudawa Camp; 4 km return trip on forest road) and **Moulawella** (5 km from Kudawa Camp to the start of this path; whole walk takes about two hours). Excursions with overnight accommodation at the Camp can be arranged by the Department of Wildlife Conservation/Wildlife Trust Sri Lanka, 18 Gregory's Rd., Colombo 7, tel. 01-696050.

UDA WALAWE

Accommodation

EMBILIPITIYA: *BUDGET:* **Centauria Tourist Hotel**, New Town (also organizes safaris), tel. 047-30104. **Saratchandra Tourist**, Pallegama, tel. 047-30044.

UDA WALAWE NATIONAL PARK: *BUDGET:* Outside the park: **Walawe Rest**, reservations though Kinjou, Colombo 5, tel. 01-591728. **Walawe Safari Village**, reservations at 33 Amarasekere Mw., Colombo 5, tel. 01-591728. Inside the Park: Four bungalows sleeping a maximum of 10 people each (**Tibirimankada** and **Gonavithagala** near the Uda Walawe Tank; **Veheragolla** and **Sinuggala** near the rock groups in the jungle), small campground (**Pilimaddhara**, east of the Walawe Ganga) in the park, and two others (**Alimenkade** and **Pansadara**); for information, contact the park ranger, tel. 047-33292; to reserve bungalows or campsites: Director, Department of Wildlife Conservation, Wildlife Reservation Center, 18 Gregory's Rd, Colombo 7, tel. 01-694241; admission US $10 plus vehicle and guide charges.

HILL COUNTRY
"The End of the World"

CHANGES IN
THE HILL COUNTRY
ADAM'S PEAK
HORTON PLAINS
NUWARA ELIYA
KOTMALE / BADULLA

CHANGES IN THE HILL COUNTRY

Powerful and steep rise the southern and eastern flanks of the hill country. Originally, dense, almost impenetrable tropical rain forest covered all the valleys and extended up the slopes, stopping just short of the highest peaks, a habitat for dangerous wild animals: elephants, leopards, wild boars, bears. For much of the year, clouds and fog shroud the peaks. The southwest of the hill country gets as much as 5,000 mm of rainfall a year, and, with altitudes averaging between 1,500 and 2,500 meters, can be unpleasantly cool for residents of the tropics, even though temperatures almost never drop below 0°C.

More than two thousand years ago, the hill country was already inhabited by the *Veddahs*, hunters and gatherers, and also served as the site of several hermitages for Buddhist monks. When the Sinhalese retreated back into the mountain country around Kandy after the 12th century, it was the adjacent highland region to the south that was now closer to them. Its eastern section, the area around Badulla, became the "granary" of the whole Kandy kingdom. However, the other parts of the region were presumably too cool, too impenetrable and too dangerous. The Portuguese and the Dutch also gave the inhospitable hill country a wide berth between the 16th and 18th centuries. For this reason, the wettest, coldest and wildest area of the hill country was largely uninhabited when the English conquered the kingdom of Kandy in 1815. But after this, changes swept through the mountain landscape at a lightning pace. First of all, the seemingly inexhaustible supply of wildlife attracted hunting parties into the green wilderness. But the lush vegetation and suitable climate also prompted the Europeans to start setting up plantations here.

Preceding pages: Tea plantation in the hill country – heritage of colonial days. Left: The Buddha of Buduruvagala, 14 meters high.

Up until the middle of the 19th century, the production of coffee was a great economic success; however, a crisis in sales on the world market and the advent of leaf disease, which affected huge areas of the plantations, almost destroyed this industry altogether in the 1880s. Subsequent experiments with *cinchona* (china bark) and even more so with tea plants proved so successful that tea cultivation took over, and still dominates large sections of the hill country to this day. This once inaccessible region of primeval forest has been transformed into

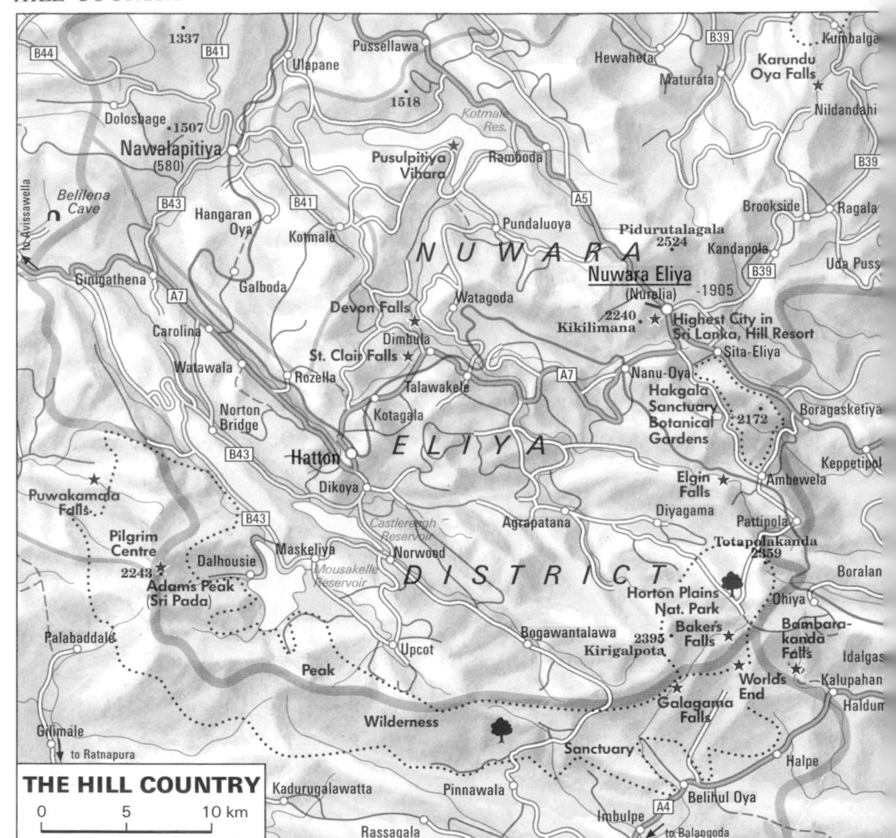

an intensively cultivated, well-tended, even picturesque artificial landscape.

Even in the days when coffee was the main crop in the area, the plantation owners had engaged – albeit only during the harvest months – migrant workers from Tamil Nadu in southern India. Cultivating tea is even more labor-intensive. Not only are tea leaves plucked the whole year round, but the bushes have to be kept trimmed to a height suitable for picking, the paths have to be carefully maintained, firewood cut, shade-providing trees and new tea bushes planted, and the land constantly fertilized. After the 1870s, therefore, the plantation owners starting bringing in whole Tamil families from southern India. For several generations, these Tamils have lived on the tea plantations in the hill country as resident laborers. The women pick the tea and the men carry out all the rest of the work involved. Their simple living quarters, often laid out in rows, with the village *kovils* (Hindu temples), are as much a part of the Sri Lankan tea estates as are the tea factories and tea bushes.

ADAM'S PEAK

Every religious person in Sri Lanka is expected to climb **Adam's Peak** at least once in his lifetime; preferably several times. As Buddha is supposed to have left his *sri patul* (footprint) here, the Sinhalese refer to the mountain as **Sri Pada**

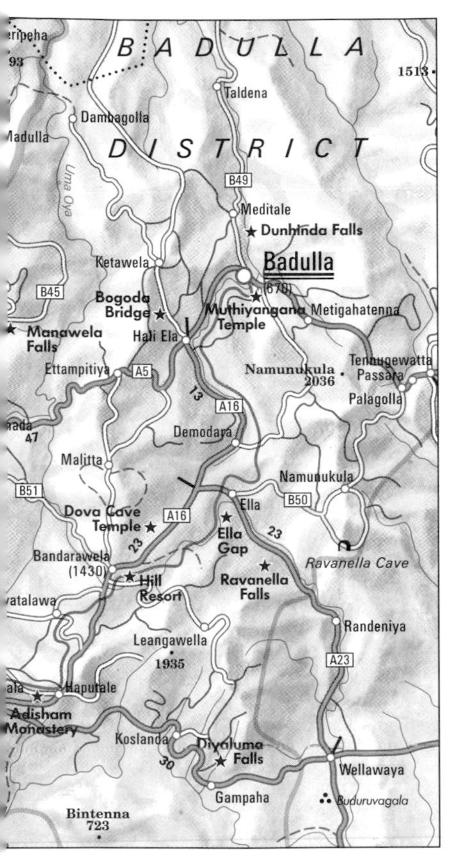

("Sacred Footprint"), and consider it one of the 16 most sacred places in the country. But adherents of other religions also make pilgrimages here: the Hindus see in Buddha an incarnation of Vishnu; the Christians believe the footprint belongs to St. Thomas; and the Muslims say it is Adam's footprint. Whatever their religious affiliation, pilgrims have been journeying to Adam's Peak for more than a thousand years. King Vijayabahu I (1055-1110) had pilgrims' shelters, or *ambalamas*, built along the routes to the sacred mountain. He granted several communities in the vicinity of the mountain royal privileges, but at the same time they were obliged to keep the pilgrimage routes well maintained. This duty did bring other advantages: then as now, tourists provided welcome extra income.

Today there is an extensive road network in the hill country, so that only the final stage up to the peak is a footpath. The two most commonly used approaches are lit by electric lights during the main pilgrimage season, as people usually make the ascent to the peak at night. This means that you experience the sunrise on the mountaintop and avoid the strenuous climb in the daytime heat.

Most often, the pilgrims use the approach from the north. You are already in the hill country when you turn off the main road, the A7 (Avissawella-Nuwara Eliya), to **Hatton**, which also has a railway station. Until you reach Nuwara Eliya, this is the most important and busiest place amid the varied landscape of the lush green tea plantations. It has a Rest House and several smaller hotels. The 40 kilometer road to **Dalhousie** (also spelt Delhouse), the starting point for the ascent, leads around the **Castlereagh** and **Moussakelle** reservoirs. In **Dickoya** and **Maskeliya** there is additional accommodation, some hotels offering magnificent views of the lakes and the imposing peak of the sacred mountain. You can't miss the starting point, since the road ends in Dalhousie. Souvenir stands, restaurants and tea rooms cater to pilgrims' needs. Then you simply follow the seven-kilometer route. Where it becomes especially steep, there are flights of stairs; looking at the pointed conical form of the peak, you can guess even before you start that there are going to be a great many steps! Whether the climb takes you two or four hours depends entirely on your physical condition, but you should try to time your departure from Dalhousie so that you arrive at the top before sunrise. And remember that atop the peak, at an altitude of 2,243 meters, it is 15 to 20°C colder than at the coast, so that an anorak or windbreaker and warm clothing are an absolute must.

The sacred site itself is not particularly spectacular. The legendary footprint is simply a one-meter hollow in the rock; it requires some imagination in order to be able to construe it as the shape of a foot at all. It is into this hollow that devout pilgrims throw their donations.

The views from here are breathtaking both by day and by night. With the first rays of the sun you can make out the reservoirs and the tea plantations at the foot of the mountain. Towards the west on the densely wooded slopes of the Peak Wilderness Sanctuary you can see the triangular shadow of the sacred mountain through the morning mist. At the sight of the sunrise and the mountain's shadow devout pilgrims excitedly chant *sadhu!* (holy!). People who have made the ascent several times ring a small bell (which can be heard over a great distance) as many times as they have made the journey.

Above: Adam's Peak, Sri Lanka's holy mountain. Right: Pilgrims await the sunrise after their strenuous climb.

The second starting point for the ascent is the village of **Palabaddale** (bus from Ratnapura; 20 kilometers, see page 123). This route from the south, almost twice as long as the northern route, passes through the **Carney Plantation** and then through mountain forest. Not only is the starting point several hundred meters lower than Dalhousie, but for large sections of the journey you have to struggle over irregularly formed stone blocks which are barely recognizable as steps. What is more, the route is so badly lit that it would be impossible to make the journey at night without a flashlight, unless there is a full moon. Despite these drawbacks, the route attracts a fair number of pilgrims on account of the peace and tranquility of its wooded surroundings.

HORTON PLAINS

The primeval forest in the hill country has not been completely destroyed. A narrow strip along the southwest flank of the hill country, 50 kilometers long, is the **Peak Wilderness Sanctuary**, which encompasses several small areas of original hill country vegetation. A single, narrow road crosses the reserve between **Bogawantalawa** and **Balangoda**; in other sections, visitors have to walk. The sacred mountain is in the west; the east section ends with **Horton Plains National Park**. Towering over these grassy plains, more than 2,000 meters high, are Sri Lanka's second- and third-highest mountains, **Kirigalpota** (2,395 meters) and **Totapolakanda** (2,357 meters), though you don't notice their height right away, as the plains are themselves so high. More surprising is the *patana*, the pale yellow plain with its coarse clumps of grass, dotted here and there with bizarre-looking trees twisted by the wind, including the red-flowering rhododendron (*Rhododendron arboreum ssp. zeylanicum*). Surrounding the highland plain is dense green primeval forest with a large num-

ber of endemic plants, including tree ferns and orchids. Rare birds are also at home here; in addition, the park provides sambhur, various monkey species, and leopards with a limited, but basically unspoiled habitat. In the 19th century, elephant herds also roamed here, but the colonial passion for hunting and the cultivation of most of the hill country have driven them away from the area.

Nature lovers and fans of Horton Plains see it as an advantage that the roads to the area are exceedingly bad. Furthermore, there is no direct means of public transportation leading here. You have a choice between three approach roads, all of them riddled with potholes: from the east via **Ohiya**, from the north by way of **Pattipola**, and from the west through **Diyagama**. The train stops in both Ohiya and Pattipola on its impressive journey through the mountain landscape. From Ohiya station, it is another six kilometers to the park entrance; from Pattipola, it's another nine. Those traveling by bus proceed through the small but lively market town of **Agarapatana**, and continue eastwards into the picturesque tea country until they reach Diyagama, the last stop. From the Diyagama Tea Estate, it is a roughly 14-kilometer walk through the plantation, then through forest until you come to the plain. Very few vehicles use these roads, making them suitable hiking trails to the national park; and you can't possibly get lost on them. Anyone coming from Nuwara Eliya by car must calculate with at least an hour's journey, even though the distance doesn't seem so long on paper (25 kilometers via Pattipola).

At the Big and Small Ends of the World

Visitors who don't have much time to spare can get to know the main sections of the national park in an approximately three-hour circular hike (once they have paid their admission fee at the park entrance). After going two kilometers across the plateau and through a diverse

area of forest, you come to **Small World's End**, a steep precipice at the southern edge of Horton Plains, which is topped, after a further 20 minutes' walk, by **Big World's End**. The almost vertical cliff walls drop down more than 1,600 meters, divided, in the lower sections, into narrow terraces for tea cultivation. The view of the land to the south, the old Sinhalese kingdom of Ruhuna with its foothills, is often shrouded in the lowland mists. Only when visibility is exceptionally good can you see as far as the island's southern coast, some 90 kilometers distant, and the Indian Ocean. And it should also be mentioned that sometimes it is even impossible to look down into the deep drop: heavy cloud cover can develop at an incredible speed around the precipice and on the plateau itself. Experience has shown that visibility is generally better during the first four months of the year and in the early morning, but one should always be prepared for exceptions to this rule and carry suitable clothing for poor weather. When the weather is good, the rocky edge of Big World's End is a favorite picnic spot.

Above: View of Horton Plains. Right: Even when the fog rolls in, the tea still has to be picked.

The **Belihul Oya** and some of its tributaries rise on the plateau. Before it crashes down to the depths at the southern edge of the mountains, this river forms several attractive smaller waterfalls on Horton Plains. About half an hour past World's End, the circular hiking trail brings you to **Baker's Falls**, and from here it takes just under an hour to get back to the park entrance.

Anyone who has grown to appreciate the tranquility, perhaps also the pleasant coolness, and even the rapidly changing weather conditions on Sri Lanka's highest plateau, will be keen to experience more of the same on similar walks. In this case it is advisable to find accommodation nearby which will shorten the strenuous walk to Horton Plains itself. You will have to sacrifice comfort for con-

venience, though. Within the park or in the direct vicinity, visitors can choose from the somewhat rundown hotel Farr Inn; the Anderson Lodge, a bungalow which has to be booked in advance through the Wildlife Department; and a very basic campground, also requiring advance booking, of which the main attraction is the Belihul Oya River running past it. Before setting out, it is wise to inquire at the office at the park entrance for information on the condition of the various trails before setting off. A further charming starting point for hikes along the southern edge of the mountains and the plateau is the World's End Lodge, a small hotel four kilometers above the main road, the A4, which runs along the edge of the mountains; the hotel (signposted from the road) sits in **Lower Ohiya** as if glued to the slope. It once belonged to the brother of the Mr. Anderson after whom the lodge on the plateau is called. The brothers used to visit each other on foot or on horseback, and the present-day visitor can literally follow in their footsteps. The area offers countless walks, but hikers should consult locals first, or engage them as guides. Another place to stay is at the Rest House in **Belihul Oya** (near the river of the same name, which the A4 crosses here). The Rest House stands at the end of the roughly 13-kilometer path which leads down from World's End to the foothills.

NUWARA ELIYA

At the center of the hill country south of **Pidurutalagala**, Sri Lanka's highest mountain (2,524 meters), there is another plain at an altitude of about 1,900 meters. Surrounding this plain, like a protective wall, is a barrier of high wooded mountains with gentle, scrub-covered hilltops. The area around today's district city of **Nuwara Eliya** ("City of Light"; pronounced *nu-REL-iya*) looks today much as it appeared to the surveyors who arrived here in the early 19th century. The lowest average temperature here is 11.4°C, while the highest average tem-

perature is 20.2 °C. Thus the climate here is much closer to that of moderate latitudes than the climate in the tropical coastal area (Colombo: 24°C and 30.4°C). For this reason, governor Sir Edward Barnes decided, in 1828, to take advantage of the cool altitudes and create a spa town in this unpopulated mountain valley. Here, Europeans suffering from malaria or other tropical illnesses could come to recuperate.

The plateau was provided with a further source of income in 1848 thanks to the enthusiasm of Sir Samuel Baker. He felt the plateau was suitable for European-style agriculture, and imported everything he considered necessary in order to get things going: seeds, animals and equipment. His initiative effectively paved the way for the extensive vegetable production that flourishes in the hill country today. Since then, a dairy industry has also successfully established itself in the hill country; in fact, even the brewery in Nuwara Eliya can be traced back to the efforts of Sir Samuel. When the hill country developed into a center for high-quality tea cultivation towards the end of the 19th century, the town became the capital of the tea industry. As for Sir Samuel, he left the island soon after the middle of the 19th century in order to search for the source of the Nile.

Above and right: The Hill Club in Nuwara Eliya, built in the 19th century as a recreational facility for British colonials.

At first sight, Nuwara Eliya appears to be just another typical Sri Lankan city with busy streets and stores as befits a district capital of 30,000 inhabitants. But on approaching it, one cannot overlook several colonial-style park areas and buildings. The 18-hole golf course, for instance, is famous, as is the **Hill Club**, set in a carefully-tended garden. The guests enjoy the historic but modernized rooms of the rustic gray stone building with half-timbered ornamentation; they are still required to wear a tie and suit at dinner (you can rent these from the reception desk, if need be), and will be

asked before going to bed whether or not they require a hot-water bottle. The neighboring **Grand Hotel**, impressive by its size and striking wood-paneled interior, is the favorite choice of package tour operators. Since 1996, a former tea factory converted into a cozy three star hotel offers an unusual night's lodging: **The Tea Factory** at **Kandapola** lies several kilometers north of the town amid lush plantations. For a small entrance fee, you can mingle with locals in **Victoria Park**, the former spa gardens. In the west of Nurawa Eliya stands a fine colonial villa for the use of Sri Lanka's President.

The fact that there has been talk of turning the attractive red-and-white half-timbered **post office** building into a museum is proof that time does not stand still here. More and more, Sri Lanka's highest city is losing its English character, as new buildings continue to spring up and some of the older buildings start to be neglected and even forgotten.

On the shores of **Lake Gregory**, an artificial lake created in the 19th century to fill up the former marshland, is the race course; ponies graze along the shore, awaiting the pleasure of those who can afford to take riding lessons. A large portion of the north side of the lake is taken up by greenhouses for flower cultivation, while the beds on the east side are used for vegetables.

Every year in the middle of April, during the week when the Buddhists and Hindus celebrate the new year, a lively fair takes over the town. Anyone who considers himself to be anyone leaves the heat of Colombo behind and comes here to see and be seen. If Sir Samuel were alive today, he would be delighted with the turnover at the brewery. Bear in mind that it can be difficult to find accommodation at this time of year.

Between Vegetables and Tea

It is no longer possible to climb **Mount Pedro** (as Pidurutalagala is also called), since a fence surrounds the radio station at the top of the mountain and a generous

chunk of the land around it. Locals will be happy to point you to alternative walks up other nearby mountains, from which there are sweeping views of the lake and the town surrounded by woodland, tea plantations and vegetable gardens. En route to the top of the 2,240 meter **Kikilimana**, a walk of about seven kilometers, you also pass through the island's highest-lying village: Shantipura.

Leaving the valley of Nuwara Eliya on the eastbound A5, after about six kilometers you see, south of the road, a nature reserve around the mountain of **Hakgala** (2,170 meters). Part of the reserve is given over to the **Botanical Gardens** which developed in the 1860s from a cinchona plantation (used in quinine) and an experimental station for acclimatizing temperate-zone plants to the tropics. Some of the original *cinchona* (china bark trees) and tea bushes are still there. In addition, the gardens have a large collection of endemic trees and orchids. Another section is devoted to ferns, and some of the gigantic tree ferns provide welcome shade.

Above: Nuwara Eliya, the district's lively capital. Right: The Kotmale Reservoir, source of electricity and irrigation.

If you want to travel to Nuwara Eliya by train, get out at **Nanu Oya** and take the bus the last eight kilometers along the A7. Going in the opposite direction you pass picturesque tea country, as well as the Tea Research Institute at **Talawalkele**, founded in 1921. En route, you also drive past the turnoff to Hatton and Adam's Peak, and some attractive waterfalls.

KOTMALE

The winding A5 Nuwara Eliya-Kandy road offers excellent views of the countryside. Moreover, you can stop off at one of the tea estates to visit the factory and sample the tea. Southwest of the road, deep in the valley below, you can see the glint of a long, narrow lake: the **Kotmale Reservoir**. Leading to it is a new, little-used road which turns off be-

tween **Ramboda** and **Pussellawa**; this road also leads past the **Information Center**, opened in 1992. Here, you can learn about the many uses of the Kotmale Project: it produces electricity, regulates the flow of the Mahaweli Ganga (the **Kotmale Oya** is a tributary of the Mahaweli), and provides irrigation. The plant was constructed with Swedish aid between 1979 and 1985. The **Kotmale Dam** is not open to the public, but you can cross the Kotmale Oya south of the Kotmale Holiday Resort, which brings you to the equally fine roads on the south side of the reservoir. Many of the villages here are fairly new: the rising water of the dam meant that villagers had to be resettled elsewhere.

Golden Pumpkin and Holy Tooth

Despite these modern developments, this area also has plenty of historical tradition. The **Pusulpitiya Vihara** ("Monastery of the Pumpkin Plain"), rising up above the reservoir, is more than two thousand years old, since the uniter of the Sinhalese, Dutthagamani, is said to have stopped here in the second century B.C. It is one of the monasteries from the kingdom of Kandy, and most of its buildings date from that time: the two-story image house with a large collection of valuable artifacts in the basement, and a small image house with well-preserved paintings. The fact that the temple is in a concealed location made it an ideal hiding place for the relic of the Sacred Tooth in times of danger. A legend surrounds the complex: the story of the monastery's founding tells that a greedy Brahman killed his son in order to get for himself a golden pumpkin from the Kotmale River.

BADULLA

Uva Province borders the hill country to the east. Though it is part of Sri Lanka's mountain country, the fact that the highest peaks shelter it from the rain means that it receives less rainfall, which gives the region a different character.

Several of the deep river valleys were already being used as transport routes during the classical Sinhalese period, forming a link between Polonnaruwa and Ruhuna. In other words, this area was known and inhabited before the arrival of European colonists. **Badulla** was, and remains, its most important town; situated at the confluence of the **Badulu** and **Kuda Oya**, it boasts around 32,000 inhabitants. It lies at an altitude of about 700 meters and is flanked by extremely steep mountain slopes which are often divided into terraces. **Namunukula**, 10 kilometers away, is, at 2,036 meters, one of Sri Lanka's highest mountains.

Badulla is also known throughout the island on account of the **Muthiyangana Temple**, which is one of the 16 most sacred pilgrimage sites in Sri Lanka. Devout Buddhists believe that Buddha consecrated the temple on one of his visits to the island. There is little in the temple to indicate its great age; in fact, there are several modern wall paintings which illustrate, rather than embody, Badulla's historical importance. Long before the kingdom of Kandy was created at the end of the 16th century, there was a small principality in this area which was able to survive due to the good harvests from its rice terraces. In the first decades of the Kandy kingdom it joined forces with the king, while remaining the seat of its own prince. After the Portuguese had totally destroyed Badulla in 1615 and 1630, the king of Kandy also struck a blow at the town by annexing it into his kingdom in 1637 and placing it under a provincial governor. For almost two hundred years the Uva Province remained an important supplier of rice, until, in the first half of the 19th century, British colonialism also took hold in this part of the hill country. The British had various reasons for establishing an important military and administrative base in Badulla: the ringleader of the revolt of 1817/18 came from here; the region was very isolated; and they wanted to expand the plantation area eastward.

Right: The colossal statues of Buduruvagala date from the ninth century A.D.

Waterfalls and Monasteries

Thanks to an extensive road network and the Badulla-Colombo railway line, the beauty of the eastern hill country is accessible to tourists today. Located on the B49 (four kilometers north of Badulla), which is an important connection for pilgrims traveling between Mahiyangana and Kataragama, the waterfalls of **Dunhinda** reward tourists at the end of a short walk (20 minutes), while the **Ravanella Falls** south of **Ella** can be seen from a distance – from, for example, the **Namunukula Massif**. If you approach these mountains from their east side on the B50, you will be rewarded by differing and incomparable views encompassing carefully-tended tea estates, the foothills, the eastern and southern plains, and continuing as far as the east coast. One famous view is through the **Ella Gap**, through which the A23 leaves the hill country heading south.

There are some spectacular sights in this mountain landscape: the **Bogoda Bridge** (signposted on the A5 in **Hali-Ela**, 12 kilometers), a wooden bridge from the Kandy era leading to an early Buddhist temple which the carpenters built without metal components; the **Dowa Shrine**, which has a statue of Buddha four meters high hewn out of the rocks (seven kilometers north of Bandarawela on the A16); the **Adisham Monastery**, three kilometers west of Haputale, actually intended as the retirement home of Englishman Thomas Lyster Villiers, completed in 1931. In this solitary mountain site, Villiers built an exact replica of a stone villa from his native town. In 1961, Benedictine monks bought the property, and they have run it as a monas-

tery and guest house ever since (if you want to stay here, apply in writing to the abbot.)

Because of the eastern hill country's scenic beauty and infrequent rainfall, towns like Ella, and especially **Bandarawela**, have developed into holiday resorts frequented by Sri Lankans, competing with Nuwara Eliya in popularity. On the southernmost point of the massif, at an altitude of about 1,400 meters, lies the market town of **Haputale** with a breathtaking view of the south of the island. Anyone wishing to prolong his sight of this magnificent view should continue on the A16 as far as Beragala (six kilometers), then turn off eastwards onto the A4. The next 32 kilometers are a steady descent down to **Wellawaya** in the lowland region, but en route you are rewarded again and again with unexpected views of the hill country, the foothills or the plains. Roughly halfway down and close to the road, the **Diyaluma Waterfall** (170 meters) is a good place to stop off.

The Uva Province extends far into the flat land of what was once Ruhuna. Just four kilometers south of Wellawaya (signposted on the A2), a sandy track four kilometers long leads to the rocks with the colossal statues of **Buduruvagala**. The central figure, a Buddha roughly 14 meters high standing in *abhaya mudra* (gesture of fearlessness), is flanked by two groups of three figures, all hewn from the same cliff.

At the center of the group on the left stands the Bodhisattva Avalokiteshvara, also referred to as the god Natha, flanked on either side by his consort Tara and the latter's son, Prince Sudanakumaru. The future Buddha Maitreya stands at the center of the right-hand group, with Manjusri on his left and Vajrapana on his right. Plaster remains on the rock face show that the reliefs were once plastered and painted. The depictions hearken back to the period when Sri Lanka was under the influence of Mahayana Buddhism, and have been dated back to the ninth century A.D.

ADAM'S PEAK

Accommodation

DICKOYA: *MODERATE:* **Upper Glencairn Bungalow**, tel. 0512-2348 (former plantation bungalow, colonial-style, with view of Adam's Peak and Castlereagh Lake, 30 km to Dalhousie and the start of the pilgrimage trail, the hotel can organize a taxi). Its affiliate **Lower Glencairn Bungalow** is nearby.

HATTON: *BUDGET:* **Frankland Hotel**, Main Street, tel. 0512-2351. **Lanka Inn Tourist Rest**, 47/6 Dunbar Road; tel. 0512-2647; (Hatton-Dalhousie 40 km).

MASKELIYA: *BUDGET:* **Maskeliya Hotel**, Main Road. **Old Post Office**, Upcot Road, Maskeliya; (Maskeliya-Dalhousie 19 km).

There's also private accommodation in every town. Officials of tea plantations are forbidden to rent out space in their roomy bungalows for commercial purposes, but no one can stop them taking in private guests. Ask, for example, in the restaurant of the **New Al Hamra Hotel**, 112 Main Street, Maskeliya.

Transportation

TRAIN: Hatton Station is a stop on the Kandy-Badulla line, with service several times a day.

BUS: Several connections a day to and from Hatton and Colombo, Nuwara Eliya, Kandy. Buses to Dalhousie leave from Hatton or Maskeliya.

TAXI: Foreign tourists are often overcharged for the ride to Dalhousie; make sure to haggle a bit.

Excursions

Adam's Peak is not the only worthwhile hiking destination. With a local guide who knows his way around (one place to organize one is the Upper Glencairn Bungalow, Dickoya, tel. 0512-2348), you can plan countless different tailor-made excursions.

Hospitals

District Hospital of Dickoya, tel. 0512-2261.
District Hospital of Maskeliya, tel. 052-7261.

BADULLA

Accommodation

BUDGET: **Badulla New Tourist Inn**, 122 Mahiyangana Road, tel. 055-23423; **Dunhinda Falls Inn**, Bandaranayake Mw., tel. 055-23028; **Riverside Holiday Inn**, 27 Lower King Street, tel. 055-22090.

Transportation

TRAIN: At least four trains a day to and from Kandy and Colombo. *BUS:* Frequent daily service to Nuwara Eliya and Kandy, several buses a day to Colombo, as well as to the south coast via Wellawaya.

Excursions / Sights

Dunhinda Falls, 20-min. on a narrow, rocky footpath from the B49 to waterfall (Badulla-Karametiya road, 4 km north of Badulla, signposted; nearly all the pilgrimage buses between Mahiyangana and Badulla/Kataragama stop here); **Bogoda Bridge**, Kandy-period wooden bridge without any metal components, 12 km from Hali-Ela (signposted); **Muthiyangana Temple**, most important Buddhist pilgrimage destination at the center of Badulla. **Namunukula**, striking 2,000 meter-high mountain southeast of Badulla; scenic circular road around it (B 50) between Passara and Ella.

Hospital

General Hospital, tel. 055-22261.

BANDARAWELA

Accommodation

MODERATE: **Bandarawela Hotel**, 14 Welimada Road, tel. 057-22501. **Prince Hotel**, Badulla Road (4 km north of Bandarawela), tel. 057-32477. **Orient Hotel**, 12 Dharmapala Mw., tel. 057-22407. **Rose Villa**, off Punagala Road (three rooms, flower garden, Sri Lankan food), tel. 057-22329.

BUDGET: **Alpine Inn**, Ellatota, tel. 057-22569. **Himalie Guest House**, Badulla Road, Bindunuwewa (4 km north of Bandarawela). **Ideal Resort**, Welimada Road, tel. 057-22476. **Rest House**, off Dharmapala Mw., tel. 057-22299.

Restaurants

Rest House, off Dharmapala Mw., tel. 057-22299; **Chinese Union Hotel**, 8 Mount Pleasant, tel. 057-22502.

Ayurvedic Beauty Farm

Suwamadhu-Suwasetha, Badulla Road (herbal baths, massage, etc., 4 km north of Bandarawela, opposite the Prince Hotel), tel. 057-22584.

Transportation

TRAIN: All trains on the Badulla-Kandy-Colombo line stop here. *BUS:* Several buses a day to Nuwara Eliya, Kandy, Colombo, Badulla, Haputale.

ELLA

Accommodation

MODERATE: **Ella Adventure Park**, Uva Karandagolla, tel. 057-87263/4, outdoor activities. **Country Comfort Inn**, 32 Police Station Rd., small old villa, tastefully renovated, two minutes' walk from train station, tel. 057-23132. **Rest House**, lovely view of Ella Gap, tel. 057-22636. *BUDGET:* **Ella Gap Tourist Inn**, tel. 057-22628. **Ravana Heights**, opposite the 27th km marker, Wellawaya Road, tel. 057-31182.

Transportation

TRAIN: All trains on the Colombo/Kandy-Badulla line stop here. *BUS:* Several a day to Badulla, Nuwara Eliya, Haputale, and the south coast via Wellawaya.

HAPUTALE

Accommodation

MODERATE: **Thotalagala Bungalow**, in tea plantation, 5 km from Haputale, restaurant, tel: 01-381644/5, 071-793706.

BUDGET: Benedictine monastery of **Adisham**, tel. 057-68030, three km west of Haputale, after about 2 km on the B 48 toward Boralanda/Keppetipola turn left and continue about 1 km along a badly-developed road. Overnight stays only possible after written request to the abbot: Father Superior, Adisham, Haputale). **New Rest House**, Bandarawela Road, tel. 057-68099. **Old Rest House**, at train station, tel. 057-68206. **High Cliffe Hotel**, 15 Station Road, tel. 057-68096. Many small guest houses. In *Haldumulla*: **Pine Village Guest House**, Uvatenna.

Transportation

TRAIN: All trains on the Colombo/Kandy-Badulla line stop here. *BUS:* Several a day to Ratnapura/Colombo, Nuwara Eliya, Badulla, and the south and east coasts via Beragala/Wellawaya.

Excursions / Sights

Adisham Monastery: Guided tours daily 9 am to noon and 1 to 4:30 pm, small specialty shop selling wine, jam and other products; **Horton Plains**: Two stops by train to Ohiya, continue on foot.

HORTON PLAINS NATIONAL PARK

Accommodation / Restaurants

BELIHUL-OYA: *BUDGET:* **Rest House**, Main Road, tel. 045-87599 (World's End Hike to Belihul-Oya is about 14 km, steep descent). Restaurant only: **River Garden Hotel**, Main Road (with lovely view).

HORTON PLAINS: *BUDGET:* **Anderson Lodge** and **campground**, must be booked in advance through the Dept. of Wildlife Conservation, Wildlife Reservation Centre, 18 Gregory Rd., Colombo 7, tel. 01-694241. **Circuit Bungalow Pattipola**, must be reserved in advance through the Forest Dept., 82 Rajamalwatte Road, Battaramulla (Colombo), tel. 01-866626. **Farr Inn Rest House,** by the park entrance, needs renovating, tel. 070-522029 (information/reservations through Ceylon Hotels Corp., tel. 01-503497.)

LOWER OHIYA: *BUDGET:* **World's End Lodge**, 4 km from the A4 between Belihul Oya and Haldummulla, signposted, tel. 071-30015, renovated, great location, ideal base for hikes.

Transportation

No public transportation to park entrance; the nearest train stations are Ohiya (6 km) and Pattipola (9 km), from here several buses a day run to Nuwara Eliya.

BELIHUL OYA, LOWER OHIYA: There are many buses every day running along the A4 toward Ratnapura/Colombo, into the mountains via Haputale, and to the east and south coasts via Wellawaya.

KOTMALE

Accommodation

BUDGET: **Kotmale Holiday Resort**, River Side, Mawatura (northwest of lake, former bungalows of the engineers of the Kotmale Reservoir), tel. 08-350558/9. **Pahala Walauwa**, Kotmale, villa with view of the reservoir, 4 guest rooms, reservations through Connaissance de Ceylan, tel. 074-610200.

Transportation

TRAIN: Nearest train station (for Kotmale Holiday Resort): **Ulapane**, several trains daily to Kandy-Badulla. *BUS:* Local buses via **Ulapane** (between Gampola and Nawalpitiya) to Ramboda/Pusselawa (for regions on the north side of the reservoir). Buses via Gampola/Nawalpitiya-Kotmale-Kotmale New Town (for regions south of the reservoir).

Sights

Kotmale Project Reservoir and Dam Viewpoint, 6 km east of Kotmale Holiday Resort, with modern information center on the Kotmale Projekt and a restaurant (both temporarily closed), view over the reservoir.

NUWARA ELIYA

Accommodation

MODERATE: **Galway Forest Lodge,** 89 Upper Lake Rd., tel. 052-23728. **Glendower Hotel**, 5 Grand Hotel Road, tel. 052-22501. **Grand Hotel**, Grand Hotel Road, tel. 052-22881-5. **St. Andrew's Hotel**, 10 St. Andrew's Drive, tel. 052-22445. **The Hill Club**, 29 Grand Hotel Road, tel. 052-23152. **The Tea Factory**, Kandapola (former tea factory, 14 km outside of Nuwara Eliya in the middle of a tea plantation), tel. 052-23600. **Windsor Hotel**, 1-2, Kandy Rd, tel. 052-22554. *BUDGET:* **Ceybank Rest**, Badulla Road (renovated), tel. 052-23053. **Chalet Du Lake**, Badulla Road (on the lake, 10 chalets), tel. 072-55519. **Haddon Hill Lodge**, 29 Haddon Hill Road, tel. 052-22345. **Princess Guest House**, Wedderburn Road, tel. 052-22462. Countless other small hotels on or near Badulla Road.

Restaurants

CHINESE: **Glendower Hotel**, 5 Grand Hotel Road, tel. 052-22749. *ENGLISH:* **The Hill Club**, 29 Grand Hotel Road, tel. 052-23152. Many cafés and restaurants along New Bazaar Street.

Transportation

TRAIN: **Nanu Oya** station 6 km toward Hatton (A 7), stop for all trains on the Colombo/Kandy-Badulla line. *BUS:* Daily service to all major cities in the country.

Excursions / Hikes

Horton Plains, 25 km, with four-wheel-drive vehicle. **Hakgala Botanical Gardens**, 4 km. Highest village in Sri Lanka, **Shantipura**, and ascent of the 2,240-meter-high **Kikilimana**, 7 km.

WELLAWAYA

Accommodation

LUXURY CAMPGROUND: **TASK Safari Camp**, Kithulkotte, Kuda Oya (25 km south of Wellawaya, off the A2 on the Kuda Oya River, guided safaris on foot, by boat and jeep in the nearby national parks: Handapangala, Uda Walawe, Gal Oya, Yala), tel. 0722-31103.

BUDGET: **Saranga Holiday Inn**, 37 Ella Road, tel. 055-74891.

Transportation

BUS: Frequent daily service from Wellawaya to Ratnapura/Colombo, to the south coast (Hambantota, Galle), east coast (Ampara/Batticaloa, Pottuvil – depending on the current political situation), and into the mountains (Ella/Badulla, Nuwara Eliya).

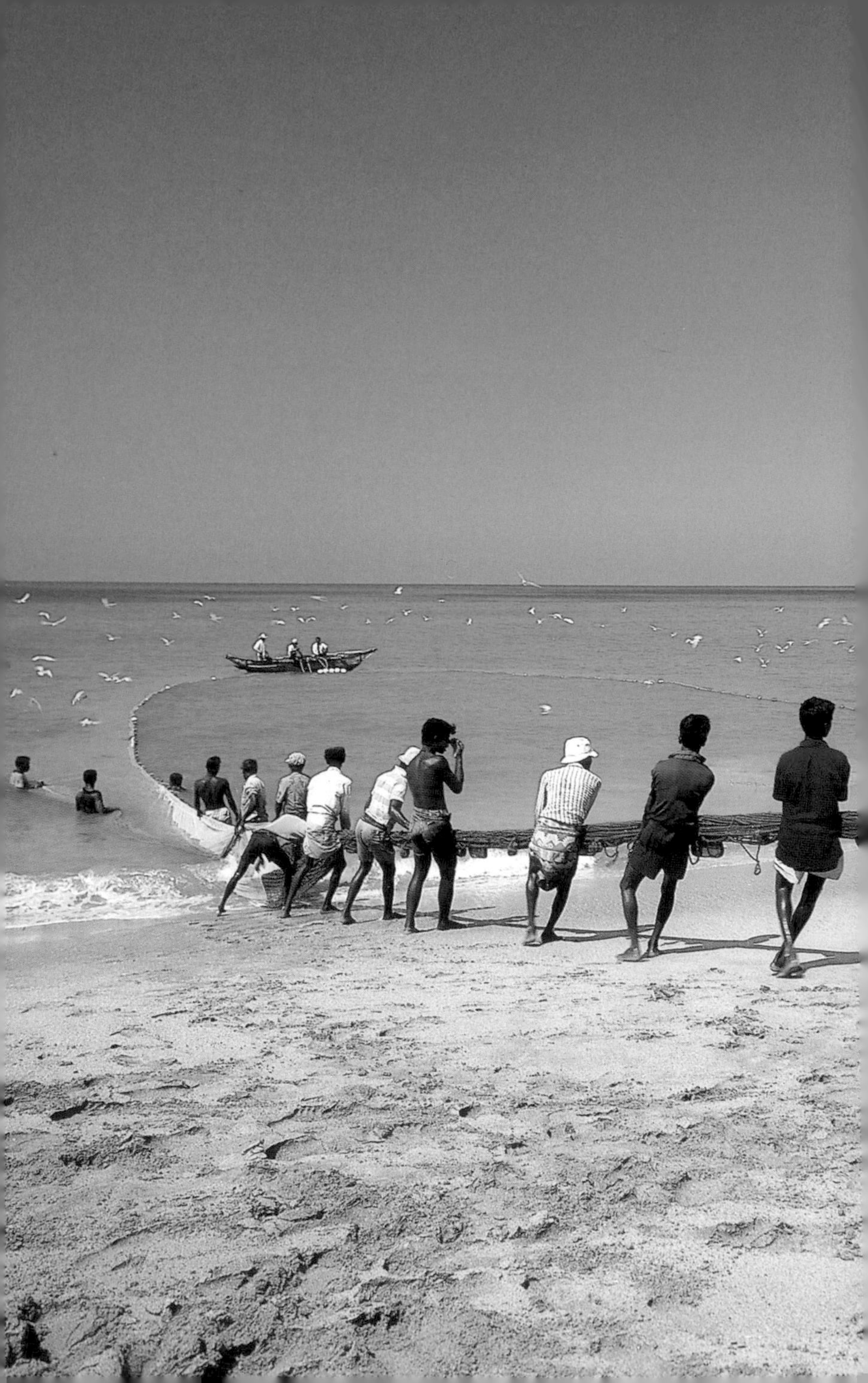

THE EAST
Destinations for Individualists

BUTTALA
LAHUGALA / POTTUVIL
ARUGAM BAY / GAL OYA
BATTICALOA
TRINCOMALEE

BUTTALA

Ruins and old temple complexes scattered all over the eastern region attest to the fact that this area was once part of Sinhalese territory in the classical period. Well-known routes existed between Tissamaharama and the north, something demonstrated by historical descriptions and *gavta* columns, milestones from the time of King Nissanka Malla (1187-1196). The old road from south to north led via **Buttala** through the eastern mountain region.

To reach the most famous shrine of the god Skanda in **Kataragama**, pilgrims still use the Buttala-Kataragama route, which has been excellently paved. Traveling by bus or car, they can stop off on their way to take in some of the other sights in the area, which the Archeology Office has conveniently signposted on both sides of the A4.

Sightseeing with the Pilgrims

About one kilometer west of Buttala, a dirt road branches off to the north and leads two kilometers to the small, well-restored monastery complex of **Culagani Vihara**. Located here are a dagoba, monks' buildings, image house and *bodhighara*, the enclosure for a sacred bo tree, all probably dating from the 12th century. A statue of Buddha that stands nearby is thought to originate from the sixth to seventh centuries.

Preceding pages: Fishermen haul in their catch. Left: Animals are included in the Hindu thanksgiving festival of Thai Pongal.

One kilometer further on is the surprisingly large, partially excavated dagoba of **Yudagannawa**; although it's covered with trees and bushes, you can still clearly see that it has a flattened top, something typical of a number of dagobas at the time of the great Parakramabahu I (1153-1186). It is thought to be the memorial dagoba erected by the king on the site where his mother Ratnavali was cremated. *Yudagana pitiya* also means "place of battle," so that this spot has also been identified as the place where Dutthagamani, who later unified the Sinhalese kingdom, defeated his brother Sadhatissa, who had seized the throne after the death of their father (second century B.C.).

From Buttala, signs direct you to the temple complex of **Dematamal Vihara**, much of which has been restored (seven kilometers east of the B53, toward **Okkampitiya**). The dagoba on the rectangular platform has been painstakingly reconstructed. In the older image house

the existing stone columns were used for the modern core of the building; a second, newer, larger image house here has the traditional ground plan. A *bodhighara*, or stone enclosure for the sacred bo tree, remains of statues, and a stone door frame all attest to the fact that the original complex was even larger.

Many Sri Lankan pilgrim tourists visit the colossal **Buddha of Maligawila** (nine kilometers from Okkampitiya), which has had major restoration work done and now once again sits upright on its lotus throne. At 12 meters in height, it is almost as tall as that of Aukana in Rajarata, and its head alone weighs around six tons. The massive stone construction is said to have been built by Prince Agghabodhi in the first half of the seventh century, while the image house surrounding it is attributed to King Dappula (659 A.D.). Only the foundation walls of the latter building have been restored, so that you can take in the full height of the statue in the open air. The building is also surrounded by a moat.

Above: Bodhighara on the grounds of the monastery at Magul Maha Vihara, near Lahugala.

Dappula was also responsible for putting up the colossal statue which comes into view near the village of **Dambegoda** after a walk of about half a kilometer through luxuriant jungle: a flight of steps leads you up to the fifth platform of a pyramid-shaped hill where a modern roof shelters a richly decorated **Maitreya Buddha**, or future Buddha. Although he only displays the small symbol of a single *Dyani Buddha* (meditating Buddha) in his crown, which, strictly speaking, indicates that he is the Boddhisattva Avalokiteshvara, Maitreya and the god Natha are traditionally also represented in this way. Both of these giant statues belong to the same monastery complex, most of which still lies buried in thick jungle. It had its heyday during the *Mahayana* period in Sri Lanka (approximately seventh to tenth centuries).

From Okkampitiya, it is around seven kilometers to the main road, the A4.

About 10 kilometers further east is the district capital, **Monaragala**. This small place, with only very basic accommodations, is dominated by the mighty mountain behind it. On its north slope, near the village of **Obbegoda**, are the remains of the former palace of **Galabedda**, assumed to have belonged to a local 12th-century ruler who had his capital, Udundora, here (signposted on the A4 and a short walk from the road). In the palace complex a particularly fine bathing pool, known as the "Queen's Bath," has been restored; this vaguely resembles the *kumara pokuna*, the pool of Parakramabahu I in Polonnaruwa.

The road now leads through a sparsely populated, forested area broken by an occasional sugar-cane field. The A4 to the coast is in good condition. The police near the important crossroads at **Siyambalanduwa**, where the A25 runs north to Ampara (57 kilometers) and Batticaloa 130 kilometers), stop drivers for inspections of vehicles, individuals and cargo.

LAHUGALA

The road soon enters the eastern province and the countryside becomes more open. Bizarre rocky hills stick up out of the jungle, the unmistakable landmarks of this area. Some of them attracted hermits more than two thousand years ago when Buddhism first came to Sri Lanka. One of the present-day jungle monasteries is called Maha Tapowanaya, where you can meditate atop a rocky hill only one kilometer north of the road.

Before the main road reaches the coast, it crosses the country's smallest national park, **Lahugala-Kitulana**. Only a bit more than 16 square kilometers in area, it was turned into a nature reserve in 1980. It's wise to drive through it slowly, since you may encounter an elephant on the road; you can also spot these animals swimming or grazing. The small park is also a treasure trove for bird lovers: 110

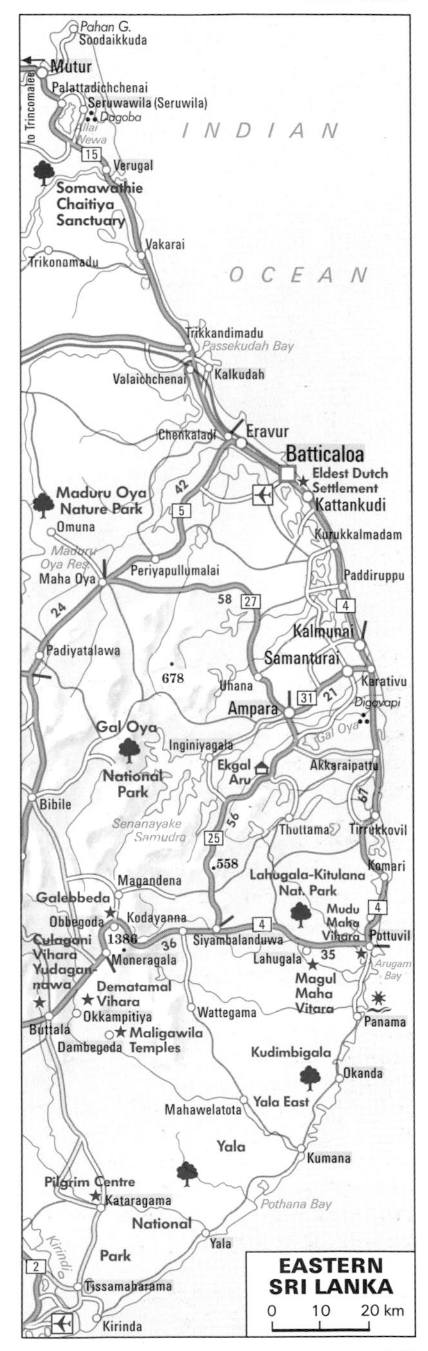

different species have been counted within its boundaries, which encompass many different habitats.

About one kilometer along a small road branching off south from the village of Lahugala is the monastery of **Magul Maha Vihara**, attributed to King Dhatusena (459-477), father of the scandalous usurper Kassapa, who built the Sigiriya fortress. Inscription plaques dating from the 14th century testify to its long history. Within the enclosing wall are the remains of the main parts of the old monastery: dagoba, image house, assembly hall, monks' buildings and a well-preserved *bodhighara*, the enclosure for the sacred bo tree.

POTTUVIL

From here to **Pottuvil**, a coastal town with a strong Moorish influence, the countryside is flat, with rice paddies and pastureland. Along the beach, a bank of dunes several meters high protects the town from the sea, but its presence also means that there is no harbor. The north-east monsoon constantly pushes the dunes further inland, burying some coastal buildings, as demonstrated by the **Mudu Maha Vihara** ("Great Monastery by the Sea"): fragments of brick scattered through the dunes, half-buried in the sand, are all that remain of the dagoba today. A wall of sand several meters high is dangerously close to the restored ruins of the image house with its richly decorated figures from the *Mahayana* epoch – the period in which the bodhisattvas found their way into Buddhism.

Above: An alternative way to transport children on the east coast. Right: Fisherman in Arugam Bay.

ARUGAM BAY

South of the bridge across the **Lagoon of Arugam**, which is abundantly stocked with fish, a number of picturesque fishing villages extend in an arc along the shore of **Arugam Bay**. Surfing connois-

seurs know the bay as a great inside tip; while the region inland holds a wealth of magnificent landscapes in store for nature lovers. Further south, there is nothing but a few tanks and rice paddies.

The paved road ends in **Panama**, as does public bus service: south of this, there are only dirt roads, which are often impassable in places during the rainy season. Local inhabitants use some of the open parkland as grazing pasturage for their large herds of cattle; nature conservation authorities also permit this in the reserves of **Kudimbigala** and the **Yala East** block of **Yala National Park**, which starts only 10 kilometers south of Panama. It is not unusual to see cattle grazing alongside the indigenous wild animals of the region.

Traversing the countryside here is a pilgrims' trail leading to Kataragama; inhabitants of the eastern and northern provinces also made use of this difficult path through open jungle country in the past. On their hike through present-day nature reserves, approximately 75 kilometers long, they made rest stops at Okanda, Madametota (near Kumana), Pothana, Yala, Warahana (by the Menik Ganga) and Katagamuwa, among others. The travelers oriented themselves first by following the coast and then by going along the river of the Menik Ganga, which also flows through Kataragama.

Once, there were countless monasteries and hermitages in this huge area, now largely reclaimed by nature; monks lived here from the third century B.C. to the tenth century A.D., concentrating especially among the massive clusters of rock that dominate the landscape. Even today, there are still a few forest monks living in the historic caves.

From Panama, it's a demanding day's hike to the striking **Kudimbigala Rocks** to the west, on the other side of the swampy **Helawa Lagoon**; pilgrim hostels and a large well serve as reminders of the fact that hordes of pilgrims periodically come through here. Deserted, by contrast, are the offices and lodgings of the gamekeepers from the Department of

Wildlife Conservation in **Okanda**, abandoned in 1985; the brackish waters of the lagoon of **Kumana**, famous for its bird life, is for the present being left to look after itself.

Little Huts, Big Waves

In contrast to all the other resorts on the east coast, which were damaged in the civil war, Arugam Bay has retained most of its – often basic – hotels, which line the single road. These are small family businesses with no aspirations to provide the standard brand of international large-scale beach-holiday comfort. A sign of this is the Arugam Bay Hilton gracing a simple guest house with a palm-thatched roof, a cheerful send-up of the conventional trappings of civilization. Arugam Bay hardly has any telephone lines. All in all it represents a kind of Gateway to Paradise for anyone able to recognize, in all its natural simplicity, the riches this place has to offer.

Activities here are governed by the annual cycle of rains and winds: the heaviest rains fall from November to mid-December, and the park-like landscape of the inland regions dons a new covering of fresh green foliage. From mid-December to April, windsurfing conditions in the bay are particularly good, while in April, according to those in the know, the waves are ideal for body-surfing. The weather becomes calmer and even drier with the onset of the southwest monsoon, which forces wild animals to congregate ever more closely around the shrinking watering holes as the summer progresses. A huge variety of bird species is to be seen during the annual migration in October.

Above: In the valley of the Gal Oya River independent Sri Lanka built its first irrigation project. Right: Many Moors live on the east coast.

GAL OYA

Rice paddies and swampy lagoons line the A4 from Pottuvil to the north. The extensive rice paddies around **Akkaraipattu** are the result of the first major agricultural project implemented by the new state following its independence in 1948. Because of the unpredictability of the northeast monsoon, the farmers on the lower reaches of the **Gal Oya River**, which is 110 kilometers long, had two problems to contend with: if there was a lot of rain, there were devastating floods, but if there was not enough rain, the rice crop suffered. To resolve this situation, between 1949 and 1951 the government built the largest reservoir in the country, 78 square kilometers in area; it was called **Senanayake Samudra** (*samudra*: sea) after the country's first Prime Minister. The intention was not only to regulate the water supply to the rice paddies that already existed, but also to make it possible to extend these fields, as well as providing a source of electricity.

Together, the reservoir and a large section of the surrounding countryside (259 square kilometers) comprise the **Gal Oya National Park**, which was established in 1954. The Department of Wildlife Conservation generally runs a bungalow in **Ekgal Aru** (though not at the present time). There are hardly any roads through the park and to continue onwards from **Inginiyagala**, by the dam, it's best to go by boat.

Ampara was built as a modern municipal center, and even has an airfield.

Digavapi – Buddha's Resting Place

The land around the lower reaches of the Gal Oya has been settled since time immemorial, and a historic pilgrim route leads through it. One place it passes through is **Digavapi**, which Buddha is said to have visited the third time he came to Sri Lanka, after he had left his famous footprint on Adam's Peak (from Ampara six kilometers to the south on the A 25, then 11 kilometers to the east; signposted). The complex at Digavapi has a

large, restored dagoba and a small, modern **archeological museum**.

BATTICOLA

The A31 passes through densely populated, flat agricultural country and connects Ampara with the A4 coastal road. The villages here crowd close together between the extensive network of lagoons and the sea. Although they have Tamil names, the composition of their population is not so simple: in the district of Ampara, Tamil-speaking Muslim Moors are in the majority, while the district of Batticaloa is dominated by Tamils who are mainly Hindu. At the time of the Tamil kingdom (13th to 16th centuries), Hindu Tamils were already living along the east coast. When the Portuguese started colonizing Ceylon in the 16th century, beginning on the west side of the island, they saw the Moors as their most dangerous adversaries: they were adherents of the Islamic faith and controlled the trade activities of Ceylon. Senarat,

king of Kandy (1604-1635) came to the aid of the Moors by making territory east of the mountains available to anyone who had been persecuted by the Europeans. Although the Moors speak Tamil, in the course of their history they tended to cooperate more with the Sinhalese, and the local administrative bodies contain a high proportion of Sinhalese officials. This region, in particular, has seen violent battles in the course of the Tamil struggle for independence.

The city center of the district capital, **Batticaloa**, which became a Dutch base in the 17th century, is located on an island in the large lagoon. Access to the government buildings in its eastern sector, as well as to the *kachcheri*, the local administrative offices, housed in the impregnable rectangular fort built in 1665, is limited to authorized persons and strictly controlled by the police. As the terminus of the railway line from Colombo, and with a population of 50,000, the town is an important regional center; however, apart from its legendary "singing fish," which you can hear – with a little bit of luck and a certain amount of indulgence, and preferably on the night of the full moon – from the bridge over the mouth of the lagoon at **Kalladi**, it has few attractions for visitors.

Above: The roads along the coast are interrupted by many rivers – ferry in Koddiyar Bay. Right: Village street near Trincomalee.

Deserted Beaches

Tourists used to flock to the beaches of the protected bays of **Kalkudah** and **Passekudah**; but that was before political unrest laid waste to the area and the hotels were all abandoned. In the 1990s, the bush and jungle completely took over this strip of coast, and the whole area is under the control of the military.

The main road and railway line veer inland at the industrial town of **Valaichchenai**. The coastal road of the A15 leads north through sparsely populated countryside, interrupted several times by ferry

crossings. Few visitors venture into this lonely region with its beautiful beaches and lagoons, as there are scarcely any tourist facilities and ferry service is often suspended.

TRINCOMALEE

Near **Verugal** begins the **Verugal Aru**, a side arm of the Mahaweli Ganga. Further north, at its estuary, the largest river in the country subdivides into further branches, which means you can't always circumnavigate **Koddiyar Bay** by car, as ferry service is sometimes suspended. Passenger ferries operate several times a day between **Mutur** and **Trincomalee**.

However, there's also a land route to the area around the estuary of the Mahaweli Ganga: from the A6, the main road between Habarana and Trincomalee, a minor road from **Kantale** runs east through the rice paddies and along the northern edge of **Somawathie Chaitiya National Park**. Thus you reach the dagoba of **Seruwawila** (Seruwila) on the east side of the **Allai Wewa Reservoir**, which may date back as far as the second century B.C. One famous artifact from here is a figure of a meditating Buddha, enthroned on a coiled cobra and protected by the snake's extended hood.

Quiet Harbor, Stormy Times

The city of Trincomalee spreads across a number of rocky promontories which surround the complex of the **Inner Harbor** on three sides. In the global monsoon wind zone, there is scarcely another harbor that is so excellently protected both from the northeast and the southwest; the bay, furthermore, is naturally deep. At the beginning of the Kandy kingdom, when the east coast was a part of the Sinhalese empire, the small harbor here, originally known as Gokanna, had already been in existence for a long time. As they explored the Indian Ocean, the Europeans were quick to see the advantages of this place, and between the early

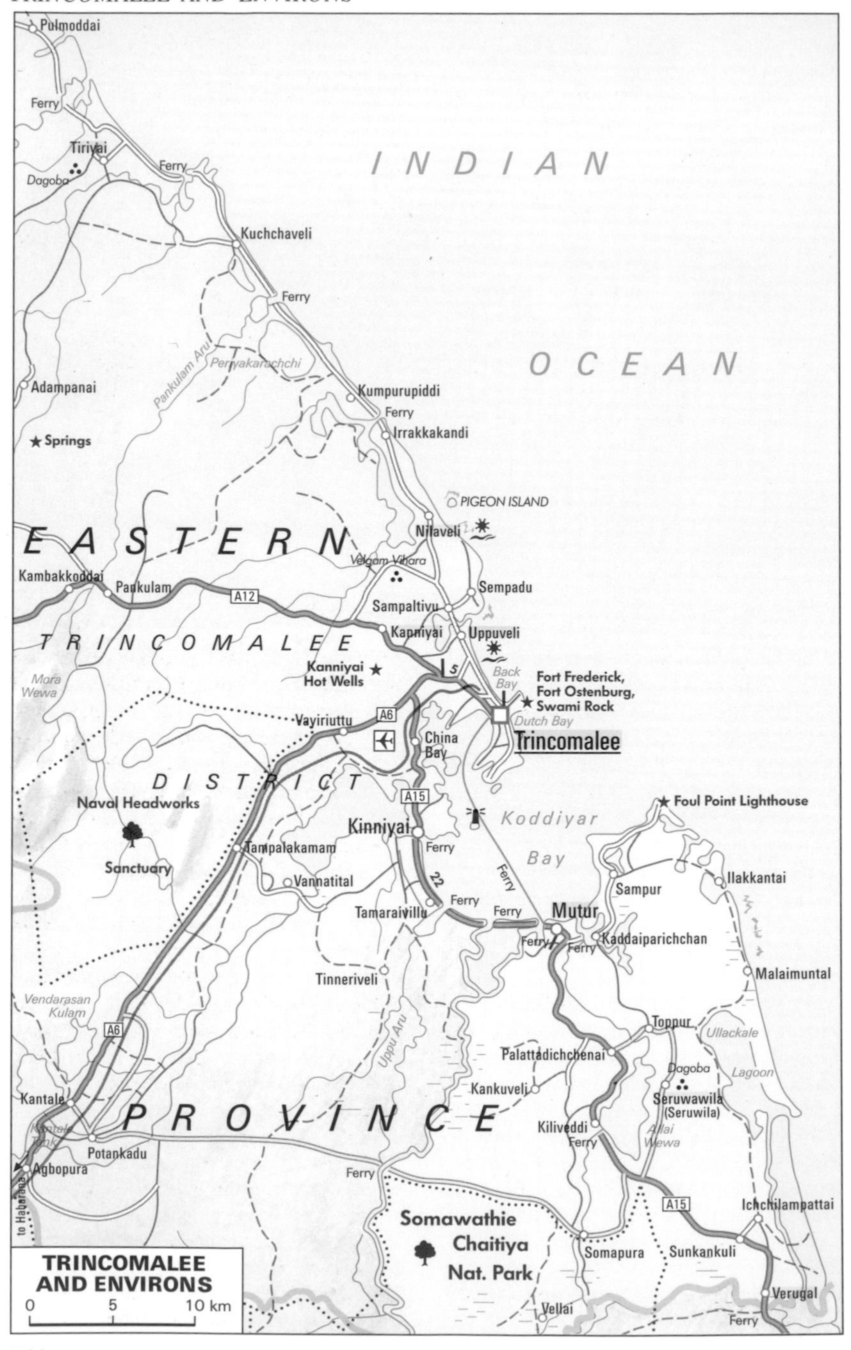
Pulmoddai
Ferry
Tiriyai
Dagoba
Ferry
INDIAN
OCEAN
Kuchchaveli
Ferry
Pankulam Aru
Periyakarachchi
Adampanai
Kumpurupiddi
Ferry
Irrakkakandi
Springs
PIGEON ISLAND
Nilaveli
EASTERN
Velgam Vihara
Kambakkoddai
Pankulam
A12
Sempadu
Sampaltivu
Kanniyai
Uppuveli
TRINCOMALEE
Kanniyai Hot Wells
Mora Wewa
Back Bay
Fort Frederick, Fort Ostenburg, Swami Rock
Dutch Bay
Vayiriuttu
A6
China Bay
Trincomalee
DISTRICT
A15
Naval Headworks
Koddiyar
Foul Point Lighthouse
Kinniyai
Ferry
Bay
Tampalakamam
Sanctuary
Vannatital
Ferry
Sampur
Ilakkantai
Tamaraivillu
Ferry
Ferry
Mutur
Ferry
Ferry
Kaddaiparichchan
Tinneriveli
Malaimuntal
Vendarasan Kulam
A6
Uppu Aru
Toppur
Ullackale
Palattadichchenai
Dagoba
Lagoon
Kankuveli
Kantale
Seruwawila (Seruwila)
PROVINCE
Kiliveddi
Kantale Tank
Ferry
Allai Wewa
Potankadu
Agbopura
to Habarana
Ferry
A15
Ichchilampattai
Somawathie Chaitiya Nat. Park
Somapura
Sunkankuli
Verugal
Vellai
Ferry
TRINCOMALEE AND ENVIRONS
0 5 10 km

17th century and the arrival of the English in 1795, Trincomalee changed hands more than 10 times. The Portuguese, the Dutch, the king of Kandy, the French and the English repeatedly fought over this strategically-located harbor, which ultimately even served as a base for the Allied fleet in World War II.

However, the town lacked the well-developed environs inland or competitive traffic connections that might have helped it to true national significance. Most of Sri Lanka's population and economic activities are concentrated in the southwest of the island, which is a long way away from "Trinco." However, with a population of some 50,000, the town is the most important on the east coast after Batticaloa. Administrative offices, schools, shops, the fishery, industries, harbor facilities and small-scale tourism provide jobs for the locals.

After passing the police control at the entrance gate of **Fort Frederick**, which was an important defence facility under the Portuguese, Dutch and English, no visitor should miss the chance to drive or walk up to **Swami Rock**. Thrusting northwards into the sea, the peninsula becomes picturesquely rugged at its tip, and, from a height of more than 100 meters, commands a splendid view of the sandy coastal strip from the town's **Back Bay** to the bathing beach of **Uppuveli**, while the beautifully clear, turquoise waters of the Gulf of Bengal foam against the rocks below. In 1887, Francina van Rhede, the lovesick daughter of a Dutch merchant, is said to have thrown herself off the cliff top.

More historically certain is that the Portuguese, full of missionary zeal, destroyed the famous Shiva temple on this spot in the year 1622. They used the building materials for their fort, and threw its holy relics into the sea. Divers rescued the Shiva *lingam* from the depths, and it is now housed in the colorful **Tirukoneswaram Kovil**, built in 1963 approximately on the site of the old Shiva shrine with its legendary thousand columns. The Buddhist monastery of **Gokanna Vihara**, which originated during the reign of King Mahasena (275-310) was also so completely flattened by the Portuguese that nothing has remained of it at all.

Above: Brightly-painted peace monument in Trincomalee.

The wooded peninsula which extends far to the south, on which the Dutch, and later the English, constructed **Fort Ostenburg** to control the harbor entrance, is naval territory and is not accessible to the public.

Although many of the city's buildings have been severely damaged in the course of the political troubles, the small streets and houses, particularly in the eastern part of town, look very welcoming. Towards sunset, the town comes to life around **Dutch Bay**, the beach near the town hall and opposite the Rest

House: this is the place where everyone gathers in the evening; it is somewhat the equivalent of Galle Face Green in Colombo – much smaller, of course, but also much friendlier.

The Advancing Jungle

Some of the areas in the district of Trincomalee were abandoned in the 1980s: fearing attacks, farmers left their villages, fishermen their beaches. There are refugee camps in the larger towns or at places further inland, where it is safer. Some well-known sights and tourist facilities have disappeared or cannot at present be reached; the road to the hot springs of **Kanniyai**, for example, is blocked from the A12.

Some 45 kilometers north of Trincomalee, the jungle has taken over the road to the restored *vatadage* (roofed dagoba) by the village of **Tiriyai**, which was abandoned years ago.

Ten kilometers northwest of Trinco, the old monastery of **Velgam Vihara** is now in an area occupied by a military camp (a 15-minute walk from Periyakulam Tank). The site is spread out over dense jungle and an adjacent rocky outcrop, and not all of it has been excavated. Inscriptions have been found dating from the second to the 12th centuries, and 18 inscriptions from the Tamil reign in the 11th century indicate that the monastery continued to function through this Hindu epoch. The large complex includes image houses, a dagoba, a *bodhighara* (bo tree enclosure) and several Buddha statues. It is surrounded by the foundations of a wall, but the monastery grounds extended beyond this.

A single hotel has remained open in **Nilaweli** in spite of the troubles. A wonderful sandy beach and **Pigeon Island**, 20 minutes away by boat, await visitors who prefer the solitude of the east coast to the crowded and touristy beaches of the west.

NOTE: Since 1996, temporary restrictions have been introduced regarding travel to the east. The following information about accommodation and transportation assumes normal political conditions in the eastern provinces. Please pay attention to the respective articles in the "Traveling in Sri Lanka" section, p. 241.

AMPARA

Accommodation

BUDGET: **Gal-Oya Safari Lodge**, 106 Kandy Road, tel. 063-2296.
WILDLIFE DEPARTMENT BUNGALOW: **Ekgal Aru**, Dhammana (16 km south of Ampara); for a maximum of 10 people, reserve in advance at the Department of Wildlife Conservation, Wildlife Reservation Center, 18 Gregory Road, Colombo 7, tel. 01-694241.

Transportation

PLANE: Flight restrictions see p. 241.
BUS: Frequent daily service to Batticaloa (where you change to the train, see p. 241), Colombo, Kandy, Wellawaya: possible restrictions.

Hospital

District Hospital, tel. 063-2261.

Museum

Ampara Archeological Museum, Digavapi, open daily 8 am to 5 pm, except closed on Tuesdays.

Excursions

Boat tours depart from the dam on Senanayake Samudra Lake in **Inginiyagala** to **Gal Oya National Park**. Four-wheel-drive vehicles recommended for access. *Attention*: Gal Oya excursions and other wilderness tours: since 1998, no touristic activities are possible in this region!

ARUGAM BAY

Accommodation

MODERATE: **Stardust**, Sinna Ullai, tel. 0722-86482 and 063-48191.
BUDGET: **Sea Breeze. Tri Star Beach Hotel. Hideaway. Arugam Hilton Guest House. Sooriya Beach Hotel. Siam View. Chutti's Place**, all along the only road and the bay. Other modest private accommodation is available in Arugam Bay and Panama.

Restaurant

Stardust, good local and European cuisine.

Transportation

BUS: Daily connections between Wellawaya and Pottuvil, and from there toward Panama there are far fewer bus connections daily. Without a 4WD-vehicle you can't travel south of Panama, while during the rainy season (from November to mid-December) it's difficult to drive toward Yala. *TAXI:* You can arrange to have the **Stardust Hotel** send a taxi for you.
ROAD CONDITIONS: The A4 between Monaragala and Pottuvil is well-developed. Speedy inspections at police checkpoints.

Doctor

In Pottuvil, tel. 067-7361.

Activities

WINDSURFING: Mid-Dec. to April. *BODYSURFING:* April to mid-September (Arugam Bay is said to be one of the 10 best places in the world). Bring your own equipment; rental facilities are limited. *DIVING:* Off the coast with the help of local fishermen and their boats, for example around the rock islands of the Little Basses. *CANOEING:* In the hinterlands between Lahugala National Park and the lagoons on the sea; canoe rental and instruction at the **Stardust Hotel**.

Excursions

Lahugala National Park (20 km): Elephants, varied bird life; south of Arugam Bay there are **forest monasteries**, such as **Kudismbigala** and **Sastravela**, between groups of cliffs in park-like areas inland from the coast. As many sites can't be reached by car, prepare youself for long walks, and take a local guide from one of the villages (such as Arugam Bay, Panama).

At the moment, there are no regulations for entering **Yala East National Park** (**Okanda**), the bird sanctuary of **Kumana**, or the **Kudimbigala Nature Reserve**, as the rangers have left their posts during the political turbulences.

BATTICALOA

Accommodation

BUDGET: **Co-op Inn**, 350 Trinco Road, tel. 065-22613. **Eastern Eating House**, 7 2nd Cross Road, Ramakrishnapuram, Kalladi. **Lake View Inn**, 6 Lloyds Avenue. **Oriental Hotel**, 87 Trincomalee Road.

Transportation

PLANE: See page 241.

TRAIN: possibly cancalled; daily service to Colombo via Polonnaruwa (nine and a half hours), possible restrictions, see page 241.

BUS: Several buses along the east coast toward Pottuvil and Amapara, Colombo daily, possible restrictions, see page 241.

Hospital

General Hospital, tel. 065-2261.

KALKUDAH / PASSEKUDAH

No hotels. At the present time the coastline is partly a restricted military zone. However, modest private accommodation is available.

MONARAGALA

Accommodation

BUDGET: **Asiri Guest House**, 8 Pottuvil Road, tel. 055-76465. **Frashi Guest Inn**, 83/1 Pottuvil Road, Yala-Safaris, pilgrimages to Kataragama and Maligawila, tel. 055-76852. Victory Inn, Wellawaya Road, tel. 055-76100.

Transportation

BUS: Daily buses to Colombo and Badulla; also via Wellawaya to the south coast.

Hospital

District Hospital, tel. 055-6261.

TRINCOMALEE

Accommodation

MODERATE: **Hotel Club Oceanic**, Samapaltivu Post, Uppuveli, tel. 026-22307, for reservations, call Colombo 01-421101 (5 km north of Trincomalee). **Nilaveli Beach Hotel**, 11th Mile Post, Nilaveli, tel. 026-22071, for reservations, call Colombo 01-343720-7 (12 km north of Trincomalee, this is the only hotel located on the country's northern east coast that has never closed during the ongoing period of political turmoil).

BUDGET: **Rest House**, Main Street (opposite the Town Hall), tel. 026-22299. **Shahira Hotel**, 10th Mile , Nilaveli, tel. 026-32224. **The Villa Guest House**, 22 Orr's Hill Road, tel. 026-22284. **7 Islands Hotel & Park**, Orr's Hill, tel. 026-22373.

Transportation

PLANE: See page 241.

BOAT: Several passenger ferries a day to Koddiyar Bay and Mutur. Irregular connections to Kankesanturai (Jaffna).

TRAIN: Daily service to Colombo (scheduled travel time is eight and a half hours), see page 241.

BUS: Frequent daily service to Anuradhapura and Colombo, if no restrictions are in effect.

Along the access roads to the east coast there are frequent police and military checks.

The coastal road north of Trincomalee (toward Pulmoddai) and south of Mutur (toward Vakarai and Valaichchenai) is often blocked when the ferry service isn't operating; there are countless military checks along this route.

Hospital

District Hospital, tel. 026-22261.

Excursions

Because of the political problems, some former sights and the roads leading to them have been reclaimed by the jungle. This is true, for example, of the *vatadage* of **Tiriyai** and the hot springs of **Kanniyai**.

Some important temples, such as the **Tirukonesvaram Kovil** above Fort Frederick or the **Velgam Vihara** complex, are located within military zones, but you are still allowed access to these religious sites.

If the four car ferries around Koddiyar Bay aren't in operation, the only land access to the temple of **Seruwawila** south of Koddiyar Bay is via **Kantale** (35 km south of Trincomalee on the A6, from Kantale 41 km to Seruwawila).

The ferry to Mutur only transports people and bicycles; Mutur-Seruwawila 14 km.

THE TAMIL NORTH

VAVUNIYA / PADAWIYA
KOKKILAI / CHUNDIKKULAM
MANTOTA / MANNAR
JAFFNA PENINSULA
JAFFNA

VAVUNIYA

During the ongoing civil war, the 400-kilometer railway journey from Colombo Fort to Jaffna stops abruptly at **Vavuniya**, 140 kilometers before its proper destination. On the map, this district capital, with a population 25,000, looks like a traffic junction where routes from all points of the compass intersect; in actual fact, however, any movements you want to undertake to the east, west or north are strictly limited.

This existence as the sole gateway to the country's northern region has conferred a certain prestige upon the town, and life here has become correspondingly hectic and expensive. While there are numerous hotels in the town, they don't expect to be serving foreign tourists; most of the business in Vavuniya comes from the military, who are present here in large numbers.

Even though the military has established a strong foothold in Jaffna, the trip here can only be undertaken by air, not via the land route. In 2000, LTTE guerillas were still operating in the hinterland of the A9 and the Elephant Pass region.

Preceding pages: Irrigation tanks make rice cultivation possible, even in the dry north. Left: Doing the laundry near Jaffna.

Our Lady of Madhu

At the end of June and beginning of July, pilgrims are allowed access to Madhu, the most important place of pilgrimage for Sri Lankan Catholics (50 kilometers west of Vavuniya). Miracles are attributed to the statue of **Our Lady of the Rosary**, and when the country was at peace, around 100,000 pilgrims came to the church in the middle of **Madhu Road Sanctuary**, a nature reserve 267 square kilometers in area, to take part in the festivities on July 2.

PADAWIYA

It is only 20 kilometers from Vavuniya on the A29 to the small rural center of **Kebitigollewa**; however, as long as this section of the road is blocked off by the military, the town can only be reached by a detour through **Medawachchiya**. The surroundings are dominated by tanks, which are once again in use, and rice paddies; uncultivated tracts of land here have a sparse covering of jungle. Many of the rocky hillocks which thrust up out of the almost flat countryside are testimony to the early days of Buddhism, containing hermit caves, inscriptions and ruins.

Farming families have settled along the route from Kebitgollewa to Pada-

wiya. They practice *chena*, or slash-and-burn methods to create clearings in the forest for their agriculture. Their vegetable and tobacco fields are fenced with dead thorn bushes to keep out wild animals.

Medieval Nature Reserve

The large tank of Padiwaya was built by King Parakramabahu I (1153-1186), something confirmed by an inscription on a column by the dam that was reconstructed in 1960. However, all this king did was to repair an existing structure which had already been renovated centuries before by Moggallana II (535-555). His successor Nissanka Malla (1187-1196) turned the area around the tank into a nature reserve.

The settlement behind the dam must have already existed at the time of Sadhatissa (137-119 A.D.). Over the course of centuries it developed into the large capital of *Uttara Passa*, the northern province. Its size is still impressive, even though it has only been partially excavated and restored; the remains include fortifications with a rampart and a moat, enclosing dagobas, image houses and indications of other monastery buildings. The southern Indian Cholas also settled here in the 11th century and left behind various Hindu shrines, including a large Shiva temple.

The land irrigated by the large reservoir of Padawiya is part of the national Mahaweli Ganga Project, and extends all the way to the lagoons of the east coast in the sparsely populated district of Mullaitivu.

Above: Yokes of oxen remain the peasants' main form of transportation.

KOKKILAI / CHUNDIKKULAM

A small road, sometimes the only transportation link when the ferries along the coast road are not running, leads from the tank to **Pulmoddai** on the coast. Individualists enthuse over this secluded

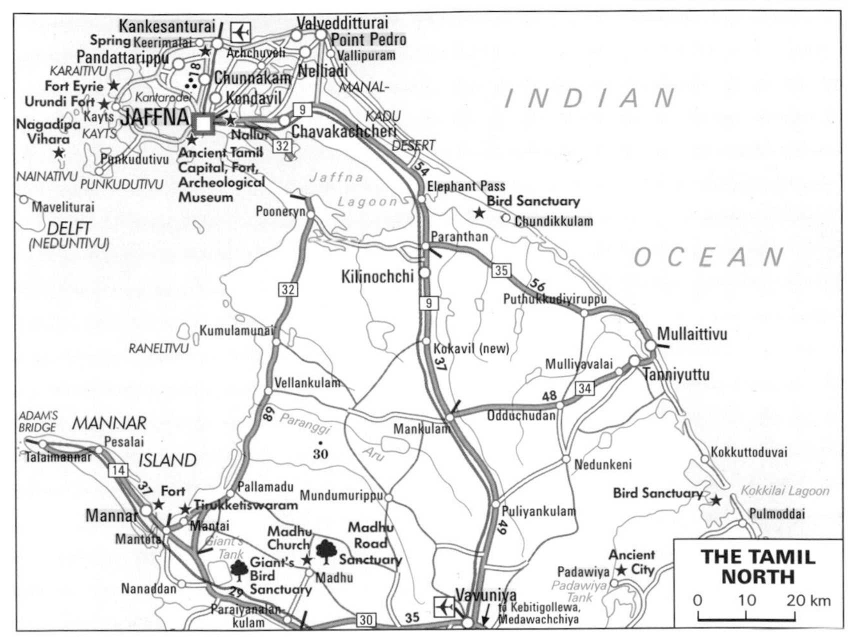

stretch of coast, while ornithologists flock to the two **bird sanctuaries** in the lagoons of **Kokkilai** and, 75 kilometers further north, **Chundikkulam**: during the winter season there are sometimes hundreds of flamingos here, as well as many other species of water fowl.

MANTOTA

Protected by the **Island of Mannar** during the southwest monsoon and not affected by the northeast monsoon, the adjacent northern bay is an ideal mooring place for small ships. Near **Mantai** is **Tirukketiswaram**, an ancient, highly venerated Shiva shrine, which may well have existed even before Buddhism arrived in Sri Lanka. Ancient sources mention **Mahatittha**, which means something equivalent to "large mooring-place"; today, it is thought that either Mantai or nearby **Mantota** might represent the successor of this first organized settlement at the gateway to the island of Lanka. Evidence of early trade activity in the harbor includes finds of Roman coins. In the *Mahavamsa*, the "Great Chronicle," Mahatittha is mentioned in connection with the shipboard arrival of the southern Indian bride of the legendary Prince Vijaya. This port may well have existed even before the arrival of the Sinhalese. It is one of the vulnerable points at which conquerors from southern India were able to attack and enter the country.

Giant's Tank

There are numerous small tanks in the hinterland along the coast, so that the largest of them all, known as the **Giant's Tank** – encompassing an area of 40 square kilometers and also a bird sanctuary – is particularly conspicuous. It is thought to be one of the large reservoirs built by Parakramabahu I (1153-1186). After tank irrigation had been abandoned for centuries, this tank was put back into use during the English colonial period. Since 1897, it has been fulfilling its orig-

inal function whenever there has been rain enough to fill it. The nature reserve was established here in 1954.

MANNAR

Like an index finger the island of Mannar points toward the Indian mainland. A railway line and a road dam lead through the shallow straits to the island and the town of **Mannar**. The district capital has a population of 20,000 and is an important station for anyone en route to India: 40 kilometers to the west is the ferry jetty of **Talaimannar**, where ferries depart three times a week for Rameswaram in the southern Indian state of Tamil Nadu.

This ferry is often an effective barometer of the political relations between Sri Lanka and India: any disagreements between the two countries, as well as bad weather conditions during the northeast monsoon from November to January, can lead to the temporary closure of this ferry service. The Sri Lankan civil war of course also plays a decisive role.

Like an extension of the flat limestone island of Mannar, a chain of islets and shallows continues toward India across **Palk Strait** and gives the impression of connecting Sri Lanka to the mainland, whence the name **Adam's Bridge**. According to the ancient Indian epic *Ramayana*, this is the place where the monkey general Hanuman crossed India to Sri Lanka with his army in a series of giant leaps in order to rescue Sita, abducted to Lanka by the demon Ravana.

In Mannar, a Portuguese-Dutch fort guards the straits between the island and the main body of Sri Lanka. Fishing, salt-mining and the service sector are the main sources of revenue for the local population. Skilled local boatmen navigate their vessels through the dangerously shallow coastal regions en route to Jaffna in the north and Kalpitiya in the south.

Above: In the north live mainly Hindu Tamils. Right: Typical tree of the region – the palmyra palm.

The districts of Mannar and Vavuniya, and the adjoining northern districts of **Killinochchi** and **Mullaitivu**, are among the least-settled areas of Sri Lanka. The expulsion of Muslim fishermen and farmers from these areas by the LTTE reduced the population further, resulting in an increased number of Tamils. In the Mannar district the proportion of Moors (more than 20 percent) was especially high. There the majority of the inhabitants are Christian, while in the other districts they are predominantly Hindu.

JAFFNA PENINSULA

Elephants once wandered through the shallow bay at the thin "neck" of Sri Lanka, which cuts the **Jaffna Peninsula** off from the rest of Lanka. The main road and railway line, blocked off at **Elephant Pass** due to the political crisis, passes large salterns, a reminder of how dry this area is. Living conditions in this northern tip of the island are extremely harsh.

The flat Jaffna Peninsula is made of limestone, unlike most other parts of Sri Lanka. The porous stone absorbs the rain very quickly and conveys it to the water table. This forms a specifically lighter layer, "swimming," as it were, on the salt water of the Indian Ocean that permeates the rock on all sides up to sea level. Open tanks are not practicable here, and fresh water has to be obtained from wells.

The Jaffna Peninsula is a little less than 1,000 square kilometers in area, including all its islands. With just under 900,000 inhabitants in 1983, the district of Jaffna is one of the most densely-populated areas of Sri Lanka, second only to Greater Colombo. In 2000, the number of inhabitants was estimated at half a million, and this former flourishing paradise has been visibly devastated by the ravages of war.

Jaffna's Palmyra Palms

The northernmost tip of the country has never been much of a magnet for tourism, but those who did visit it found it to be a pleasant surprise. The countryside is flat, and water – whether sea or lagoons – is never very far away. Most of the area is dry and sandy, and the most common tree is the palmyra palm with its elegant fan-like fronds. Locals here tap it for *toddy*, the sap from its cut flowers. Like the sap of the coconut or kittul palms, this liquid can be distilled to make *arrack* or processed into *jaggery*, palm sugar. The leaves of the fan palm can be skillfully folded to make a beaker for *toddy*, but more often you see them used as decorative fences.

In the desert-like dunes of the **Manalkadu Desert**, there are occasional groups of palmyra palms silhouetted attractively against the deep blue of the Gulf of Bengal. The northeast shoreline stretches away into the distance; at its far end is the little port of **Point Pedro**, almost the northernmost point of the country.

In 1936, in the village of **Vallipuram**, six kilometers south of Point Pedro, an inscription was found engraved on a thin gold plaque referring to the construction of a Buddhist monastery during the reign of King Vasabha (67-111). The small village, in which there is a venerated Vishnu temple, may have been the forerunner of the capital of the kingdom of Jaffna.

Keerimalai – Fresh Water by the Sea

The deep blue sea is constantly in view along the northern coast road, but it is not particularly suitable for swimming, as there are shallow coral reefs along almost the entire length of the shore. The airport is located near the modern industrial town and port of **Kankesanturai**. A wide road and the railway lead south to the capital, which is 18 kilometers away. However, if you opt to continue further west along the coastal road, you will eventually pass into a much quieter rural area. In **Keerimalai**, which is right next to the beach, there is an unusual open-air swimming pool, or rather, two large, pleasantly deep bathing pools (one for men and another for women), containing clear, fresh water: something very special in a country with a water shortage! In the eighth century, or so it's told, this miraculous water helped an ugly Chola princess with a face like a horse to completely transform her appearance. Out of gratitude, she built the Skanda *kovil* of **Maviddapuram**.

Right: The Kandaswamy Kovil in Nallur, a Hindu religious center, includes a shrine to Murugan, the god of war.

Island Fates

In the current civil war, the garland of islands southwest of the capital is functioning as a strategic wall which protects the peninsula. The former colonial overlords of times past also used these islands for this precise purpose, something clearly demonstrated, for example, by **Urundi Fort**, which the Portuguese built on **Kayts**; the island stronghold of **Fort Hammenhiel**; or **Fort Eyrie** on **Karaitivu**. Not until the traces of the 20th-century military action have disappeared will visitors be able to enjoy once again the quiet sandy beaches and the clean, friendly villages with their neat palm-leaf fences.

It is particularly hard for Hindu and Buddhist pilgrims alike not to be allowed to visit the small island of **Nainativu**, southwest of Kayts. The Hindus go to the temple of Minakshi, as the consort of the god Shiva is known in southern India, to petition for the well-being of new-born babies; the name Minakshi means "fish-eyed," as this deity was originally a Tamil fishermen's goddess and princess from Madurai. The temple festival in June/July attracted tens of thousands of pilgrims. For the Buddhists, **Nagadipa Vihara** is the place where the Buddha landed when he visited Sri Lanka for the second time. It is thus one of the 16 most

important pilgrimage destinations of Sri Lankan Buddhists.

Christian pilgrims from Sri Lanka and India also have to wait for more peaceful times before they can once again make the journey to the tiny island of **Kachchaitivu**, 20 kilometers southwest of **Neduntivu**, which is the proper name of the large island of **Delft**, for the festival of Saint Anthony.

JAFFNA

This sprawling city, once home to 130,000 inhabitants, used to make a cheerful and well-ordered impression in times of peace; with the artistically carved blinds on its houses and the severity of the closed rows of fences in some districts, it had an almost reserved, although not unfriendly air. The main municipal facilities are distributed between several centers. West of the train station are markets and shopping streets. In the south, on the other side of the wide esplanade surrounding **Jaffna Fort**, are the post office, court, police station and hotels; while the *kachcheri* or local administrative offices, tax office and agricultural authority form a small center around two kilometers further east, an area which was also the administrative center during the English colonial period. The university quarter is located on the northern edge of the town. The old royal city of Jaffna is in **Nallur**, around four kilometers from the fort.

Jaffna Fort – Bastion of the Military and the Church

Star-shaped Jaffna Fort was once the best example of Dutch fortress architecture in Sri Lanka, but has suffered heavily from the war. Its southwest side faces Jaffna Lagoon. The first fort was built by the Portuguese; it was taken by the Dutch in 1658 and was rebuilt between 1660 and 1680 to its present size, with three bastions on the landward side. In 1792, the complex acquired an additional outer rampart, shortly before the English took

power in 1796. From the southeast, a drawbridge led into the spacious inner courtyard, in which even the **Groote Kerk**, built in 1706, looked lost in spite of its great size. The floor of this rather austere Baroque church is covered with memorial tombstone slabs bearing the names of Dutch colonial officials and their families. Other buildings of the fort functioned as a prison, police quarters and the occasional residence of the president, until the Sri Lankan military took it over during the civil war at the end of the 20th century.

Nallur – Temple of the God of War

A spectacular festival is held on a massive scale in Nallur between the full moons in July and August. Like numerous other *kovils*, the present **Kandaswamy Kovil** has splendidly-decorated floats, brought out for the festival honoring the fearsome god Murugan (Skanda, Kataragama; god of war) and his two wives, in a procession accompanied by thousands of faithful followers. The present ornate temple was not built until 1807, and has been enlarged several times since then. The Portuguese had destroyed both the original *kovil* on the site of the royal palace and the town itself.

Above: Votive dagobas at the excavation site of Kantarodai.

Dagobas in the Land of the Hindus

Halfway between the city of Jaffna and the port of Kankesanturai, west of **Chunnakam**, the administrative official P.E. Pieris made an unusual archeological discovery in the village of **Kantarodai** in 1913: in an area of more than 8,000 square meters, the Archeology Office excavated almost 70 dagobas; some 50 of these, however, measured a mere two to four meters in diameter. These are taken to be votive dagobas. Statues, ruins and inscriptions on the site indicate that there was a monastery here between the second and seventh centuries.

NOTE: As long as there are travel restrictions in effect in the north, there is no point in making a complete listing of hotels, restaurants and the like in the restricted area. Since 1997, civil flights have been servicing Colombo and Jaffna again. These flights are only available to residents and personnel holding required official permits. Towns and accommodations which were accessible at the time of the printing of this book follow below (see also page 241).

MADHU

Accommodation

Simple pilgrim hostels during the pilgrimage season (two weeks at the end of June/beginning of July), or you can sleep out in the open.

Transportation

PLANE: At present there are no connnections from Ratmalana (Colombo) to Anuradhapura or Vavuniya. *TRAIN:* Daily connections to Anuradhapura, Medawachchiya and Vavuniya; from there, take the bus to Madhu. *BUS:* Countless charter buses from the major cities, especially from the west coast, where there's a high Catholic population. Local buses from Anuradhapura, Medawachchiya, Vavuniya.

MEDAWACHCHIYA

Accommodation

BUDGET: **Rest House** of the Ceylon Hotel Corporation (only four rooms, can also be reserved through Ceylon Hotels Corporation, 411 Galle Road, Colombo 4, tel. 01-503497), tel. 025-5699.

Restaurant

Queen's Chinese Rest, 14/1 Rajarata Mandiraya, tel. 025-5615.

Transportation

TRAIN: Station located 5 km east of town on the A 14; four trains daily to/from Colombo and Vavuniya. Rail service to Mannar/Talaimannar has been suspended. *BUS:* Numerous connections to the east: Kebitigollewa/Horowupotana: ask there and then. To the west: Cheddikulam, to the Madhu festival to Madhu Road. To the north: Vavuniya. To the south: Mihintale, Anuradhapura and Colombo. No service to Mannar/Talaimannar.

Doctor

Dr. A. Thangarajah, tel. 025-5661.

Excursions

To visit **Tantirimalai**, take the A 14 toward Mannar until you reach Mankulam-Neriyakulam, where a smaller road branches off south. Another 12 km will bring you to the rock monastery; there's also a military camp on the site. You can get permission to visit the large rock area from the head of the monastery.

From **Padawiya** via Kebitigollewa, it is about 60 km. There are numerous military controls. To get to the ruins, turn off before the southern entrance to Padawiya toward the dam of Padawiya Wewa; from the notable bend in the dam, it's several minutes northwards into the jungle on foot. The access west of the town center of Padawiya leads along a dirt road in poor condition. The site is quite large; a guard lives on the premises.

To the bird sanctuary of **Kokkilai**: south, before Padawiya, take the turnoff to Pulmoddai on the east coast (this is the only access when ferry service on the coast road to Trincomalee is suspended). West of Pulmoddai's town center, the coastal road leads north to the bird sanctuary.

It's a good idea to get information about the condition of the roads in Pulmoddai and the current level of safety and security before you set out. Bird-watching from boats is another rewarding option (rubber rafts or local fishing boats).

VAVUNIYA

Accommodation

BUDGET: **Rest House**, Station Road (quite noisy; part of the building is used as cheap accommodation for Tamils who want to travel further north or are coming from the north; the regular rooms are generally booked out in advance, and the price inflated), tel. 024-2299. It's quieter in Medawachchiya, located 20 km south.

Transportation

PLANE: During limitations in domestic air traffic: no flights – otherwise approximately five times weekly.
TRAIN: Up to four trains daily to/from Colombo via Anuradhapura (the Vavuniya-Colombo stretch takes about six hours); there's no service on to Jaffna.
BUS: Only southwards toward Medawachchiya/Anuradhapura; to Trincomalee via Medawachchiya and Horowupotana or via Anuradhapura.
The A30 toward Mannar is only open for the annual Madhu festival in July, and then only as far as Madhu Road.

Hospital

Vavuniya District Hospital, tel. 024-2261.

MANNAR / TALAIMANNAR

The district of Mannar is currently a restricted area (off limits).

Transportation

BOAT: Ferry service to Rameswaram (India) has been suspended. Occasional private boats run sporadically between **Kalpitiya** (Puttalam district) and **Mannar**.
TRAIN: Train service from Medawachchiya to Mannar/Talaimannar has been suspended during the civil war.
BUS: Local buses run between Medawachchiya and Madhu Road; a continuing journey on to Mannar is not possible.

RAJARATA
Heart of the Sinhalese World

RAJARATA / MIHINTALE
ANURADHAPURA
AUKANA / YAPAHUWA
SIGIRIYA / DAMBULLA
POLONNARUWA

RAJARATA

Sri Lankans refer to the area most important to their history and culture as the "Cultural Triangle," and with good reason; this region is especially recommended to visitors to their country. It is delineated by the three most important historic capitals: Anuradhapura in the north, Polonnaruwa in the east and Kandy in the south. Centers of interest are the north and east; here lay Rajarata, the heartland of Sinhalese irrigation civilization. Ravaged by wars, the area was abandoned in the 13th century, and most of the magnificent buildings and shrines were soon buried in the jungle. Many of them had been forgotten when the British started to take a closer look at the interior in the 19th century. There followed a wave of excavations; the tanks and irrigation system were again set into operation, enabling renewed use of the rice paddies that had been swallowed up by jungle.

MIHINTALE

Only 12 kilometers east of Anuradhapura, near the junction of the A9 and A12, in the midst of bizarre rock formations and frangipani groves, is the place of conversion: **Mihintale**. It is one of the 16 most important pilgrimage destinations in the country; the *Poson* (June) full moon festival, in particular, attracts thousands of pilgrims. According to the *Mahavamsa*, the "Great Chronicle," the ruler Devanampiya Tissa (250-210 B.C.) was here on a hunting expedition when he saw a white deer. He pursued it, but the deer vanished; in its place stood the monk Mahinda, who tested him, found him worthy and converted him to Buddhism.

When you climb up to the shrine you are treading steps constructed by generations of monks and pilgrims. Turn right at the first landing, where a flight of steps leads up to the **Kantaka Dagoba**. Named after Buddha's horse, this is one of the oldest dagobas on the island (second century B.C.). *Vahalkadas*, projecting structures before the altar – brick at their core, but decorated with marvelous limestone reliefs – face in the four directions of the compass. On limestone steles placed next to them are sculptures of the corresponding animal symbols: the elephant is the east, the bull south, the horse west and the lion north. The reliefs, which are best preserved on the east and south sides, consist of horizontal rows of *gana* (dwarves), *hamsa* (geese), and the trunks

Preceding pages: The Ruvanveliseya Dagoba. Left: A fifth-century beauty (Sigriya).

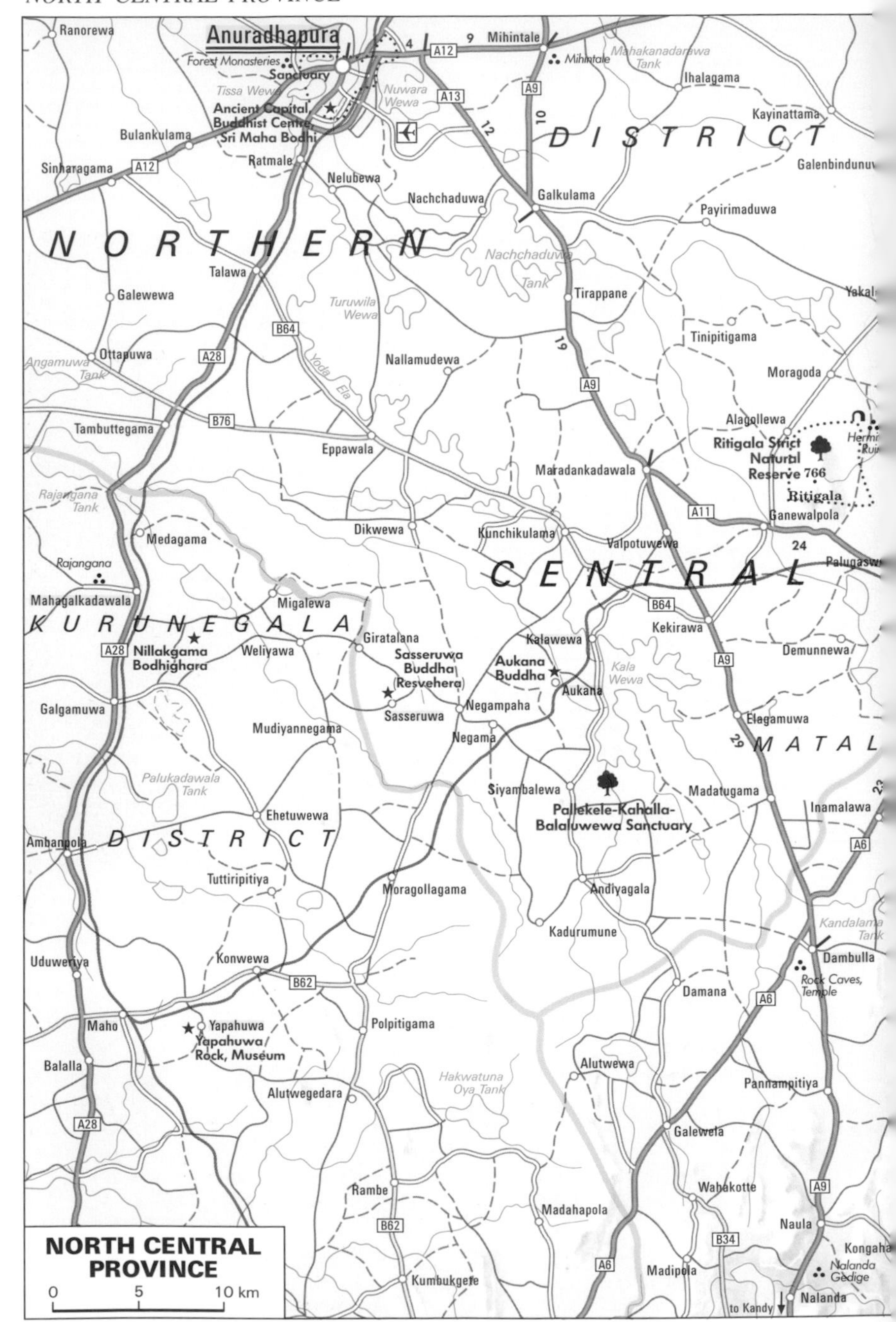

Anuradhapura
Forest Monasteries
Sanctuary
Tissa Wewa
Ancient Capital, Buddhist Centre, Sri Maha Bodhi
Nuwara Wewa
Mihintale
Mahakanadarawa Tank
Ranorewa
Bulankulama
Sinharagama
Ratmale
Nelubewa
Nachchaduwa
Galkulama
Ihalagama
Kayinattama
Galenbindunu
Payirimaduwa
NORTHERN
DISTRICT
Talawa
Galewewa
Nachchaduwa Tank
Tirappane
Turuwila Wewa
Tinipitigama
Ottapuwa
Angamuwa Tank
Nallamudewa
Yoda Ela
Moragoda
Tambuttegama
Eppawala
Alagollewa
Ritigala Strict Natural Reserve 766
Ritigala
Maradankadawala
Rajangana Tank
Dikwewa
Kunchikulama
Valpotuwewa
Ganewalpola
Medagama
Rajangana
Palugaswe
CENTRAL
Mahagalkadawala
Migalewa
KURUNEGALA
Nillakgama Bodhighara
Weliyawa
Giratalana
Sasseruwa Buddha (Resvehera)
Kalawewa
Aukana Buddha
Aukana
Kala Wewa
Kekirawa
Demunnewa
Galgamuwa
Sasseruwa
Negampaha
Negama
Elagamuwa
Mudiyannegama
MATAL
Palukadawala Tank
Siyambalewa
Pallekele-Kahalla-Balaluwewa Sanctuary
Madatugama
Inamalawa
Ehetuwewa
Ambanpola
DISTRICT
Tuttiripitiya
Moragollagama
Andiyagala
Kadurumune
Kandalama Tank
Uduweriya
Konwewa
Dambulla
Rock Caves, Temple
Damana
Maho
Yapahuwa
Yapahuwa Rock, Museum
Polpitigama
Balalla
Alutwewa
Hakwatuna Oya Tank
Alutwegedara
Pannampitiya
Galewela
Rambe
Wahakotte
Madahapola
Naula
Kongaha
Madipola
Nalanda Gedige
Kumbukgete
Nalanda
to Kandy
A12
A13
A9
A28
B64
B76
A11
B62
A6
B34
NORTH CENTRAL PROVINCE
0 5 10 km

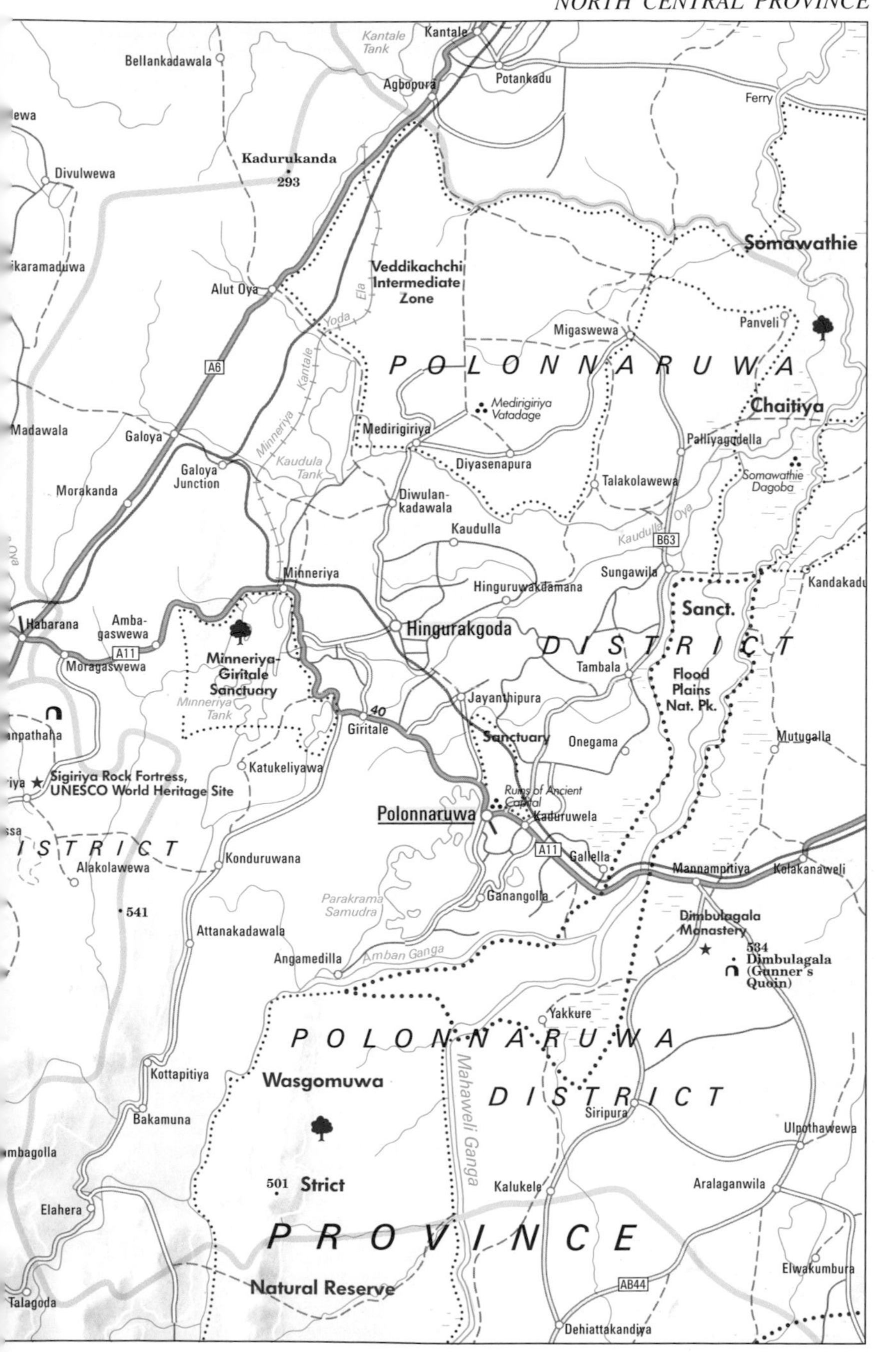
Kantale Tank
Kantale
Bellankadawala
Agbopura
Potankadu
Ferry
Kadurukanda
293
Divulwewa
Somawathie
Veddikachchi Intermediate Zone
Alut Oya
Panveli
Migaswewa
A6
POLONNARUWA
Medirigiriya Vatadage
Chaitiya
Madawala
Galoya
Medirigiriya
Palliyagodella
Kaudula Tank
Diyasenapura
Galoya Junction
Somawathie Dagoba
Morakanda
Talakolawewa
Diwulankadawala
Kaudulla
B63
Minneriya
Sungawila
Kandakadu
Hinguruwakdamana
Sanct.
Habarana
Amba-gaswewa
Hingurakgoda
DISTRICT
A11
Moragaswewa
Minneriya-Giritale Sanctuary
Tambala
Flood Plains Nat. Pk.
Minneriya Tank
Jayanthipura
40
Giritale
Sanctuary
Onegama
Mutugalla
Katukeliyawa
Sigiriya Rock Fortress, UNESCO World Heritage Site
Ruins of Ancient Capital
Polonnaruwa
Kaduruwela
Gallella
Konduruwana
Alakolawewa
Mannampitiya
Kolakanaweli
Parakrama Samudra
Ganangolla
541
Dimbulagala Monastery
Attanakadawala
534
Dimbulagala (Gunner's Quoin)
Angamedilla
Amban Ganga
Yakkure
POLONNARUWA
Mahaweli Ganga
Kottapitiya
Wasgomuwa
DISTRICT
Siripura
Bakamuna
Ulpothawewa
501
Strict
Kalukele
Aralaganwila
Elahera
PROVINCE
Elwakumbura
AB44
Natural Reserve
Talagoda
Dehiattakandiya

of *makara*, legendary animals. Around the dagoba are a number of *sri patul*, stone slabs symbolizing the footprint of the Buddha.

Caves for the Holy Men

West of the dagoba, rounded chunks of rock piled one on top of the other form **caves**. Projecting **drip ledges** at the upper edge of the caves, laboriously chiseled by hand out of the hard stone, show which of these were used as dwellings: the ledges prevented the rainwater from running into the cave, diverting it instead to the outside.

Brahmi **inscriptions** below the drainage ledges bear the names, titles and occupations of the caves' donors. It was considered meritorious to make such hermit dwellings available to the *arahants*, the holy men; 68 of them have been counted in Mihintale. The style of the Brahmi symbols here has enabled archeologists to date them back to the third century.

Above: Historic staircase up to the shrine of Mihintale. Right: Even today, monks' lives are governed by strict regulations.

Monastery Regulations

From the Kantaka Dagoba, a flight of steps on the south leads down to a small area with a few ruins which give some indication of what monastic life was like: there are several rectangular monks' dwellings with rough stone pillars that have been replaced in their original upright position and probably supported roofs, and *Sinha Pokuna*, the **Lion Bath**. The water that poured from the mouth of this sitting stone lion flowed in from the catchment basin behind his back. Ritual baths of purification were among the duties of a monk.

A few steps higher, to the east, is a spacious platform shaded by several large trees; the main flight of steps also leads to this level, giving onto the platform through a kind of gatehouse.

East of this platform was the center of monastery life, protected on the valley side by a massive wall of stones. The monks assembled for their daily meal in the *dana salawa*, the **Alms Hall** (refectory); the rooms for storing, preparing, distributing and eating the food were arranged around a pool in the open courtyard. A system of clay pipes kept the building, which measures about 35 by 25 meters in area, supplied with fresh water, which flowed from the lowest part of the pool.

In addition to the ingenious plumbing system, there is also a colossal *bat oruwa*, or **rice boat**, a giant stone trough for cooked rice, with, set at a right angle to it, the *kanda oruwa*, a trough to contain the side dishes, generally curries. This facility could feed more than a thousand monks.

To the south are the foundations of the **image house**, which have been restored. The two upright inscription slabs dating from the time of King Mahinda IV (956-972) to the left and right of the entrance are a fountain of information about monastery life; they give a detailed description of daily routines and monastery regulations, from the monks' morning teeth-cleaning to payment of the servants who were responsible for getting the flowers for sacrifices.

Next to this is the third important building of the monastery, the *sannipata salawa*, or **Assembly Hall**. Standing in the middle of this square room is a raised platform for the abbot; from here, he spoke or preached to the assembled monks.

Missionary's Landing and Bed

As you continue on up the stairs, you can see old Sinhalese inscriptions chiseled in the bare rock (south side). Behind the modern monastery entrance is the "conversion platform" with the **Ambastala Vatadage**, built in the first century as a roofed dagoba and said to contain the ashes and relics of Mahinda. From the platform, shaded by palm trees and circled by rocks, a path leads east down the slope to **Mahinda's Bed**, a cave with a smooth couch of stone.

Further up the cliff is the **Sila Rock**, where Mahinda, who flew by miraculous means to Sri Lanka, is said to have first touched ground. Reward for the strenuous climb up to "Mahinda's Landing Place" is the splendid view over the tanks, rice paddies and irrigation channels of the plain to the large dagobas of Anuradhapura.

West of the rock is the large **Maha Seya**, or "Great Dagoba," dating from the first century, which is said to contain the hair from the base of the Buddha's nose. The less conspicuous **Mihindu Seya** immediately behind it is even older, probably dating from the second century B.C.; in the relic chamber, which was opened up in 1951, a number of unusual votive dagobas were found, examples of early stupa architecture.

Up here on the bare rock there is no shade, and few visitors climb the paths and steps south leading to **Et Dagoba** with its incomparable view. More pleasant is the walk to **Naga Pokuna**, the **Snake Pool** (signposted from the monastery entrance), a natural reservoir in a cleft of rock which supplied the lower-lying parts of the monastery, such as Sinha Pokuna and the refectory, with water.

Plunder and Meditation

On the way down to the parking lot, east of the main path, is the counterpart of the Kantaka Dagoba, the **Giribandhu Dagoba** ("Nameless Dagoba"). Its relic chamber was plundered, but fragments of wall paintings have remained. All this is documented in the small modern **museum**, only a short distance from the parking lot, as are other finds from the hill of Mihintale: the **hospital**, the **Indikatu Seya**, the dagoba from the Mahayana period, and the **Kaludiya Pokuna**, the "Black Water Pool" near the A9, which is about half a kilometer south of the parking lot.

Above: The bo tree in Anarudhapura, one of the most sacred places on the island. Right: 344 elephants bear the Ruvanveli Dagoba.

The meditation center of the monks, in its splendidly isolated setting, radiates such peace that even today time seems to stand still. Even the monkeys, who pester visitors for food outside, seem to submit here to the order's regulations.

ANURADHAPURA

None of **Anuradhapura's** many buildings, scattered over an area of 40 square kilometers, is in its original condition. This is scarcely surprising, since the town was destroyed and rebuilt many times before finally losing its function as a capital in 1017. Almost all of the ruins left today are those of monastery buildings. The main monasteries, as well as the royal palaces, were located west of

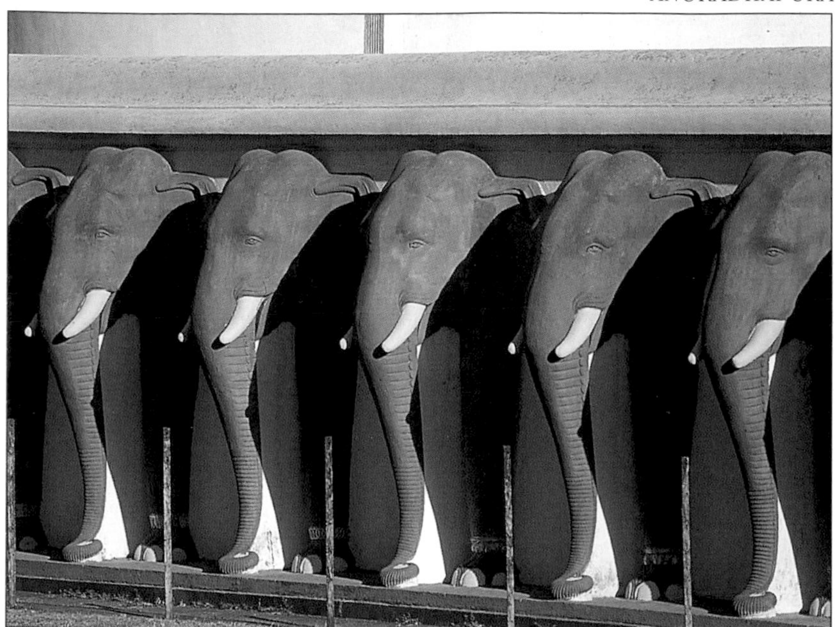

the **Malwatu Oya River**, beyond the present-day modern town and near the three large tanks to the west.

The three most important monastery complexes are the **Mahavihara**, dating back to the time when Buddhism was introduced in the third century B.C., the **Abhayagiri Monastery**, built under Vattagamani (89-77 B.C.), and the **Jetavana Vihara**, which split off from this last in the fourth century A.D. All of the other monasteries were subsidiaries of these large monasteries, in spite of their independent existence.

Mahavihara – Mother of all Monasteries

Immediately after his conversion, Devanampiya Tissa (250-210 B.C.) built a temple of the sacred bo tree, the **Sri Maha Bodhi**, which was probably located in his own royal garden. The cutting from the fig tree under which Buddha attained enlightenment was brought to this special place by Mahinda's sister Sanghamitta. From here, the king laid out a procession route across his garden to the **Thuparama Vatadage**. According to legend, Mahinda took personal responsibility for the architecture, marking the location of the future **Mahatupa** with a large stele.

The Temple of the Bo Tree is still one of the holiest places on the island. It may even be true that it has never been destroyed, as the tree is also sacred for the Tamil Hindus. All that is left of the original temple is the platform bearing the tree and parts of the surrounding wall. The smaller temples, moonstones, guardstones and *makara* balustrades are all later additions. You can join the line of pilgrims before one of the smaller temples to have, in return for a small donation, a cotton thread wound around your wrist, which is supposed to bring luck and enlightenment. Picking up, let alone plucking, leaves from the bo tree is strictly forbidden.

The northern exit from this holy place leads to the procession route, which has

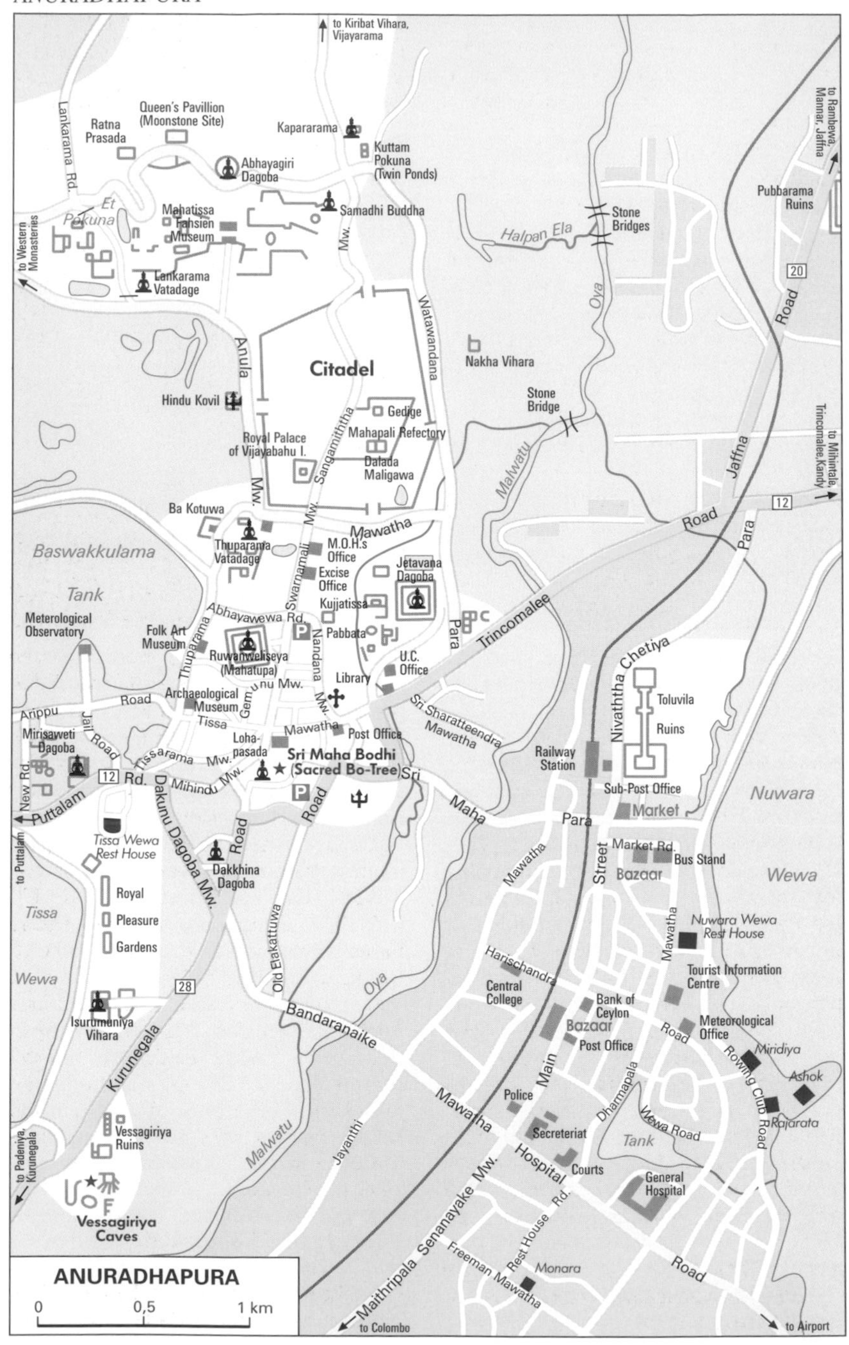
ANURADHAPURA
0
0,5
1 km
to Kiribat Vihara, Vijayarama
Queen's Pavillion (Moonstone Site)
Ratna Prasada
Lankarama Rd.
Kapararama
Kuttam Pokuna (Twin Ponds)
Abhayagiri Dagoba
Et Pokuna
Mahatissa
Fahsien Museum
Samadhi Buddha
Lankarama Vatadage
to Western Monasteries
Stone Bridges
Halpan Ela
Oya
Pubbarama Ruins
to Rambewa, Mannar, Jaffna
20
Citadel
Watawandana
Anula
Mw.
Nakha Vihara
Hindu Kovil
Gedige
Mahapali Refectory
Royal Palace of Vijayabahu I.
Dalada Maligawa
Sangamiththa
Stone Bridge
Malwatu
Jaffna
Road
to Mihintale, Trincomalee, Kandy
12
Ba Kotuwa
Mawatha
Thuparama Vatadage
Baswakkulama
Tank
M.O.H.s Office
Excise Office
Jetavana Dagoba
Kujjatissa
Swarnamali
Abhayawewa Rd.
Pabbata
Nandana
Para
Trincomalee
Meterological Observatory
Folk Art Museum
Thuparama
Ruwanweliseya (Mahatupa)
U.C. Office
Library
Nivaththa Chetiya
Toluvila
Ruins
Archaeological Museum
Gemunu Mw.
Arippu
Road
Jail Road
Tissa
Mawatha
Post Office
Sri Sharatteendra Mawatha
Railway Station
Mirisaweti Dagoba
Loha-pasada
Tissarama Mw.
Sri Maha Bodhi (Sacred Bo-Tree)
Sri
Maha
Sub-Post Office
Nuwara
12
Rd.
Mihindu Mw.
New Rd.
Puttalam
Road
Para
Market
Tissa Wewa Rest House
Dakunu Dagoba Mw.
Road
Dakkhina Dagoba
Mawatha
Market Rd.
Bus Stand
Street
Bazaar
Wewa
to Puttalam
Royal
Pleasure
Gardens
Tissa
Wewa
Mawatha
Nuwara Wewa Rest House
Old Elakattuwa
Harischandra
Tourist Information Centre
Oya
Central College
Bank of Ceylon
Bazaar
Post Office
28
Isurumuniya Vihara
Bandaranaike
Road
Meteorological Office
Kurunegala
Miridiya
Rowing Club Road
Ashok
Mawatha
Police
Main
Dharmapala
Rajarata
Vessagiriya Ruins
Malwatu
Jayanthi
Secreteriat
Wewa Road
Tank
Hospital
Courts
to Padeniya, Kurunegala
General Hospital
Maithripala Senanayake Mw.
Rest House Rd.
Vessagiriya Caves
Freeman Mawatha
Monara
Road
to Colombo
to Airport

been restored and is now paved with red stones. To the right, east of where it starts, is the forest of stone pillars which once supported the roof of the **Lohapasada**, the "Brazen (or bronze) Palace." Although they were only gathered together and set upright again a few years ago – this is why they differ in style – the 1,600 columns spread over an area of 2,500 square meters give a good idea of the dimensions of the original nine-story monastery building, which was erected during the reign of Dutthagamani (161-137 B.C.).

The wooden construction with a copper roof which rested on the columns burned down after only 15 years. There were subsequent buildings, seven, five and three stories high, but none of these rivalled the original building's dimensions. When, in the third century A.D., serious conflict arose between Mahavihara and the Abhayagiri Vihara and the monks of Mahavira were forced to flee, their opponents used the Brazen Palace as a quarry. In the ninth century, 32 monks were still living in the historic building. Along the procession route are the remains of monks' and service buildings belonging to the large monastery.

The huge dome of the Mahatupa or **Ruvanveliseya** (Ruvanveli Dagoba) towers above the ruins and the tree-studded parkland. Approximately 90 meters high and almost the same measurement in diameter, it was in its day the largest stupa in the world. Dutthagamani had it built on the spot indicated by Mahinda. The present dagoba is a reconstruction of the one Parakramabahu I (1153-1186) had built in the style of the period, and the impressive elephant pedestal around the square platform is also his work: 344 elephants, which were once fitted out with real tusks, "bear" the dagoba. Over the last century, it has been completely restored. As well as small votive dagobas and a few statues of Buddha and royal personages, there are, in a small building left of the entrance, images of Dutthagamani and Elara which look for all the world like waxworks.

Above: The stone columns of the Thuparama Vatadage (Anuradhapura) once supported a roof.

A little further west of the Mahatupa is the first tank in Anuradhapura, the **Bawakkulama**, constructed around 430 B.C. The Mahavihara grounds extend further to the northeast with the ruins of an image house, a shrine and a hospital, and end in the north with the Thuparama Vatadage, the city's oldest building apart from the Temple of the Sacred Bo Tree, and the relic house for Buddha's right collarbone. Four rows of 176 pillars with ornate capitals supported a domed or conical roof which protected the dagoba and its ambulatory.

The Citadel

To the north, adjacent to the grounds of Mahavihara, is the **Citadel**, the king's

preserve, surrounded by a rampart which was originally five meters high. The wall is a total of five kilometers in length, broken by gate openings at all four points of the compass. At the gates, 10 percent of the foodstuffs passing through were collected as tithes, to the benefit of the **refectory** east of the road, where as many as 6,000 monks could fill their bowls and stomachs.

Next to this is the oldest **Dalada Maligawa** ("Temple of the Tooth"). The Sacred Tooth of Buddha was kept in India until the beginning of the fourth century; as Hinduism advanced through that country, the tooth came from Kalinga in East India into the possession of the Sinhalese king Sirimeghavanna (301-328). *Peraheras*, processions in honor of the tooth, were already held in Anuradhapura; similar festivities still take place in Kandy today.

Above: The Baswakkulama (fifth century) is the oldest tank in Anuradhapura. Right: The Kuttam Pokuna ("Twin Ponds").

A road leads from the east gate to the **Royal Palace** west of the Citadel. The only palace visible today, which can be identified from its foundations, originated from the reign of Vijayabahu (1055--1110); this king was already ruling in Polonnaruwa and had a country residence built here. All the earlier palaces on this site lie beneath this one – the building grew up from the rubble of its precursors. The oldest traces of settlement, dating from 500 B.C., were discovered at a depth of nine meters.

Abhayagiri Monastery

The **Abhayagiri Monastery** is located north of the Citadel area. Originally called **Uttara Vihara**, "Northern Monastery," it was subsequently renamed after the king who built it, Vattagamani Abhaya (103/89-77 B.C.). This king was deposed by Tamils in the year 103, and obliged to live in hiding for many years; one of his refuges was the caves of Dambulla. The monk Mahatissa, who had

Waterford City Library
Ardkeen Library
13 JUN 05 03:46pm
Library Receipt

For renewal/enquiries phone 051 849755

Fine Payment

Patron Name: Gaynor, Geraldine

ollected - overdues
A room with a view
30005003195255 3.60

Waterford City Library
Ardkeen Library
13 JUN 05 03:46pm
Library Receipt

For renewal/enquiries phone 051 849755

Checkout

Patron Name: Gaynor, Geraldine

lew Loan: Sri Lanka
0005002442872 Due: 04 JUL 05 *

been expelled from Mahavihara, helped him to regain his throne; in return, the king gave him land north of the city wall. When people began to criticize the expulsion of this monk in orthodox Mahavihara, 500 other monks took his part and ultimately founded Uttara Vihara, where Mahatissa became abbot. He accepted the tenets of Mahayana Buddhism and Tantrism, which were new at the time, and permitted the worship of *Bodhisattvas* (Buddhist saints).

Although they both worshiped Buddha, the monasteries of Mahavihara and Abhayagiri were at ideological odds from this period on. The latter was assured of royal support, especially since in the fourth century it was given custody of the relic of the Sacred Tooth, and it became a leading theological institution with contacts as far afield as China, Burma and even Java. After the fifth century A.D., it was purely Mahayana. Like all the monasteries of Anuradhapura, it experienced a renaissance after liberation from the Cholas in the 11th century, but in the 12th century, under Parakramabahu I (1153-1186), it was forced to unite with the other monasteries. A few monks lived there right up to the 16th century, but it was then given up altogether.

Encompassing an area of 240 hectares, it accommodated as many as 7,000 monks. Unfortunately, the chronicle of this monastery has been lost, and Mahavihara, which produced the historical chronicle the *Mahavamsa*, was understandably silent about its rival.

However, the excavations, supported by UNESCO, have meanwhile shed more light on this huge monastery complex. The excellent **Mahatissa-Fahsien Museum** (named after the monastery's founder and a fifth-century Chinese traveler, whose writings include a record of his visit to Anuradhapura), located in the modern complex south of the monastery's huge dagoba, provides information on the historical context and internal

functioning of monastery life, and displays a good selection of more recent excavation finds (from the Thuparama Vatadage, follow Anula Mawatha Road north).

If you start your tour of inspection at the east side of the monastery complex, you'll encounter a fine example of architecture designed to fit in with the landscape at the place where **Vatavandana Road** (Outer Circular Road) curves to the west: the **Kuttam Pokuna**, or "Twin Ponds" consist of two rectangular pools (the northern one, 30 by 17 by 5 meters, is 12 meters shorter and about one meter shallower than the southern one), their walls comprised of stone slabs arranged like stairs so that the monks could always bathe, regardless of the water level.

The four entrances to the ponds are decorated with *kumbakalasa*, solid stone vases with lotus buds sticking out of them. An imposing *naga* stele guards the flow of water into the northern basin, which runs through a sophisticated filter system. There's a small pool at the northern edge

of the bathing complex into which the water flowed underground from the nearest tank. Skillfully arranged overflows held back the sediment, enabling clear, filtered water to fill the bathing pools themselves.

If you follow the main route, the Outer Circular Road, a few hundred meters further west, you'll come to a fenced-in and guarded plot of land south of the road, the site of a temple still venerated by Buddhists today. The **Samadhi Buddha** (meditating Buddha) from the fourth century, protectively sheltered by a modern concrete construction of dubious aesthetic value, is the only one left of an ensemble of four Buddha statues originally grouped at the four cardinal points around a bo tree, which has also since vanished.

Pandit J. Nehru, Prime Minister of India from 1947 to 1964, was a great admirer of Buddha and meditated before this statue.

Above: Detail of the famous Moonstone. Right: A vendor of sacred offerings, Anuradhapura.

Further west is the vast bulk of the **Abhayagiri Dagoba**, the second-largest on the island with a height of 115 meters and a diameter of approximately 90 meters. It is the successor of an older dagoba, which Vattagamani, on his return from exile, had built on the site of the hermitage of a *Jaina* (member of the Indian Jain sect) who had taunted him before his flight. Under King Gajabahu I (114-136 A.D.), the building assumed its final form.

Today, however, this dagoba is an overgrown ruin, and most of its richly decorated side temples have crumbled away. Only the south side has two remarkable steles of Padmanidhi and Samkanidhi, the well-nourished companions of Kubera, the Hindu god of prosperity, who is also the symbol of the north. This is, on the one hand, evidence of the symbiosis of Hindu and Buddhist religious thought, and on the other, an example of the adaptation of Hindu deities to local conditions: prosperity is water, which in India usually comes from the north; in Sri Lanka, however, water is more plentiful in the south, so that the gods of prosperity here faced the opposite direction.

Grouped around the dagoba in an open park setting are the ruins of the monasteries; excavations are in progress in many different places. One building which has been brought to light is the **refectory** with its large "rice boat," a stone trough for the rice which was the staple of the monastic diet, and a smaller one for the curries, the side dishes. More than 5,000 monks had to fill their bowls by noon, as they were allowed no further meals for the rest of the day. Only such a huge rice boat could allow this number of monks to serve themselves at the same time – a system not unlike that of a modern cafeteria.

Also in the park south of the road was a *bodhighara*, a shrine for a bo tree, which, like the temple with the Samadhi Buddha on the Outer Circular Road, also had Buddha statues located at the four cardinal points. Three of these were found with their *asana*, or thrones; one of them was left *in situ*, while the others were taken off to the museum. Two stone inscription slabs which were excavated here praise the beauty of the nearby "Gem Palace."

The **Et Pokuna**, or "Elephant Pond," which is surrounded by numerous *kuti*, or monastic dwellings, is one of the largest bathing complexes for monks in Anuradhapura. Supporting the walls of the pool were hewn stone pillars arranged in a honeycomb pattern.

Further south is the **Lankarama Vatadage**, a dagoba originally sheltered by a roof. This was the center of the Lankarama Monastery, a subsidiary of the Abhayagiri Monastery, also built by Vattagamani. Three concentric circles of pillars supported the original wooden roof. Lankarama is an important place of pilgrimage for Buddhists.

From the peaceful park, return to the crowded Outer Circular Road, with its tourists and souvenirs. A few hundred meters northwest of the Abhayagiri Dagoba, at the entrance to an image house (confusingly called Mahasena's Palace), is the famous **Moonstone**, ornamented in classic Abhayagiri tradition. Its outer band depicts the flames of desire, while the second band has a sequence of animals – elephant, bull, horse and lion – repeated three times and concluding with a further elephant, symbolizing human life and its trials from birth to death. If one overcomes these, as Buddha did, one achieves the vitality represented by the climbing plants and leaves in the next band, and finally becomes like the geese in the next band, who have the ability to separate water and milk – to distinguish, that is, between good and evil. If you're able to overcome the next decorated band, which represents enlightenment, you come to the lotus at the center, a symbol of nirvana. The flight of steps above the Moonstone are decorated with

gnomes, while the entrance is flanked by the companions of Kubera, the god of prosperity, and two Sinhalese lions.

A little further to the west is the **Ratna Prasada**, the "Gem Palace," as the chapter house of the monastery is called. These ruins date back to the time of King Mahinda II (777-797), who allegedly had the palace built for 300,000 bronze coins. Of this building, which was constructed mainly of wood, only the stone foundations remain. Beneath the ruins, a previous building from the first century B.C. was found, probably the first chapter house of the Abhayagiri Monastery.

The **Guardstone** at the entrance is one of the most splendid in Sri Lanka: the Naga King (water god) holds in his hands the horn of plenty and the flowering branch of prosperity; he is protected by a hooded cobra and accompanied by a gnome.

Above: The toque macaque, a coquettish escort of pilgrims and tourists. Right: The Jetavana Dagoba is being restored.

The Forest Monks

If you leave the Abhayagiri Monastery grounds toward the west, the Outer Circular Road will lead you along a section of the shore of the historic **Bulankulama Tank**. Scattered throughout the jungle region around this area are 14 monasteries which once belonged to the forest monks, who subjected themselves to particularly rigorous disciplinary rituals in the solitude of the jungle. They were known as *Pamsakullika*; the name, meaning "shrouds," refers to the robes they wore, which were made of funerary cloths and which were intended to emphasize their freedom from material needs.

In accordance with this philosophy, a **forest monastery** tends to be very basic, if not without certain refinements: some of them are equipped with walkways for meditation, and one even has an ingenious air-conditioning system whereby the double platform of rock on which the monastery buildings were perched was cooled by a ditch full of water that was dug around it.

The surprisingly ornate **Urinal Stones** are a complete puzzle: one, for example, boasts a lotus table crowned by a *makara* arch over an open drain; another, next to it, is sculpted with lions. Were these perhaps intended as an expression of scorn for worldly luxuries? Immediately below the urinals are three overlapping clay containers in which the urine was purified in succession by gravel, sand and charcoal.

It has never been proved that drinking filtered urine was part of a kind of self-purification ritual and thus a special form of meditation, although there are known to be modern-day adherents of this (rather unsavory) practice. More recent excavations have demonstrated that such urinal systems were in fact extremely common throughout the classical Sinhalese empire.

Jetavana Vihara

The largest complete dagoba in the world was built as a result of conflict between the religious leaders and royalty in Anuradhapura. King Mahasena (274-301) came down on the side of a monk and his followers who were expelled from Mahavihara, and dedicated the **Jetavana Monastery** east of Mahavihara to him. After suffering severe reprisals, the orthodox monastery of Mahavihara managed to regain its influence to some extent; the king then publicized his personal preference for the rebellious monastery by building the huge **Jetavana Dagoba**. Approximately 120 meters in height, it towers over all the other buildings in the city, and its massive weight requires a brick foundation several meters deep to support it. The dome is still overgrown and is currently being restored. The monastery district is located mainly to the west and south of the huge dagoba and includes the remains of some impressive buildings. Among these are the **image house** with the imposing door frame opening to the east; it has lost its Buddha figure, but the lotus throne has been restored. Revealing for modern visitors is a deep opening which enables you to look under the throne, where you can see a huge *garbhagrha*, a type of case for various relics, indicating that this was the most sacred place in the building.

South of this are most of the *panchakavasa*, rectangular accommodation units each with four *kuti* (monk's dwellings) and a central meditation room. The monastery also had a system of pipes to supply the monks with a hot bath. A good example of simulated wood construction techniques in stone edifices is a **Buddhist fence** in the southern part of the grounds. Adjacent to this on the east are the **chapter house** and the **refectory**.

Museums and Rest House

From the sacred bo tree, the center of the so-called Sacred Area of the city of Anuradhapura, it is only a short walk to

two long-established museums, located close together on Thuparama Mawatha, the road which runs along the east side of the Baswakkulama Tank.

The **National Museum for Archeology** collects the most important finds of the Anuradhapura district and has a small archeological library. The book of tickets for the whole Cultural Triangle can also be purchased at the cash desk.

The **Folk Art Museum**, unfortunately often overlooked given the dominance of archeology in this area, has a fine, well-ordered collection of traditional everyday objects and folk art.

The largest of the three historical tanks in the west of the city, the **Tissa Wewa**, is located south of the museums. The nearby **Tissa Wewa Rest House** named after it is a solid old building from the British colonial period. Since the hotel is within the Sacred Area, no alcohol can be served here. It is an ideal place from which to explore the historic sites.

Above and right: Secular adornment on the Isurumuniya Monastery – "The Lovers" (now in the museum) and an elephant relief.

On *poya* days, every month, it is an unforgettable experience to mingle with the pilgrims at full moon and follow a procession route thousands of years old by the light of numerous flickering oil lamps.

Small Monasteries and the Royal Park

West of the Rest House is the **Mirisaweti Dagoba**, which is said to have been built by Dutthagamani. A rice boat from the refectory and a few imposing columns from the chapter house have been preserved from the monastery which belonged to it.

The **Dakkhina Dagoba**, about half a kilometer southeast of the Rest House, is also among the pre-Christian buildings. It was rebuilt in its present form in the second century and is said to have contained the ashes of Dutthagamani. At the time of the religious wars, this monastery produced the founders of the Mahayan Jetavana Monastery.

Immediately behind the high dam of the Tissa Wewa Tank are the **Royal Gardens**. The tank originally irrigated the park, providing the water for its pools and cascades. Most of the buildings were wooden pavilions; but one room, hewn out of the living rock, was cooled by water and contained stone couches, and was probably also originally painted. The gardens themselves were ornamented with an abundance of lotus and goldfish ponds, and lavish plantings of flowers and trees.

To the south is the **Isurumuniya Monastery**, where caves for hermits were provided by Devanampiya Tissa at the time when Buddhism was first introduced into the country. A more secular tone is struck by the elephant reliefs which flank a bathing pool on the east side of the group of rocks. A human

form, peeking out from behind a horse's head, is interpreted as representing the Indian forest god Aiyanar. Among the numerous secular reliefs which were also found in the monastery grounds are **The Lovers**, the best of the numerous works in the Indian Gupta style that was prevalent in the seventh century. They have been given a place of honor in the small museum located next to the modern temple complex.

The **Vessagiriya Monastery**, also dating back to the beginning of Sri Lankan Buddhism, is a fine example of the architecture here, linking natural rock formations with skillfully designed buildings. It took on its final splendid form in the fifth century, when Kassapa, builder of the rock fortress of Sigiriya, had the complex, which had already been destroyed, completely rebuilt. Flights of stairs cut directly into the stone led up to the three large rock formations; the walls on either side were covered in plaster and decorated with a type of fresco, traces of which can still be seen today.

Old Monasteries, Modern Airport

Anuradhapura has numerous other old monasteries, some of them outside the Sacred Area of the old city. They were built between the third and tenth centuries, and all follow the same regular pattern, designed round a square platform. Dagoba, chapter house, image house and bo tree form the core, with the monks' buildings adjacent to it and a ditch round the whole complex.

East of the train station, for example, is the **Toluvila Vihara**: its famous meditating Buddha is the first thing you see when you enter the National Museum in Colombo.

The modern city of Anuradhapura, the busy capital of the largest district in Sri Lanka, has a population of 40,000. Most of the city's hotels are here, many of them near the huge tank of **Nuwara Wewa**, which was already irrigating the rice paddies east of the Malwatu Oya in classical times. For visitors with little time to spare, flights to Anuradhapura

will be available after resumption of domestic air traffic.

AUKANA

Around 50 kilometers southeast of Anuradhapura, and 10 kilometers off the A9, the rural town of **Kalawewa** is located on the northern edge of the huge **Kala Wewa Reservoir**, which was built by King Dhatusena (455-473). A road runs along the top of the high dike here, commanding a a fine view over the lake. Today, the tank again supplies more than a hundred villages with water, including **Aukana**, located three kilometers west of the dam.

This town is famous for its monastery, which boasts the **Aukana Buddha** at its center. Measuring 12 meters in height – 14 meters if you count the lotus throne – it is the largest monumental sculpture in Sri Lanka. Looking towards the Kala Wewa, the sculpture, while hewn out of the living rock, is only joined to the rock at the back. It depicts Buddha with his right hand in the *asisha mudra* position, a gesture of benediction, while he gathers up his robe with his left hand as he prepares to step over the eternal river of the cycle of rebirths.

The age of the statue has long been disputed, as has the reason just why it was made, but it is assumed to date from between the sixth and eighth centuries. The statue was originally protected by an image house, of which only the foundations remain; more recently, a massive brick arch was built over it in order to protect it from the vagaries of the weather. The monastery is a popular place of pilgrimage.

Above: The hand of the Aukana Buddha makes a gesture of blessing. Right: Communal meeting-place – the village spring.

The Buddha of Sasseruwa

Only 10 kilometers west of Aukana as the crow flies is the **Buddha of Sasseruwa**, almost the same height and prob-

ably dating from the same epoch. It is rather difficult to get to on account of the potholed roads; the approach roads from various directions are signposted to **Resvehera**, the name of the monastery where it is located, which sits idyllically at the edge of a tank. When a visitor arrives, rather a rare occurrence, a friendly monk usually approaches with a huge key to open the doors to the painted image houses, which are located in rock caves.

The standing Buddha chiseled out of the rock on the eastern slope of the hill once also stood inside an image house that has since fallen into ruin, as holes for beams in the rock round the figure show. For unknown reasons the figure was never completed.

Ten kilometers west of Sasseruwa – best reached from the B126 (the A28 from Galgamuwa going east) followed by six kilometers of minor road from Gallewa and a 15-minute walk – the beautifully decorated **Bodhighara of Nillakgama** sits in solitude in the midst of the jungle. The square platform of the ambulatory for this tree temple, which originally had a wooden roof, is decorated on the outside with relief slabs featuring geese, bands of trailing plants, and, above all, lions. You can enter the sanctuary from two sides through unusual door frames; positioned at the cardinal points around the bo tree inside are empty *asana*, or thrones, as symbols of the Buddha.

Anyone interested in architecture should examine the unusual *vatadage* of the monastery of **Rajangana**, about three kilometers west of Mahagalkadawala (A28). Since the monastery was abandoned at an early stage and no changes were ever made to it, you can still see a dagoba (originally roofed) in an early form, standing on a square platform.

YAPAHUWA

Instead of ruling from Dambadeniya like his predecessors, Bhuvanekabahu I (1272-1284) found an even more imposing rock outcropping for his fortress at

Yapahuwa. This site had already proved to be an excellent observation post for the Sinhalese during the rule of Magha (1215-1236); it now acquired two stalwart ring walls, one within the other (they have since been restored) with moats on the southern side of the rock, while the rock itself, reaching a height of some 100 meters, completed the protective ramparts.

Today, it's believed that houses for the townspeople were located in the spacious area between the two walls, while the more important buildings for the ruler and his immediate retinue were located within the inner ring. The foundations of large rectangular buildings have been preserved.

The **Temple of the Tooth** stands out dramatically on a natural platform on the southeast slope of the rock, reached by a steep, open-air staircase. Among the figures adorning the richly ornamented staircase are two lions resembling watchdogs. The stairs end at a stone door frame, flanked by two window openings. These were originally fitted out with stone grilles, which have now found a more sheltered home in the museums of Colombo and Yapuhawa. Little has remained of the actual building, apart from the brick foundations.

In 1284, Southern Indian Pandyas stole the precious reliquary from the temple of Yapahuwa. The fortress was destroyed and never occupied again.

A footpath leads from the platform to the summit, where you can survey the countryside like the watchmen of old. If you're more interested in the artistic side of things, you can study the influence of Indian art in the reliefs and sculptures of the staircase and the exhibits in the modern **Museum** (above the ticket office). A cave on the east side of the rock has been used by monks since the second century; today, it's part of a modern monastery which welcomes visitors.

Above: Fetching water is women's work. Right: Visible from afar – the cliffs of Sigiriya, once surrounded by water gardens.

Yapahuwa is five kilometers east of **Maho** (railway junction for the lines north and east; about two kilometers east of the A28 between Kurunegala and Anuradhapura). This distinctive landmark towers above all the other hills in the surrounding area, and can be seen from several kilometers away.

SIGIRIYA

Throughout the ages, murder and manslaughter were a common method of determining the succession to the throne. Nowhere else, however, did a serious crime of this nature result in such an original building as the palace complex of Sigiriya.

Its builder was Kassapa I (478-497), who walled his father Dhatusena up alive because he refused him the succession to the throne and the riches he demanded. Kassapa saw his revenge and punishment as fully justified, given that his father had had his own sister burned as a consequence of an insignificant family quarrel. The legal successor to the throne, Kassapa's half brother Moggallana, fled in horror to India.

Kassapa did not dare rule from Anuradhapura; instead, he chose for his residence the gneiss rock of Sigiriya ("Lion's Maw"), 200 meters high and steep on all sides, 60 kilometers southeast of the capital. He had 18 years in which to build and enjoy his palace fortress, until Moggallana returned with a Southern Indian army and forced him out. Kassapa stabbed himself; his brother had the buildings pulled down, handed over the rock with its caves to monks, and ruled again from Anuradhapura.

The whole complex extended across the entire rock as well as the land around it to the west and east, and was fortified with triple and double ramparts with moats in between. The innermost moat on the west side has been restored; this is also where the only original entrance was located.

More recently, however, an additional entrance has been created from the south,

so that you can reach the complex directly from the parking lot.

Kassapa's Palace in the Clouds

Before reaching the main rock, the path ascends between massive blocks of stone, past caves with draining ledges which served as **monks' dwellings** before Kassapa took over the area and redesigned it for his own purposes. Remains of plaster and painting in the **Cobra Cave**, formed out of a block of stone rearing up like a snake, and the **Asana Cave**, a small cave with a chiseled stone throne, indicate that they were used in Kassapa's time. In the rock above is a cleverly integrated **well**, and the smaller block of stone near it with a carefully smoothed surface suggests that this was originally the location of an **audience** or **court room**. Post holes in the ground are an indication that this building was originally roofed.

Above: The ascent to the Palace of the Clouds starts between the paws of a giant lion. Right: A beggar at the monastery of Dambulla.

Continuing further up the stairs, you come to the rock itself. On its west side you can see the ocher-colored **Mirror Gallery**, the outer wall of the path clinging to the rock face that leads to the upper parts of the fortress. This protective wall is covered with a mixture of pulverized quartz, oil and glue to give a glass-like surface with reflecting properties rather like a mirror. The mixture is ideal for tropical conditions, as the excellent state of the gallery shows. Sinhalese graffiti has been found on the inside of the wall, the oldest secular writing in this language. Between the seventh and 12th centuries, tourists scratched their comments and observations into the wall, praising the scenery, and, above all, the **Cloud Damsels**. Large areas of the rock were probably originally covered with paintings of pairs of splendidly bejeweled, lightly-clad ladies. They may have involuntarily reminded earlier visitors here of the cloud-covered Mount Kailasa, home of the pleasure-loving god Kubera, with dark cloud damsels and light storm princesses dancing round it. It is possible that Kassapa was trying to shore up his kingdom or legitimize his seizure of the throne with this reference to the gods.

Even though numerous questions remain unanswered (why are the girls only depicted from the waist up, even though they are evidently dancing? Why is the dark-complected girl always in the pose of a servant (lowered head, proffering a bowl of flowers) while the fair one is always the mistress (raised head, richer jewelry)? Why are they always in pairs? These freely drawn figures are fine works of art. The colors were applied on a base of glue and oil which combined with the plaster, creating a similar effect to that of Italian frescoes. Today, fewer than 20 of the damsels remain, protected by a natural overhang. You can reach them by means of a narrow winding staircase leading from the gallery.

The Mirror Gallery leads up to a platform on the north side of the rock. From here, there is a modern flight of steps between two huge **lion's paws** made of brick, which are all that is left of the original *sinha* or lion, the symbolic animal of the Sinhalese.

The surface of the rock is covered with the ruins of the palace complex, which was destroyed in the sixth century. It is almost impossible to identify the function of the individual buildings. At the highest point, in the north, was the **Royal Palace**, while a cistern the size of a swimming pool is visible on the south side of the grounds, which slope gently downwards. Most points up here afford a magnificent **panoramic view**. You can look down over the symmetrical **Pleasure Gardens** in the west; to reach them, return down the Mirror Gallery and descend the steps on the west side. A straight path leads past fountains and ponds to the **west gate**

on the inner moat. This is the location of another parking lot, kiosks and a small **museum**.

Sigiriya opens at 7 a.m. and is very popular. It is thus advisable to make the ascent of the rock early in the day.

DAMBULLA

The **Cave Monastery of Dambulla** has been in operation for two thousand years. Just south of **Dambulla** itself there is a rocky path with steps, thronged with beggars and traders, leading to the monastery located halfway up a huge rocky hill. The panoramic view of the plain and mountains is worth the climb. This was probably the place where King Vattagamani hid after fleeing from Tamil invaders in 103-89 B.C.

An account of the founding of the monastery is recorded in a first-century Brahmi inscription over the entrance to the first cave. This cave is dominated by the 14-meter statue of the dying Buddha, hewn out of the rock. It has been re-

painted countless times in the course of its history, and probably received its last coat of paint in the 20th century.

At his feet is Buddha's favorite pupil, Ananda; at his head, Vishnu, said to have used his divine powers to create the caves. The first one is called **Devarajalena**, or "Cave of the Divine King."

In the second and largest cave, in addition to 16 standing and 40 seated statues of Buddha, are the gods Saman and Vishnu, which pilgrims often decorate with garlands, and finally statues of King Vattagamani, who honored the monastery in the first century B.C., and King Nissanka Malla, responsible in the 12th century for the gilding of 50 statues, as indicated by a stone inscription near the monastery entrance. This cave is accordingly called **Maharajalena**, "Cave of the Great Kings." The Buddha statue hewn out of the rock on the left side of the room is escorted by wooden figures of

Above: The gods Vishnu and Saman in the Maharaja cave of the Dambulla Monastery.

the *Bodhisattvas* Maitreya (left) and Avalokiteshvara or Natha (right). There is also a dagoba and a spring which drips its water, said to have healing powers, out of a crack in the ceiling. Valuable tempera paintings on the cave ceiling dating from the 18th century depict scenes from Buddha's life, from the dream of Mahamaya to temptation by the demon Mara. Further pictures relate important events from the country's history (make sure to bring a flashlight).

The third cave, the **Maha Alut Vihara**, the "Great New Monastery," acquired ceiling and wall paintings in the typical Kandy style during the reign of King Kirti Sri Rajasinha (1747-1782), the famous Buddhist revivalist. In addition to the 50 Buddha statues, there is also a statue of the king. The fourth and fifth caves are smaller; they date from a later period and are not of such high quality. A small **Vishnu Devale** between the first and second caves attracts many worshipers. Ever since a woman tourist caused great offence by having herself photographed sitting on a Buddha statue, photography in the monastery area has been strictly forbidden. All visitors should wear appropriate clothing (no shorts; skirts should cover the knees).

Nalanda – The "Abu Simbel" of Sri Lanka

Twenty kilometers south of the Dambulla Temple, about one kilometer east of the A9, is the attractive **Nalanda Gedige**. The unusual image house was transferred to this spot near the town of **Nalanda** when the **Bowatenne Tank**, which is part of the Mahaweli Ganga Program, was built.

The small building is designed like a Hindu temple with a *mandapa*, an entrance hall (originally roofed), a short passage to a bare *cella*, and an ambulatory round the holy center. There is no sign of Hindu gods, however, and the temple is said to have been used by Buddhists.

The richly decorated facade sections, laboriously reassembled in 1975, are predominantly in the South Indian style, and may have originated in the eighth to 11th centuries, but cannot be precisely dated. However, the god Kubera appears on the south side of the tympanum over the sanctuary, and this is a feature only to be found in Sri Lanka. The temple, nestled in a marvelous setting, is hard to tear yourself away from.

POLONNARUWA

After the southern Indian Cholas stormed the city of Anuradhapura in 933, they established a new capital in **Polonnaruwa**, 90 kilometers to the southeast. Only 10 kilometers further east, the Maheweli Ganga forms the border with the historic province of Ruhuna, where the Sinhalese were constantly massing their troops in order to retake their country. One king who was successful in doing

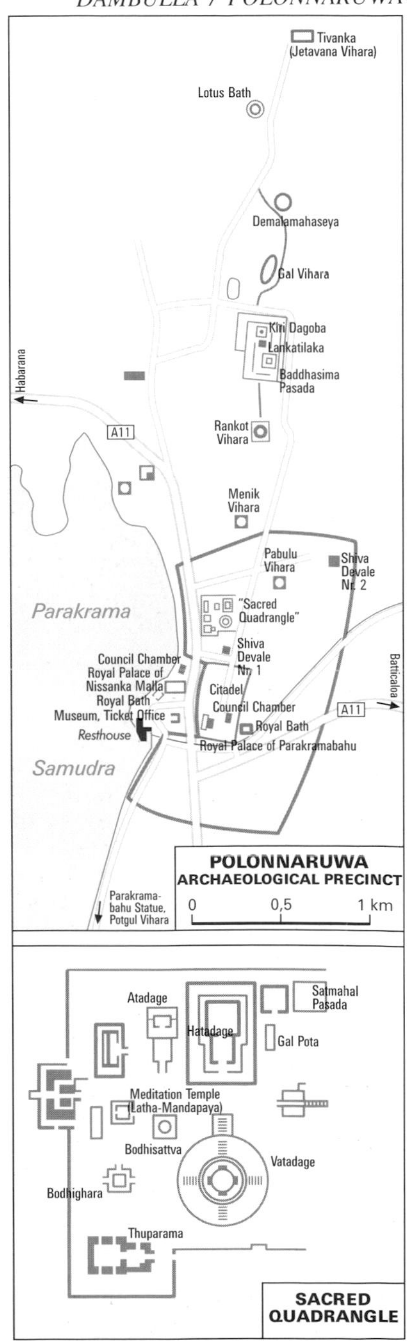

this was Vijayabahu (1055-1110), who also made the capital built by the Southern Indians his own. Two further Sinhalese kings, Parakramabahu I (1153-1186) and Nissanka Malla (1187-1196), also contributed to the architecture of Polunnaruwa. In the 13th century, however, it was abandoned and the palaces and monasteries were swallowed up by the jungle.

By the Sea of the Great Parakrama

The few thousand inhabitants of the district capital of Polonnarawa still get their water from the huge reservoir of **Parakrama Samudra**, the "sea" of the great (*-bahu*) Parakrama, who, by imposing some exceedingly tough measures, succeeded in uniting the old Sinhalese kingdom one more time and renovating the irrigation system. The dam, several kilometers long, borders the historic city in the west. The city itself extends five kilometers from north to south, while the part of it that's been excavated to date measures about nine square kilometers in area.

Above: At Kandalama Tank near Dambulla. Right: Statue of Parakramabahu, the greatest king of Polonnaruwa.

Near the south end of the dam is a dignified stone sculpture which is assumed to represent the great king. Whether what he holds in his hands is a yoke or a palm-leaf manuscript, symbolizing either royal dignity or wisdom, is unclear. The larger-than-life **statue** of Parakramabahu looks through sparse jungle to the **Potgul Vihara**, the "Library Monastery," a couple of hundred meters away.

On the last of four walled terraces is the sanctuary, which is a remarkable round building with an entrance corridor. It was here that the holy books were preserved: the great king is said to have built a monastery in which *jatakas*, legends from the Buddha's former lives, were recited. On the third platform monks' buildings were grouped around the central terrace. If you walk north along the top of the dam for about two kilometers, you'll come to a small peninsula jutting out into the lake, once the site of the Pleasure Gardens of Parakramabahu. On the southern shore is the **Rest House**, boasting a splendid view. It was built on the occasion of a visit by the Queen of England in 1954.

Two Kings – Two Palaces

Located immediately behind the Rest House, there is an old dam floodgate. A small path crosses the adjoining canal and leads past the pool of the **Royal Baths** and to the **Palace Precinct of Nissanka Malla**. Some hundred meters further on, near the lake shore, is a windowless building several stories high, which some have identified as the **Mausoleum** of this king.

Behind the remains of a dividing wall is his **Palace**, of which only the foundations remain, and his **Audience Hall** on a long rectangular platform, which has lost almost all the relief slabs that comprised its exterior decoration. You can still see, however, the sturdy, rough-hewn columns, each bearing the name of the courtier who sat beside it. The wooden roof has disappeared. At the southern end is the massive **Lion Throne**.

A second palace district, that of Parakramabahu, lies within the massive walls of the Citadel. It forms the central part of the old city area, which was also surrounded by a wall. A modern boundary of barbed wire and barriers seals off the restricted **archeological precinct**, which encompasses the Citadel, the eastern part of the old city and the monastery areas adjoining it to the north. Entrance tickets are available at the **Museum** near the Rest House.

The Citadel is located south of the signposted entrance to the archeological precinct. Its high brick walls surround a spacious area in which the highest and

most striking building is the **Palace of Parakramabahu**. His residence was surrounded by two walls, which formed a gallery enclosing the square palace (50 meters on each side) and the equally large courtyard. In the massive walls of the ruin you can still see the holes for the ceiling made of wooden beams, as well as the stone staircase leading to the second floor, the pillars of the atrium, a further large hall and the servants' cells along the outside wall. There is nothing left of the other six floors of the palace, which is said to have had a thousand rooms.

About a hundred meters further east is the **Audience Hall of Parakramabahu**, the outer walls of which are covered with friezes bearing reliefs of elephants, lions and gnomes. To enter, visitors walk over Polonnaruwa moonstones (the cow or Nandi bull is absent from the animal symbols on these stones, a gesture of consideration for the numerous Hindus in the country), while the balustrades are decorated with *makaras* and lions. Pain-

stakingly worked columns once supported a wooden roof.

Outside the wall of the Citadel, near the main canal in the south, the great king could pause to take a refreshing dip in the **Kumara Pokuna**, or "King's Bathing Pool." It is square with elegantly shaped corners, and at one side of it there is a **bathing pavilion** decorated with reliefs of lions.

The Citadel has only one entrance from the north. Facing this is the **Shiva Temple No. 1**; most of the niches for statues in the lower part of the elaborate facade are empty, but the cella still houses the *lingam*, the phallic symbol of the god Shiva. Only fragments of the tiled roof remain.

A large collection of bronze gods were found in this temple; these can now be seen in the National Museum in Colombo.

Above: Lingam in the Shiva Temple No. 1, Polonnaruwa. Right: Temple guard at the vatadage of Polonnaruwa.

The Sacred Quadrangle

On a raised surface approximately 100 square meters known as the **Sacred Quadrangle**, some way away from the city's monasteries but close to the Citadel, are several temples that were connected with the reigning kings. After the relic of the Sacred Tooth became the main symbol of royal dignity, the rulers each made sure they built their own *Dalada Maligawa*, or "Tooth Temple."

The circular building left of the main steps is the **Vatadage**, roofed dagoba, and is the Tooth Temple of Parakramabahu, but it was later altered by Nissanka Malla, who added an inscription tablet that claimed he had built it himself. Three circles of columns supported the wooden roof of the central dagoba and the ambulatory, the outer one enclosed by a fine Buddhist railing. A massive brick wall supported the construction. Around the dagoba, four meditating Buddhas sit at the four cardinal points, and in front of each of them is an entrance artistically decorated with *makaras*, guardstones and moonstones.

Opposite this, to the north, is the Tooth Temple of Nissanka Malla. The **Hatadage** ("House of 60 Relics") is surrounded by a stone wall. The stone staircase which you see in the entrance hall used to lead to the wooden upper floor with the tooth relic chamber.

On the west side of this is the **Atadage**, or "House of Eight Relics," which Vijayabahu built for the tooth relic. The king assigned Tamil mercenaries to guard the temple in order to provide them with an income, as an inscription near the building indicates.

The **statue of a Bodhisattva**; the **Meditation Temple of Nissanka Malla** decorated with dainty columns; an image house with the brick remains of a reclining Buddha; and a *bodhighara* (bo tree enclosure) are to be found north of the massive 12th-century image house known as the **Thuparama**. This building's facade, with its niches and pilasters, garlanded with a frieze of elephants and buildings, was clearly influenced by Southern Indian art.

The inner dome is a "false vaulting," where the walls become thicker towards the inside and meet in the middle. There are only a few brick remains of the colossal Buddha statue which used to stand in the inner sanctum, and the other statues displayed here were actually found in the course of excavations in other parts of the city. On the northeast edge of the sacred area are the **Gal Pota**, the "Stone Book," in which the glorious deeds of Nissanka Malla are engraved, and the **Satmahal Pasada**, the seven-story building that Laotian monks erected as a memorial.

Temples and Monasteries in the Jungle

Within the city walls are Hindu temples to Shiva, Vishnu and Ganesha, which were either built during the time of

the Sinhalese kings for their Tamil wives or date from the Chola period, such as the small 11th-century **Shiva Devale No. 2** in the northeast corner of the city area, which is usually closed. Completely intact, it is surrounded by four Nandi bulls; Hindu pilgrims visit it every year on two days in June.

Some of the queens were Buddhist and had striking dagobas built, such as the **Pabulu Vihara** near the Shiva Devale, or the huge **Rankot Vihara** outside the city walls, near the small monastery of **Menik Vihara**.

North of the large Rankot Dagoba, a broad footpath leads through the extensive **Alahana Pirivena** ("Monastery by the Cremation Grounds"). It continues past numerous *kuti* (monks' dwellings) and a hospital, recognizable from a stone herbal bath shaped like a human form, to the highest part of the area and the foundations of the **Baddhasima Pasada**, the assembly hall. A platform in the middle of the extensive building marks the place where the preacher stood. The image house below this, **Lankatilaka**, the "Jewel of Lanka," was originally almost 30 meters high but consisted of only a single story, even though the facade looks as if there are several floors to it. The huge figure of the standing Buddha, originally 13 meters high, could be circled by a procession walking round an ambulatory in the wall or viewed from the *mandapa*, the **meditation building** decorated with lion friezes opposite the entrance.

The **Kiri Dagoba**, or "Milk Dagoba," thus named because of its white lime plaster, and a few smaller memorial dagobas are the final buildings located along the northernmost edge of the monastery grounds.

At this point, you rejoin the main path and come to a parking lot and picnic area by a small tank. A footpath along the top of the dam branches off (right) to the **Gal Vihara**, or "Stone Monastery." For many people, the ensemble of four statues chiseled out of the gneiss rocks are the real highlight of any visit to Polonnaruwa. At the time of Parakramabahu, under whom the monastery was built, the statues were painted and each one stood in its own image house, as is indicated by the holes for the beams that can be seen in the rock and surrounding walls.

The larger of the two meditating Buddhas, on the left, has a finely worked halo, and his lotus throne is decorated with lightning bolts and lions. This five-meter figure decorates the front of the rock; for the seated Buddha next to him, only one and a half meters high, however, a cave was chiseled into the rock. He is protected by a stone shade and flanked by servants bearing palm-frond fans. The cave still has traces of plastering and paint. To the right, the front of the rock has been smoothed and contains an inscription referring to the council which Parakramabahu summoned in the year 1160 in order to unite the Buddhist orders.

The standing statue in the *tivanka* position (triple bow) to the right is puzzling on account of the unusual way his arms are crossed; it's open to question whether this really is a figure of Buddha. The final figure in the group is the impressive reclining Buddha, a good 14 meters long, depicted in the process of departing this life for nirvana. The sculptor's masterful ability to work in this difficult material is particularly evident in the decorated pillow with a depression in it, the position of the arms, and the folds of the garment.

A few minutes' walk from here along a narrow footpath through the jungle is the completely overgrown giant stupa of **Demalamahaseya** ("Tamil Dagoba"), unfinished and resembling a flat-topped hill, on top of which sits a small dagoba. Both may have been built by Tamil prisoners of war in the 12th century. The footpath rejoins the main path after a few yards. West of the road north is the charming **Lotus Pond**, a ritual monks' bathing pool in the form of an eight-petalled lotus blossom. The road ends at the image house of the **Jetavana Monastery**. The building acquired the name **Tivanka**, "Thrice Bent," from the position of the Buddha statue, which curves three times from the perpendicular posture. It is famous for its 12th-century paintings, which illustrate a number of different *jatakas*.

Right: Two of the four impressive statues of Buddha in the Gal Vihara, Polonnaruwa.

Places of Pilgrimage in the Land of the Elephants

North of the A11, halfway between **Habarana** and Polonnaruwa, is **Medirigiriya**, reached by way of **Hingurakgoda** along many picturesque irrigation canals. About three kilometers north of this is the remote local monastery built on rock foundations in the midst of the jungle, with a particularly fine **vatadage**.

It dates from the 12th century and is similar to that of Polonnaruwa, but set in much more beautiful surroundings. Four image houses adjoin it to the west, and ancient stone steps lead up to a small dagoba on the rock to the north. Outside the monastery, which is known to have existed since the second century, are the ruins of a hospital and a picturesque lotus pond.

Although the road is in bad condition due to frequent flooding, it's worth negotiating the main A11 in the valley of the Mahaweli Ganga, east of Polonnaruwa, to visit the old province of Ruhuna. **Elephants** feel at home in this sparsely-populated area and can occasionally be spotted here; they also frequent the nature reserves west of Polonnaruwa.

Dimbulagala, a massive rock 543 meters high towering up out of the plain on the far side of the wide river valley, is visible from a long way off; its advantages as a look-out point for military commanders and a secluded refuge for hermits were already recognized and exploited two thousand years ago. In recent years, as a result of the Mahaweli program in the area east of the big river, numerous new rice paddies and villages have appeared, and Japanese development aid has gone into the construction of excellent roads. As a result, the journey from **Mannampitya** on the A11 to **Dimbulagala Monastery** on the western ridge of the mountain now takes only a few minutes; if you have no time to stop, you can get to Mahiyangana, 90 kilometers away, in just over an hour.

Until a few decades ago, parts of the now intensively cultivated countryside were the traditional territory of the indigenous *Veddah* peoples. The monk Silalankara devoted himself for 40 years to integrating this local population and the thousands of immigrants from other parts of the country, until he was murdered by the Tamil Tigers in 1995.

The caves of the monastery, which dates back to the fifth century, have now been modernized and are visited by numerous pilgrims.

ANURADHAPURA

Accommodation

MODERATE: **Hotel Palm Garden Village**, Puttalam Road, Pandulagama, tel. 025-23961/2. **Miridiya Hotel**, Rowing Club Road (quiet, lovely garden), tel. 025-22112. **Nuwara Wewa Rest House**, New Town (at the dam of the tank), tel. 025-22565. **Rajarata Hotel**, Rowing Club Road (quiet location), tel. 025-2578. **Tissa Wewa Rest House**, Sacred City (in park-like grounds in the sacred city, no alcohol served, colonial-style building, bike rental), tel. 025-22299.

BUDGET: **Ashok Hotel**, 20 Rowing Club Road, tel. 025-22753. **Cottage Tourist Rest**, 38/388, Harishandra Mw. **Hela Inn**, New Town (near the bus station), tel. 025-22642. **Hotel Lion's Den**, 523/11 D.S. Senanayake Mw., tel. 025-22270. **Hotel Randiya**, Rowing Club Road, tel. 025-22868. **Kondamalee Guest House**, 42/388 Stage 1, Harishandra Mw., tel. 025-22029. **Monara Tourist Guest House**, 63 Freeman Mw., tel. 025-23043. **Shanti Guest House**, 891 Mailagas Junction, tel. 025-22515. **Swan Chinese Rest**, 310/1 Harishandra Mw., tel. 025-22058. **Hotel Jananie**, 280A Main Street, tel. 025-22979.

Transportation

PLANE: Providing there are no flight restrictions: several flights a week to/from Ratmalana via Sigiriya, and to/from Vavuniya and Trincomalee. See page 241.

TRAIN: Daily service to Colombo/Matara; change in Maho to Trincomalee.

BUS: Frequent service toward Colombo; direct connections to the west coast (Puttalam), Kurunegala/Kandy, Dambulla/east coast.

Sights

Sacred City: The main roads can be navigated by car, but by bike or on foot you'll be able to explore things in far greater detail. Even if you are in possession of an admission ticket for the whole Cultural Triangle, some of the holy sites require additional admission.

Archeological Museum: Thuparama Mw., (sells general admission tickets for the Cultural Triangle; small library), open daily from 8 am to 5 pm.

Folk Art Museum: Thuparama Mw., open daily from 8 am to 4:30 pm except Thursdays and Fridays, Cultural Triangle ticket not valid.

Mahatissa Fahsien Museum (also called **Abhayagiri Museum**): Entrance from the south, Anula Mw., open daily 8 am to 4:30 pm.

Hospital

General Hospital, Hospital Road, tel. 025-22261.

DAMBULLA

Accommodation

LUXURY: **Kandalama Hotel**, Kandalama (8 km east from the A9 in Dambulla, at the edge of the jungle, view of the tank and Sigiriya cliffs, guided tours into the jungle), tel. 066-84100, fax 84109.

MODERATE: **Culture Club**, Kandalama (7 km east from the A9 in Dambulla, on the tank's western shore, individual bungalows in the park, nature tours), tel. 066-31822/24/25. **Eden Garden Hotel**, Sigiriya Road, tel. 066-85230.

BUDGET: **Gimanhala Transit Hotel**: 754 Anuradhapura Road, tel. 066-84864. **Hotel Laxapana**, Matale Road, tel. 066-84803. **Sun Flower Inn**, Ratmalgahaela Road, Temple Junction (50 meters east of the A9, near the ascent to the rock temple).

Transportation

BUS: Frequent service daily to Colombo, Kandy, Anuradhapura; buses to the east coast: ask for information. See page 241.

Sights

Cave Temple: Open daily, admission fee: donations requested, strict prohibition on photographing, both men and women may only enter the temple precinct in appropriate clothing (no shorts; knees covered!).

Dambulla Arboretum, Kandalama Road, visiting the wealth of flora indigenous to the monsoon forest only possible after advance registration at: Sam Popham Foundation, Mr. F. H. Popham, Kandalama Road, Dambulla.

Wasgomuwa National Park: The Culture Club and Kandalama hotels organize safaris; there are three bungalows in the park: **Kadurupitiya** (maximum of eight people), **Gale** and **Angamadilla** (six people each), reservation information: Department of Wildlife Conservation, 18 Gregory Road, Colombo 7, tel. 01-694241.

Rock Fortress of Sigiriya, located about 15 km from the Kandalama Hotel along inland routes, 20 km along the main road from Dambulla.

HABARANA

Accommodation

MODERATE: **The Lodge** (bungalows and rooms in row houses in an extensive park by the tank; tennis courts, bird-watching, bike rental, elephant rides), tel. 066-70011/2. **The Village** (next to The Lodge, rooms somewhat simpler), tel. 066-70046/7. *BUDGET:* **Habarana Inn**, Dambulla Road. **Rest House**, at the junction of the A11 and A6, tel. 066-70003.

Transportation

TRAIN: At the present time no regular services between Colombo-Batticaloa (station about 2 km from the hotels). For services to east coast see page 241.

BUS: Several buses a day to Colombo, Kandy, Anuradhapura.

Excursions

Habarana is centrally located with regard to the main sites of classical Sinhalese culture: Sigiriya 17 km, Dambulla 22 km, Aukana 32 km, Medirigiriya 35 km, Polonnaruwa 45 km, Mihintale 50 km, Anuradhapura 57 km.

Ritigala: Nature reserve and pre-Christian cave monastery on a wooded mountain more than 700 meters high, 15 km west of Habarana, hard to reach in the rainy season.

Ayurvedic Doctor

Dr. S.M.H. Wijesinghe, nationally-known orthopedist, specializes in broken bones and explains Ayurvedic methods; complex includes a very simple hospital and a pharmacy: "Siriwedaniwasa," Horiwila, Palugaswewa, 12 km from Habarana on the A 11 toward Maradankadawala/Anuradhapura, then turn south.

MAHO / YAPAHUWA

Accommodation

BUDGET: **Yapahuwa Rest House** near the Maho train station.

Transportation

TRAIN: Several trains a day to Colombo. Train junction for lines to Anuradhapura/Vavuniya, Trincomalee.
BUS: Several buses a day to Anuradhapura, Colombo, Kurunegala, Kandy; local buses run the 5 km to Yapahuwa.

Museum

Archeological Museum, Yapahuwa, open daily 8 am to 5 pm except Tuesdays.

MIHINTALE

Accommodation / Restaurant

MODERATE: **Hotel Mihintale**, Anuradhapura Road, tel. 025-66599.

Transportation

BUS: Frequent service to Anuradhapura, 12 km.

Museum

Archeological Museum, located between the ascent to the temple and the A12, open daily except Tuesday 8 am to 5 pm.

POLONNARUWA AND ENVIRONS

Accommodation

GIRITALE: *MODERATE:* **Giritale Hotel**, National Holiday Resort, tel. 027-46311. **The Deer Park Hotel**, tel. 027-46470, new, overlooking the Giritale Tank. **The Royal Lotus**, above the Giritale Tank, tel. 027-46316.
HINGURAKGODA: *BUDGET:* **Rest House**, Medirigiriya Road, tel. 027-46267. **Gold Flower Hotel**, 54 Airport Rd., tel. 027-46339.
POLONNARUWA: *MODERATE:* **Hotel Sudu Araliya**, New Town (new), tel. 027-24848. **Hotel Seruwa**, New Town (quiet, 2 km south of the entrance to archeological precinct), tel. 027-22411. **The Village Polonnaruwa** (formerly **Amalian Nivas**), New Town (quiet, well-tended place near the lake, 2 km from archeological precinct), tel. 027-22405.
BUDGET: **Gajaba**, Kuruppu Gardens, Lake Road, tel. 027-22394. **Rest House**, Lake Road (on the lake, built in 1954 on the occasion of the visit of Queen Elizabeth II, rooms and restaurant with lake view, good food), tel. 027-22299 and 01-503497.
WASGOMUWA NATIONAL PARK: **Angamedilla Bungalow**, maximum of six people, entrance at the southern Parakrama Samudra, reservation through Dept. of Wildlife Conservation, Wildlife Reservation Center, 18 Gregory Road, Colombo 7, tel. 01-694241.

Transportation

TRAIN: Station is in Kaduruwela, 4 km east of the entrance to the archeological precinct, at the present time no regular service between Colombo-Batticaloa. See p. 241 for further information.
BUS: Several buses a day to Colombo, Kandy, Anuradhapura; change in Habarana and Dambulla for countless other destinations.

Sights

Archeological Precinct: Except for the area south of the dam of Parakrama Samudra Lake (Potgul Vihara etc.) and the palace area of Nissanka Malla (by the Rest House), the precinct is strictly off-limits to the public. Entrance tickets (or general-admission Cultural Triangle tickets) sold in the **museum**, a few hundred meters toward the Rest House, open 8 am to 4:30 pm; after 9 am, except Sun, you can also get special permission to enter the restricted area on the same day (there are no restaurants in this area).
Woodworking: There are legal regulations about foresting the valuable woods of the surrounding jungle; a number of workshops (wood-carving, furniture-making) are located around the western exit from the archeological precinct and along the B11 west of Polonnaruwa.

Hospital

Base Hospital, Batticaloa Road, tel. 027-22261.

SIGIRIYA

Accommodation

MODERATE: **Hotel Sigiriya**: tel. 066-84811. **Sigiriya Village Hotel**, lovely facility in well-tended park, tel. 066-31803/4/5.
BUDGET: **Rest House**, tel. 066-31899.

Transportation

PLANE: There are no flights at the present time.
BUS: Direct service daily from Colombo and Matale, hourly from Dambulla.

Sights

Rock Fortress open 7 am to 5 pm, Cultural Triangle general admission ticket valid, entrance from the south, near all the hotels, or from the west through the inner fortress moat. **Archeological Museum**, daily except Tue 8 am-5 pm. **Cave Temple of Dambulla**, 20 km, the tanks and the jungle in the area offer countless opportunities for **nature observation**.
There are **hikes** and **bike tours** off the main roads to Kandalama, Dambulla and Habarana.

KANDY
Sacred Tooth, Tamed Mahaweli

THE KINGDOM OF KANDY

The Sinhalese name for their former capital is not **Kandy** but *Maha Nuwara*, "Great City," even though there are larger cities on the island. And, as no visitor can fail to notice, the Sri Lankans are extremely proud of it. The name Kandy comes from *Kanda Uda Pasrata*, the former kingdom in the mountains, which was divided into five regions. In order to appreciate Kandy's greatness, past and present, you have to see the old royal city in the context of its surroundings.

Malayarata was the Sinhalese name for the hill country as early as the classical period; today, it remains an impressive sight, regardless of which side you're approaching from. It was an ideal retreat for the Sinhalese when threatened by foreign invaders; however, it did not become a political or cultural stronghold until the 14th century.

Although the Sinhalese at first avoided the mountains when they created their new capitals in the 13th century, the rock fortresses of Dambadeniya, Yapahuwa, and Kurunegala – as well as Beligala, where the Sacred Tooth relic of Buddha was kept – show that the kings attached great importance to places which were strategically protected. It was thus only logical, after Kurunegala was given up, that **Gampola** should become the next capital (1341-1408), located as it was near the upper reaches of the Mahaweli Ganga on the edge of a network of deep, crevassed mountain valleys.

Preceding pages: Fantastic scene – perahera in Kandy. Left: Music accompanies the elephant procession.

Even as early as the Gampola period, there was a ruler's residence called **Senkadagala** on the site of what was later to become the city of Kandy, which King Vimaladharmasuriya made his capital in 1593. Much to the satisfaction of the Portuguese colonial overlords, he married a Catholic. This did not, however, prevent him from remaining true to Buddhist traditions: he built a temple for the Sacred Tooth relic, the symbol of the legitimate ruler of the country. Seven other kings were to follow him until 1815.

From the 18th century on, there was a revival of Buddhism in *Kanda Uda Pasrata*, and the kings of Kandy built and renovated a large number of temples. Whenever they felt threatened, they fled with their retinue into even narrower mountain valleys and took the Sacred Tooth with them to keep it safe.

During the rule of the English, large sections of the jungle were cleared to make way for plantations, and modern

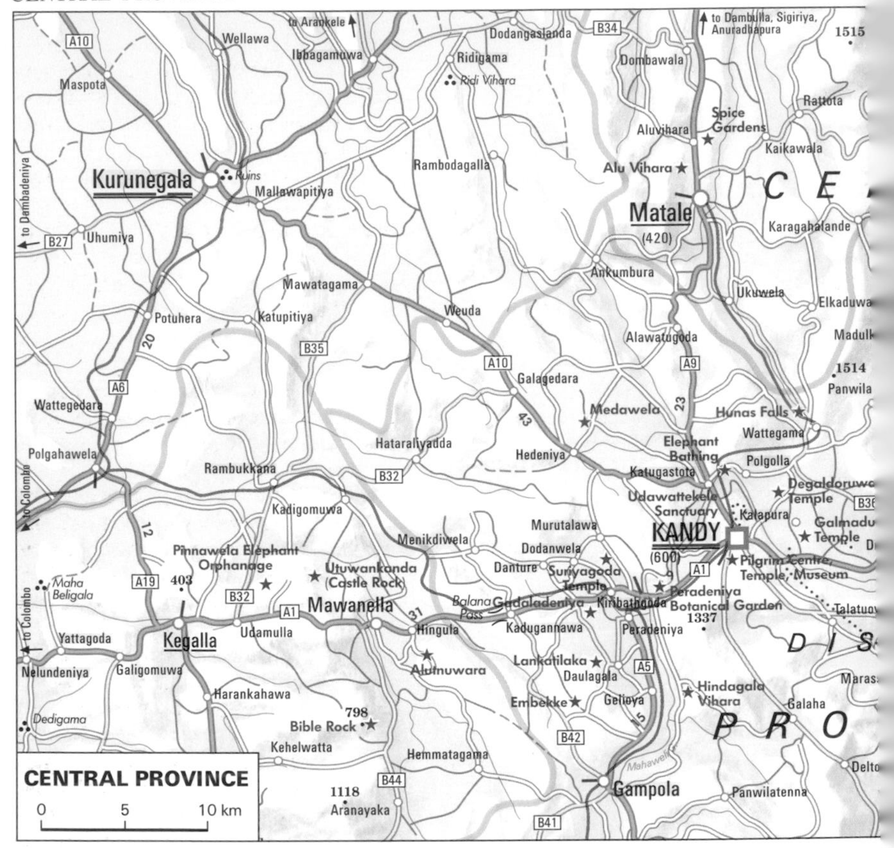

roads were built. Most recently, the reservoirs along the Mahaweli Ganga have changed the landscape east of Kandy, underlining the beauties of this mountainous region.

THE MAHAWELI GANGA

East of Kandy, you can cross the Mahaweli Ganga at three places. The simplest and most direct crossing is the new **Tennekumbura Bridge**, around three kilometers from the city center; the most romantic is the **Lewella Suspension Bridge**; and the most interesting, if you get permission from the guard, is the **Polgolla Dam**. Since 1976, some of the Mahaweli River's yellow water has been channeled underground for eight kilometers from here to the **Ukuwela Power Station** south of Matale. At the information center in Polgolla you can find out more about the ambitious Mahaweli program to provide energy and irrigation in Sri Lanka, and the results it has already achieved. Three reservoirs and power plants have been built in the last few years between Kandy and Mahiyangana, only 40 kilometers away as the crow flies. The main road to Mahiyangana has now been rerouted higher up on the north shore of the **Victoria Reservoir**, which was built with British aid. A good minor road leads to the **Victoria Dam**, 520 meters long and 122 meters high, which has an impressive **information center**.

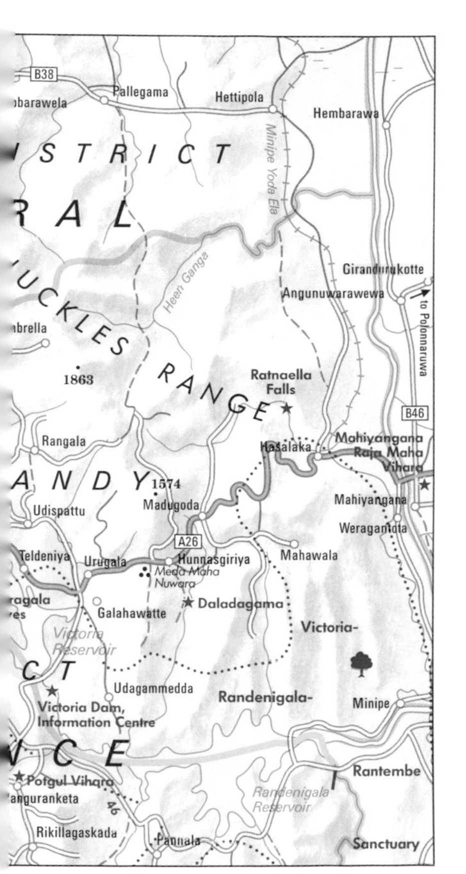

Below the dam, in the narrow rocky bed of the Mahaweli, is the powerful hydroelectric power plant (210 megawatt). The river water collects downstream in the reservoirs of **Randenigala** and **Rantembe**, built with German aid, and electricity is also produced behind their dams (126 and 50 megawatts respectively).

Royal Routes to the East

After the A26 leaves the Victoria Reservoir, it rises continuously until it reaches the southern foothills of the **Knuckles**. Several Kandy kings fled to the safety of this magnificent countryside. For the last one, Sri Vikrama Rajasinha, flight was in vain: the British caught up with him and his wives in Galahawatte on February 18, 1815. His surrender marked the end of the succession of the Sinhalese kings, which had lasted for thousands of years.

On the western slope of the **Hunnasgiriya Cliffs** are the ruins of the fortress of **Meda Maha Nuwara** ("Middle Great City"): King Senarath (1605-1635) fled here to safety from the Portuguese persecutors, but he was later obliged to move on to Alut Nuwara (Mahiyangana). The ruler's symbol, the Sacred Tooth of the Buddha, was also taken into exile. Today, the Maliga Vihara is still tucked away in **Daladagama** ("Tooth Village") east of the ridge.

A poor road from **Hunnasgiriya** to the north leads to the east flank of the Knuckles ridge, just under 2,000 meters high (signposted "Looloowatte 14 km"). The magnificent view right to the eastern shore of the island makes up for the potholes that you have to negotiate to get there. At the end of the road, you have to continue on foot: this trail is for seasoned hikers only. You have to know how to use a compass and be confident of finding the paths used by the cardamom pickers and herb gatherers. If you are prepared for a two- to three-day walk and are afraid neither of sudden downpours nor hordes of leeches, you will be rewarded by some of the most beautiful scenery in Sri Lanka: the mountainous region between **Corbett's Gap** and the tea plantations of the western Knuckles.

As the A26 continues on its winding route eastward, there are further dramatic views of the Dumbara Valley, until dense forest swallows up the view. Only after the 17 hairpin turns on the east side of the hill do you have a panorama of the rice paddies east of the Mahaweli Ganga. This is where **Mahiyangana** is located. The spot where the **Great Dagoba** now stands marks the place where Buddha is said to have visited Sri Lanka for the first time. It has been repeatedly enlarged by

successions of rulers; its most important relic is the hair that the Buddha pulled out of his head to give to the newly converted as a souvenir. One especially important discovery was the paintings in the relic chamber from the time of King Vikramabahu (12th century). Otherwise, the temple complex is modern.

East of Mahiyangana one can observe and acquaint onesself with the back-to-nature lifestyle of the *Wedda* communities and pay a visit to the **Maduru Oya National Park**.

Irrigation on the Mahaweli

Mahiyangana lies like a link in a chain between the mountainous region and the plains that formed the heart of classical Sinhalese irrigation culture. The fastest route north to Polonnaruwa is the excellent secondary road (AB 44) to the north.

Above: The Temple of Medu Dumbara in the Dumbara Valley. Right: Beware of wild elephants!

The modern irrigation system of the Mahaweli subsidiary canals with additional tanks has made huge areas available for rice cultivation. The new farming settlement of **Girandurukotte** is rather like a modern garden city, and has attracted 20,000 families since 1970. Here, an excavated dagoba and a colonnade decorated with lions both date from the classical Sinhalese period.

In times past and still at present, at **Minipe** south of Mahiyangana, a dam diverts Mahaweli water onto the fields around the river. The superbly-paved road along the picturesque southern shores of the three new reservoirs of Rantembe, Randenigala and Victoria, however, belongs very much to modern times. Signs warn you to beware of wild elephants, which may wander across the road in this sparsely populated jungle area. Minor roads lead up into the highlands; one of them goes to **Hanguranketa**, another refuge of the kings of Kandy. The palace was destroyed in 1818 and the rubble was used to build the

Potgul Vihara. This monastery is today the central feature of this sleepy little town. The image house and the treasury are open to the public on *poya* days.

KURUNEGALA

The main roads, the A9 and A10, lead from the north, the traditional heartland of Sinhalese civilization, to Kandy, converging at the bridge over the Mahaweli Ganga in Katugastota. From here it is approximately 40 kilometers to **Kurunegala**, the busy capital of the northwest province, with a population of 30,000. According to legend, the dark rocky hills east of the city were once animals which threatened to drink the tanks dry during a drought; a sorceress averted the misfortune by turning them into rocks. Kurunegala is the last capital of the Sinhalese kings (1291-1326) in the dry zone, close to where the mountains begin. A few ruins by the **Ibbagala** rock are all that remain to attest to the former city's importance.

Sixteen kilometers to the northeast, near **Ridigama**, is the cliff-top monastery of **Ridi Vihara**. Whether there is any substance to the legend that a vein of silver was found here in the second century B.C. is a matter of conjecture, but the caves were certainly in use in the pre-Christian era and were beautifully decorated with paintings under the Kandy king Kirti Sri Rajasinha (1747-1782).

Leave the A6 at **Ibbagamuwa**, 16 kilometers northeast of Kurunegala, and take the B62 north, toward Polpitigama, to the tank of **Pansalamulla Wewa**, 18 kilometers further on, which marks the start of the extensive forest monastery of **Arankele**. The rocky outcrops jutting out into the water are decorated with reliefs, and there are also smooth slabs of stone which are thought to have been used by monks and visitors to enter the water for ritual ablutions. On the other side of the tank, a flagstone path leads for about 400 meters through the jungle, past a stone

pavilion surrounded by a moat, which was once an idyllic retreat for forest monks, shaded by *na* trees (*mesua ferrea*, ironwood tree). Other monks lived in three caves with drainage ledges, separated by dividing walls, which are undoubtedly extremely old. Holes in the rock wall, however, also indicate that wooden constructions were put up in front of the caves at a later date. There are no inscriptions, and the simplicity of the interior makes it difficult to date this large monastery complex in its attractive, isolated setting.

MATALE

Matale, the new district capital on the A10, surrounded by mountains, developed from an English fort. In the mid-19th century, the English destroyed the monastery of **Alu Vihara**, three kilometers away, during their pursuit of local rebels; the monastery was rebuilt, however, in the 20th century because of its historic importance. For it was here, in

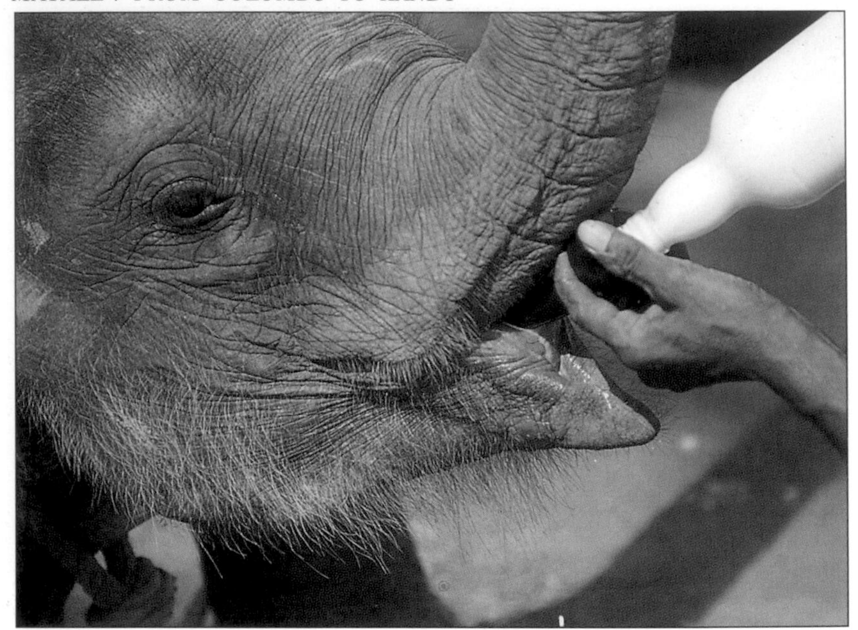

the first century B.C., that around 500 Buddhist monks assembled at a council and made the decision to commit the *tripitaka* (three baskets) to paper. Up until then, there had been no complete written record of the *sutta* (Buddha's teachings), *vinaya* (monastic order regulations) and *abhidhamma* (interpretations). In Pali, these three important works of the *sangha*, the Buddhist community of brothers, were engraved into the smoothed leaves of the talipot palm (*corypha umbraculifera*) and kept in *pitaka*, or baskets. In the small monastery museum, a curator or monk can explain the stages in the production of the *ola*, or palm-leaf manuscripts.

Before the A10 – the most important route to the classical Sinhalese territory with its royal cities – reaches the irrigated plain around Nalanda, it passes through shady plantations and mountain forests with numerous spice gardens, which offer instructive tours for visitors. Batik factories have now also been set up along the routes most frequented by tourists. The simple lime works serve the local building trade.

Above and right: The elephant orphanage at Pinnawela is a favorite with local as well as foreign visitors.

FROM COLOMBO TO KANDY

There are two ways to get from Colombo to Kandy; by driving on the A1 or else taking the train. The fastest rail connection by Inter-City Express takes about two hours to cover the distance of 126 kilometers. After the varied scenery of the flat countryside with its rice paddies between Colombo and Rambukkana, there come breathtaking views as the line enters the mountains; here, the panoramic carriage hitched to the back of the train proves its merit.

You'll find that traveling by your own means of transportation will provide you with maximum flexibility for stopping for rests and sightseeing off the beaten track. It is 116 kilometers by road from

Colombo to Kandy on a very busy route that passes through many towns and villages and misses out on the beautiful scenery. Among the places of interest in the mountain region past **Ambepussa**, where the A6 (to Kurunegala) branches off from the A1 (to Kandy), is **Dedigama**, reached on a small road which branches off to the south from **Nelundeniya** (four kilometers). The famous king Parakramabahu I (1153-1186) immortalized his birthplace with the flat-topped **Kotavehera Dagoba**, which encloses an older, smaller dagoba. The unusually large relic chambers yielded some remarkable finds, now displayed in a small **museum** which also includes models of the interior of the dagoba.

Only two kilometers further along on the A1, in **Yattagoda**, a steep road leads north to the **Maha Beligala** (three kilometers). On this bare rocky hill rising from the midst of a rubber forest, the Sacred Tooth of Buddha was kept in the 13th century when the king was reigning in Dambadeniya, 25 kilometers away. There is an impressive view of the rounded foothills from this secure summit.

Today, travelers can pass **Utuwankanda Hill** without a second thought, unlike their precursors in the 1860s. In those days the highwayman Saradiel was in the habit of attacking, with the help of the local people, any heavily laden carriages that ventured past his hilltop hideaway.

A few kilometerss further on, you can't miss the turnoff to the **Elephant Orphanage** at **Pinnawela** (five kilometers). This is a rewarding detour, especially at noon when the *mahouts*, or elephant keepers, scrub the baby elephants, as well as a few fully-grown animals, in the river.

Many pilgrims, but few foreigners, come to the well-tended temple complex of **Alutnuwara**, four kilometers from Hingula. The image of the deity Dedimunda (Upulvan/Vishnu) from Dondra, the southern tip of the island, was brought here to the safety of the mountains after the Portuguese destroyed its temple in the 16th century. Today, it has found a permanent abode in the Maha Vishnu Devale of Kandy. From the winding A1, you now have a view over several kilometers of foothills, with the **Bible Rock**, flat-topped and almost 800 meters high, the most dominant feature.

The **tunnel** cut through the rock when the road was laid, as well as the 38-meter **memorial tower** for the road engineer Dawson in **Kadugannawa**, are reminders of how difficult it was to build this road in 1827. The small **open-air museum** at the **Kiribathgoda** railway crossing also spotlights the achievements of transport technology.

KANDY

Maha Nuwara, the Great City

Travelers' ecstatic descriptions of the wonderful location of **Kandy** (*Maha Nuwara*) date mainly from the 18th and 19th centuries. Since then, the population of the city has grown from a few thousand to more than a hundred thousand. It is thus very much to the city's credit that the truly lovely ensemble of the **Lake of Kandy**, with the grounds of the **Palace** and **Temple of the Tooth** against the green backdrop of **Udawattekele Park**, has managed to remain unspoiled.

South of the lake, on the slope of the mountain, old villas, new buildings – including numerous hotels – and the **Malwatte Monastery** lie tucked away behind huge trees and flowering shrubs. The market, prison, bus station and train station crowd together below the dam of the artificial lake, which was not built until the reign of the last Kandy king. The modern statue of Buddha on the **Bahiravakanda**, the hill bordering the city center on its west side, symbolizes the spread of buildings across the hillsides of Kandy, especially towards the end of the 20th century. But the kings designed the core of the city itself with great care and significance, not merely to serve as a commercial or residential city, but rather to be the residence of the king, the gods, dignitaries and subjects. It was damaged by the Portuguese in 1610 and the Dutch in 1765, and underwent a major change of orientation with the abdication of its king in 1815; it subsequently became the center of the developing plantation economy in the region. Kandy is on the UNESCO World Cultural Heritage List.

The Royal Palace and Temple of the Tooth are located at the foot of the wooded Senkadagala Hill, separated from the city by a moat. The complex is additionally protected by two pierced stone walls the height of a man, but nevertheless rather fragile in appearance. The lower one symbolizes the motion of waves, the upper one drifting clouds. Out of this garland of clouds, the last king used to appear to his subjects from the *pattirippuwa*, the octagonal building by the moat. Not until the 20th century did this become part of the temple complex.

The Temple of the Tooth, where the precious tooth relic is kept, is a small two-story building that dates from the 18th century; in 1988, it was fitted out with its striking roof, of which the gleaming golden tiles are visible from afar. On the upper floor, Buddha's left eyetooth is enclosed in seven golden caskets in the shape of dagobas. The outer one is draped with precious hangings, presents to the temple.

At *poya* times (6:30 a.m., 9:30 a.m. and 6:30 p.m.) those believers who have made a large donation to the temple can go and stand directly in front of the altar, which is strewn with jasmine flowers. For all other visitors, a monk opens a small door in the upper floor of the Temple of the Tooth so that the large outer casket, which is at least half a meter high, can be seen from a distance of several meters and can be photographed. The long line of visitors often extends right

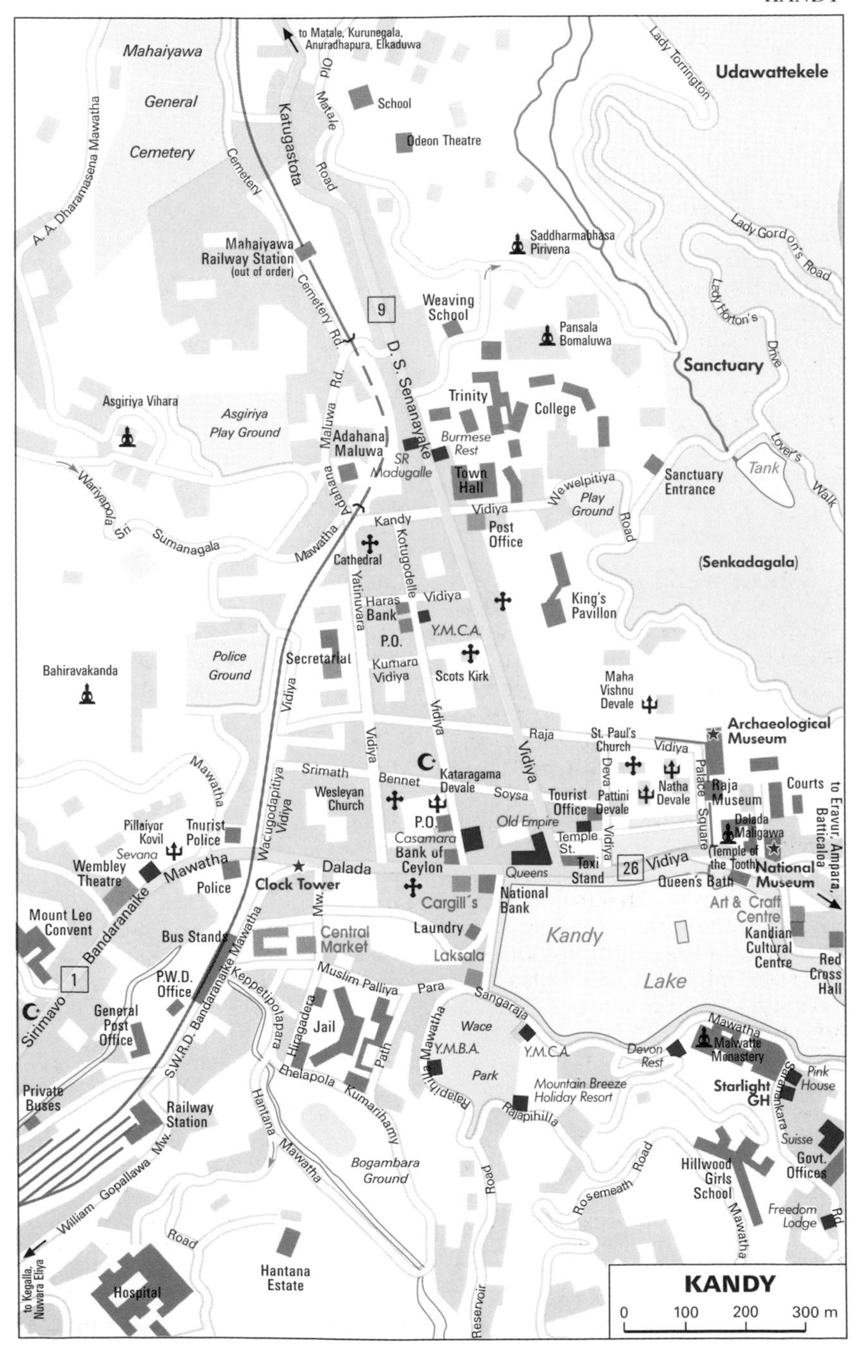
KANDY
0 100 200 300 m
to Matale, Kurunegala, Anuradhapura, Elkaduwa
Mahaiyawa General Cemetery
School
Odeon Theatre
Udawattekele
Lady Torrington
Lady Gordon's Road
Lady Horton's Drive
Sanctuary
Saddharmabhasa Pirivena
Mahaiyawa Railway Station (out of order)
Weaving School
Pansala Bomaluwa
Trinity College
Asgiriya Vihara
Asgiriya Play Ground
Adahana Maluwa
SR Madugalle
Burmese Rest
Town Hall
Sanctuary Entrance
Tank
Lover's Walk
Wewelpitiya Play Ground Road
Post Office
Cathedral
(Senkadagala)
King's Pavilion
Haras Bank
P.O.
Y.M.C.A.
Secretariat
Police Ground
Kumaro Vidiya
Scots Kirk
Bahiravakanda
Maha Vishnu Devale
Archaeological Museum
St. Paul's Church
Natha Devale
Raja Museum
Courts
Kataragama Devale
Wesleyan Church
Tourist Office
Pattini Devale
Dalada Maligawa (Temple of the Tooth)
National Museum
to Eravur, Ampara, Batticaloa
Pillaiyar Kovil
Tourist Police
Sevana
Old Empire
Casamara
Bank of Ceylon
Temple St.
Taxi Stand
Queen's Bath
Wembley Theatre
Police
Clock Tower
Cargill's
National Bank
Art & Craft Centre
Mount Leo Convent
Bus Stands
Central Market
Laundry
Kandy Lake
Kandian Cultural Centre
Red Cross Hall
Laksala
P.W.D. Office
General Post Office
Jail
Wace Park
Y.M.B.A.
Y.M.C.A.
Devon Rest
Malwatte Monastery
Pink House
Starlight GH
Mountain Breeze Holiday Resort
Private Buses
Railway Station
Suisse
Govt. Offices
Hillwood Girls School
Freedom Lodge
Bogambara Ground
Hantana Estate
Hospital
to Kegalla, Nuwara Eliya
D. S. Senanayake Vidiya
Dalada Vidiya
Bandaranaike Mawatha
Sirimavo Bandaranaike Mawatha
S.W.R.D. Bandaranaike Mawatha
William Gopallawa Mw.
Hantana Mawatha
Rosemeath Road
Reservoir Road
Rajapihilla Mawatha
Kumarihamy
Ehelapola
Sangaraja Mawatha
Kandy Vidiya
Kotugodelle Vidiya
Yatinuvara Vidiya
Raja Vidiya
Srimath Bennet Soysa
Deva Vidiya
Palace Square
Queens
9
26
1

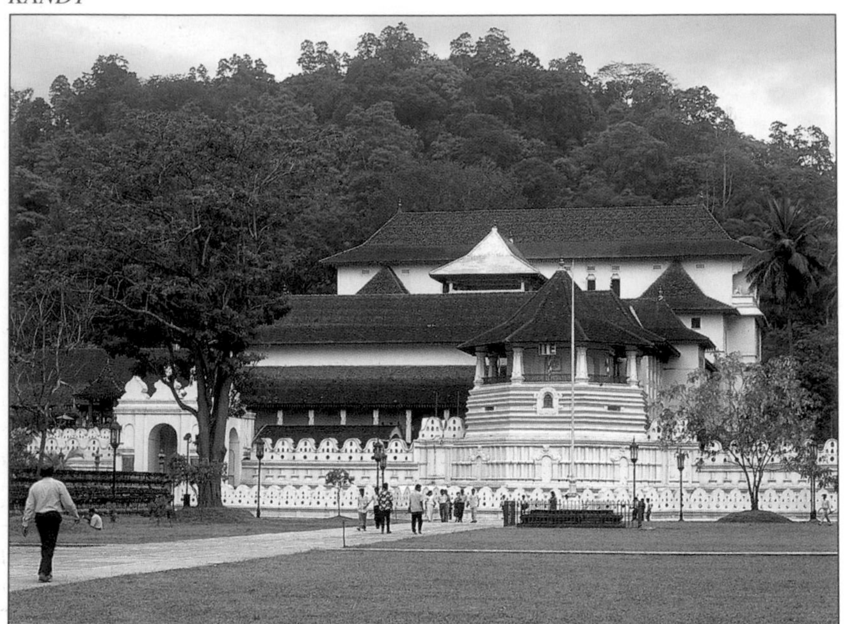

down to the lower hall, where musicians announce the ceremony with muffled drum rolls and shrill notes on the flute.

By comparison with the temple complex, the **Royal Palace District** next to it is rather unassuming. The former harem behind the temple today houses the **National Museum** (with objects from the Kandy period), while the **Queen's Residence** is now occupied by the Archeology Office. The adjoining court building originates from the British colonial period, and the small district court holds its sessions in what was once the **Royal Armory**. The former **Royal Palace**, with its long imposing facade fronting the moat, houses the **Archeological Museum**.

One of the most attractive buildings is the open **Audience Hall** in the middle of the Palace District, with an elegant roof resting on carved wooden pillars. On the lake shore, outside the Palace District, you can see the *ulpenge*, or **Queen's Bathhouse**, now housing a department of the police. The white buidling, half of which rises from the water, is an interesting sight, but is not open to the public.

Above: In the Temple of the Tooth at Kandy, the relic of Buddha's left eyetooth is preserved. Right: Rhythm at the perahera.

Three of the four most important *devales* are located in the immediate vicinity. Opposite the palace, a high stone wall encloses the **Natha Devale**; its main shrine is in traditional 14th-century Hindu style and is the oldest building in Kandy. Natha is the local god of Senkadagala Hill, as well as the *Bodhisattva* Avalokiteshvara or Maitreya worshiped by Mahayana Buddhists. North of this is the **Maha Vishnu Devale**, where the image of Alut Nuwara (Dedimunda, Upulvan) has found a new home. The **Pattini Devale** is the smallest temple: the goddess of fertility is highly esteemed in Sri Lanka, and is especially popular with women.

Two roads over to the west is the unusual **Kataragama Devale**. Peacocks (the mount of Kataragama, the god of

war) decorate the entrance, which is concealed between shops on the **Kotugodelle Vidiya** (road). The priests here are Hindu Brahmins.

The Kandy Perahera

These four devales play an important role in the annual *Esala Perahera*, the July festival procession. The origins of this famous parade are as scintillating as the event itself is exciting and multifaceted.

The *kap* ceremony marks the beginning of the festivities: the ritual felling and quartering of a young jack tree at new moon in July; this probably hearkens back to an ancient rain-making ceremony. Inside the temple, each part of the jack tree is set up and decorated in turn and circled by ceremonious processions in the temple grounds on five successive nights. This is followed by the five nights of the *Kumbal Perahera*, when crowds of whip-crackers, musicians, dancers, dignitaries and splendidly decorated elephants leave the four temples and join up with a further procession from the Temple of the Tooth. The largest elephants with the biggest tusks carry the most important relics: the four swords from the devales, in memory of Gajabahu's liberation of 12,000 Sinhalese prisoners from southern India in the second century A.D., and a replica of the relic cask from the *Dalada Maligawa* ("Temple of the Tooth"). This splendid *perahera*, however, only progresses a short distance through the city. The spectacle reaches a climax during the *Randoli* (palanquin) *Perahera* on the last nights before the full moon, continuing for hours by the light of hundreds of coconut-oil torches.

Originally, the king also participated in the procession, riding or driving in all his finery, together with his highest dignitaries. The Temple of the Tooth was first involved in 1775, when monks from Thailand, who had come to Sri Lanka to revive the Buddhist faith, were horrified by the heathen festival they found. King Kirti Sri Rajasinha brought about a clever

compromise: he simply integrated the Sacred Tooth of Buddha into the procession together with the Hindu gods, the highest dignitaries in the land in all their splendor, rain-making ceremonies, the celebration of military victories and, above all, fantastic displays of acrobats and performers.

Crafts, Temples and Science in the Kandy Hills

Hidden away in the countryside around Kandy are numerous temple buildings centuries old. Along the minor roads leading to them are villages with a long tradition of handicrafts. East of Kandy, still within the municipal district, is the **Gangarama Temple**, a branch of the Malwatte Monastery, with a Buddha hewn out of the rock and valuable paintings in the image house dating back to the reign of King Kirti Sri Rajasinha (1747-1782). The fine paintings decorating the cave temple of **Degaldoruwa**, east of the Mahaweli Ganga, also date from approximately the same period. Only three kilometers away is the unusual **Galmaduwa Temple**, with a pyramid-shaped central building where one might expect to find a Hindu divinity rather than a seated Buddha. Nearby, in the village of **Kalapura**, skilled craftsmen produce articles made of brass.

The caves at **Bambaragala** (five kilometers on a good minor road from **Digana** on the A26) are around two thousand years old. There are steps and paths up to the summit, 682 meters high, with a splendid view of the Victoria Reservoir. You can also see the modern villages which were created when the reservoir was built and the old ones had to be moved, such as **Teldeniya**. In this town, in the district of **Udawela**, the textile designer Nazha Sehawer-Hewawasama demonstrates how craft skills can adapt

Above: Pedestrians make use of the train tracks (Kandy). Right: Quality silk fabric is produced in Teldeniya under the eye of designer Nazha Sehawer-Hewawasama.

to suit modern tastes. Some two hundred talented women help to realize her designs in silk, spinning, dying, weaving, or knitting, many of them working at home.

North of Kandy, in a rather concealed spot, is the well-kept temple complex of **Medawela** (A10 to Hedeniya, then four kilometers east). The *tempita* (built on columns) image house, decorated with valuable paintings, dates from 1755 and competes with later buildings on a peaceful hill in a landscape of luxuriant gardens and woods.

The **Suriyagoda Temple** (A1 to Kiribathgoda, then four kilometers north), also in an idyllic setting, has a meditation ambulatory leading round the *tempita* image house. For those who want to spend longer in this area there is a hotel in **Murutalawa**. Good walkers can hike from there to the splendid avenue of *na* trees (*mesua ferrea*, ironwood tree; the national tree of Sri Lanka) of **Dodanwela**, which ends at an excellently restored *ambalama* (roofed resting place for travelers and pilgrims) with a **Vishnu Devale** behind it. King Rajasinha II (1629-1687) made a vow to build this temple after a victory over the Portuguese.

Continue via **Danture**, three kilometers away, with its two-story temple, to Pilimatalawa on the A1: some 600 meters further on, toward Kandy, there is a sign indicating the way to three famous temples from the Gampola period (minor road to the south).

The whole temple complex of **Gadaladeniya** is perched on a small rocky outcrop. The image house, made of stone blocks, looks Hindu, but shelters a meditating Buddha, and a Vishnu Devale is integrated on one side of the entrance. The dagoba is crowned with a fine roof. The village at the foot of the outcrop is the scene of a small local *Esala Perahera* (annual festival procession in July).

Many craftsmen working in brass can be seen at work along the path to the **Lankatilaka Temple**. Even from some distance away, you can see this temple's elegant roof construction at the end of an outcrop of rock. This temple is also a *budu-ge* (house with a Buddha statue, entrance from the east) and a *devale* with five Hindu or local divinities (entrance from the west): Ganesha and Kataragama are represented in the niches facing east, while Saman, Vishnu and Vibishana face north, west and south. The *hewisi mandapa* (drum hall) looks out over the dramatic highland scenery. The *devale* of **Embekke** is dedicated to Kataragama. The drum hall is aesthetically very pleasing: its roof rests on imaginatively carved wooden pillars which are said to have originated in the palace of the royal city of Gampola, which was pulled down. In the village, the craft of artistic wood carving is still very much alive.

Under the British in the 19th century, the royal forest in the large bend of the Mahaweli Ganga, west of the municipal district of Kandy, was turned into the world-famous **Botanical Gardens of Peradeniya**. Its main attraction are its numerous trees from all over the world, including a palm garden illustrating the variety of this particular species. Massive bamboos thrive along the banks of the Mahaweli, while around the central circular flower bed are memorial trees planted by dignitaries from all over the world. The gardens also include a small orchid section; and you can even drive through the extensive complex. Opposite it is the spacious, modern campus of Sri Lanka's first **university**, founded in 1942, which now has more than 7,500 students.

South of this, the narrow road above the Mahaweli Ganga is lined by steep cliffs. A long flight of stone steps leads up to the **Hindagala Vihara** monastery. In addition to paintings from the Kandy period, some of which were painted over in the 20th century, a few poorly-preserved traces of paint and plaster, probably dating from the fifth century, indicate that the monastery was already in use in the classical Sinhalese period.

KANDY

Accommodation

LUXURY: **Hunas Falls Hotel**, Elkaduwa (in a tea plantation 45 minutes northeast of Kandy), tel. 08-476402/3. **Le Kandyan Resorts**, Heerassagala, Peradeniya, tel. 08-233521/2. **Mahaweli Reach Hotel**, 35 P.B.A. Weerakon Mw., tel. 08-232062. **The Citadel**, 124 Sirimath Kuda Ratwatta Mw. (on the banks of the Mahaweli Ganga), tel. 08-234365.

MODERATE: **Babylon**, Mount Franion, Muruthalawa (10 km west of Kandy, signposted on the A 1), tel. 071-764876. **Chalet Hotel**, 32 Frederick De Silva Mw. (Gregory's Rd.), tel. 08-234571. **Casamara Hotel**, 12 Kotugodella Vidiya, tel. 08-234327. **Hotel Hilltop**, 200/21 Bahirawakanda, Peradeniya Road, 08-234 317. **Hotel Suisse**, 30 Sangarajah Mw., tel. 08-233024. **Hotel Thilanka**, 3 Sangamitta Mw., tel. 08-232429. **Hotel Topas**, Anniewatte, tel. 08-224150. **Hotel Tourmaline**, Anniewatte, tel. 08-233099. **Janaki Hotels**, 40/1 2nd Rajasinghe Mw., tel. 08-224261. **Queens Hotel**, Dalada Vidiya (colonial hotel near the Temple of the Tooth), tel. 08-222813. **The Swiss Residence**, 23 Bahirawakanda Lane, tel. 074-479055. **Tree of Life**, Yahalatenna (10 km northwest of Kandy, in a tea plantation, signposted on the A 10), Ayurveda, tel. 08-499777. **Kings Park Hotel**, 34 Sangaraja Mw., Lake Road, tel. 08-225806.

SMALL HOTELS, PENSIONS: **Bonavista**, 117/14 Anagarika Dharmapala Mw., tel. 08-223190. **Castle Hill**, 22 Rajapihilla Mw., tel. 08-223506. **Freedom Lodge**, 30 Saranankara Road, tel. 08-223506. **Grassmere Holiday Home**, Alupothuwela, Ukuwela (45 minutes' drive northeast of Kandy, in a coffee plantation with an exotic garden), tel. 078-668329. **Hotel Sunray**, 117/8 Anagarika Dharmapala Mw., tel. 08-222207. **Kandy Holiday Home**, 30/51 Bangalawatte, Lewella Road, tel. 08-232739. **Lake View Rest**, 71A Rajapihilla Mw., tel. 08-232034. **Regent Lodge**, 172 Riverdale Road, Anniewatte, tel. 08-232032. **Riverdale Tourist Hotel**, 32 Anniewatte Road, tel. 08-223020. **Royal Tourist Lodge**, 93 Rajapihilla Mw. tel. 08-233364. **The Palanquin**, 253/2 Katugastota Road, tel. 074-472747.

BUDGET: **Y.M.C.A.**, 116A Kotugodella Vidiya, tel. 08-223529.

During the *Kandy Perahera* in July/August, keep in mind that most hotel prices will be considerably higher than usual.

Restaurants

The Pub, 36 Dalada Vidiya, tel. 08-234341, bar, restaurant and internet café. **Peradeniya Resthouse**, Kandy Road, tel. 08-288299. **Queens Hotel**, Dalada Vidiya, tel. 08-22121. **Paivas** and **Shangrila**, 37, Yatinuwara Vidiya, tel. 08-34493.

There are numerous restaurants between the market and Queens Hotel along Dalada Vidiya Road.

Museums / Exhibitions

National Museum, Dalada Vidiya (behind the Temple of the Tooth), open 8:30 am to 5 pm, objects from the Kandy period, 16th to 19th centuries, Cultural Triangle general admission ticket valid; **Archeological Museum**, in the former Royal Palace next to the Temple of the Tooth, open daily except Tue 8 am to 5 pm, Cultural Triangle ticket valid; **Museum for the Elephant Rajah**, next to the Archeological Museum, a long-time participant in the *Kandy Perahera*, now stuffed, has a place of honor here and is particularly admired by locals; open sporadically; **Upper Mahaweli Environment Exhibition Hall**, near the Polgolla Bridge, exhibits about the Mahaweli program and region environmental concerns, Mon-Fri 8 am to 4:30 pm.

Dance Performances

Before visits to the Temple of the Tooth (*poya* 6:30 pm), dance performances for tourists begin daily at 5 pm (Kandy dances, Kolam dances, walking on coals, etc.) at the following venues: **Kandyan Cultural Centre**, 72 Sangaraja Mw., on the eastern section of the lake, near the Temple of the Tooth; right next to this, at **Red Cross Hall**; the best (advance reservations advised), qualitatively speaking, are at **Kandy Lake Club**, 7 Sangamitta Mw., tel. 08-223505; many tourist shops give out free tickets.

Shopping

The old and new Central Markets south of Dalada Vidiya Street are two-story edifices which seem to be bursting at the seams. Huge selection of fruit and vegetables, meat and fish, spices, household goods, textiles, and many other things.

Most of the souvenir and jewelry shops are located along Peradeniya Road. Some of them take particular pains to organize interesting presentations and small exhibitions, such as **Crest Jewels**, 329 Peradeniya Road, tel. 08-222502; handicrafts at the state-owned **Laksala**, west of Kandy Lake, even larger and better selection at the **Arts & Crafts Center** east of the lake. You'll find mainly specialty stores in the streets of the city center: silk designer goods: **Bombyx Mori**, Kande Walauwa, Udawela, Teldeniya (25 km east of Kandy, developmental aid project), tel. 078-70603; best book store: **Vijitha,** Kotugodella Vidiya, opposite the Casamara Hotel; devotional objects, Buddhist flags, shoulder bags like the monks wear: several shops at the east end of Bennett Soysa Vidiya.

Transportation

TRAIN: Train station south of the market, tel. 08-234222, twice daily *Inter-City Express* to and from Colombo, as well as many additional passenger trains; trains into the mountains and Badulla also leave from Peradeniya.

BUS: Bus stops between the market and the train station, government buses run to Colombo about every half hour, private buses are more frequent, daily direct connections to major destinations in the Cultural Triangle, larger towns in the mountains, and the east.

TAXI: For excursions, ask at the taxi stand opposite the Queens Hotel or at travel agencies, such as **Maurice Travels**, 143 1/1 Senanayake Vidiya, tel. 074-470317, or **Queens Tours & Travels** in the Queens Hotel, tel. 08-233290.

Parks

Botanical Garden of Peradeniya on the A1 immediately east of the bridge over the Mahaweli Ganga, 6 km west of the city center of Kandy, open daily 7:30 am to 5:30 pm, significant collection of tropical trees, orchid house, restaurant; **Udawattekele Nature Reserve** (Sanctuary), follow the Kande Vidiya eastward, up the hill, open daily, mainly indigenous trees with a wealth of bird life.

Hospital

General Hospital, William Gopallawa Mawatha, tel. 08-233337/42.

Pharmacies

Government Pharmacy in **Cargill's** department store, Dalada Vidiya, near the Queens Hotel.

Tourist Information

Headmans Lodge, 3 Deva Vidiya (at the parking lot opposite the Queens Hotel), tel. 08-222661, open 9 am to 4:45 pm.

KURUNEGALA

Accommodation

BUDGET: **Kandyan Reach Hotel**, 344-350 Kandy Road, tel. 037-24218. **Oliver's Inn**, 2 Bamunugedara Road, off North Lake Road, tel. 037-23567. **Hotel Surasa**, Negombo Rd., Alakoladeniya, tel. 037-23993.

Restaurant

Diya Dahara, 7 North Lake Road, tel. 037-23452. **Situmedura**, 21 Mihindu Mw., tel. 037-22335.

Excursions

The cliffs at the northeastern edge of the city command magnificent views of the surrounding area. **Ridi Vihara**, 20 km east of Kurunegala, near Ridigama, pre-Christian monastery complex with Kandy-period paintings; **Arankele**, 35 km northeast of Kurunegala, 18 km north of Ibbagamuwa, extensive forest monastery with hermit caves.

AROUND MAHIYANGANA

Accommodation

BUDGET: **Rest House Gurulupotha**, Hasalaka (on the A26, 10 km west of Mahiyangana). **TREE Center Bungalow**, Randenigala, reservations through Wildlife Trust of Sri Lanka, 18 Gregory's Rd., Colombo 7, tel. 01-696050. Accommodations in Mahiyangana are not to be recommended. Excursions east of Mahiyangana: to the **Weddas** and into the **Maduru Oya National Park.**

TEA FOR THE WORLD

It can't have been tea from Ceylon that "brewed" in Boston Harbor at the Boston Tea Party, for in 1773 the country's most important export was cinnamon. And a hundred years later, Sri Lanka was a veritable coffee country, with some 1,200 square kilometers of land occupied by plantations. But the coffee industry began to decline in 1869, when the first case of leaf disease (*hemileia vastatrix*) was diagnosed. Within a few years, this disease attacked almost all of the country's plantations, sealing the fate of its coffee production and export.

As if he'd had some forewarning of this catastrophe, the Scottish plantation owner James Taylor was experimenting with a wide variety of domestic plants on his plantation, Loolecondera Estate, as early as the 1860s. In 1867, before the start of the coffee catastrophe, he planted some eight hectares with tea, thereby leading the way for other local plantation owners to do the same.

Preceding pages: Tea-pickers wait for leaves to be weighed. Hindu bridal pair. Above: Tamil tea-picker settlement on a plantation. Right: Young shoots only!

Ceylon's mountainous regions proved ideal for tea cultivation, and thus, just as coffee plantations had spread like wildfire in the few decades between 1823 and 1873, tea now took over the island. Tea cultivation initially centered on those areas where coffee had once flourished, and which now lay fallow; but more and more land was taken over for tea growing. The rate of growth was dizzying: in 1880, 38 square kilometers of land were occupied with tea plants; in 1900, it was more than 1,550, and in 1910, more than 2,350 square kilometers.

In the years since, however, any growth has been due to better-organized use of extant land rather than taking over additional territory. In the two decades before the turn of the millenium, the land used for tea cultivation had settled at a constant 2,200 square kilometers.

As you survey the carefully tended rows of bushes on a tea plantation, you could easily forget that tea actually grows on trees. Originally from China, the plant *camellia sinensis* would reach heights of some 10 meters and produce delicate white flowers with numerous yellow stamens, which would develop into a tripartite fruit, if it weren't cultivated in another direction. But on the plantations, the plants are, throughout their life (which can last more than a hundred years), pruned and cut back to make them branch out close to the ground; furthermore, they aren't allowed to grow higher than the reach of the tea pickers, who pluck the young shoots with their nimble hands. Planting and maintaining a plantation – to say nothing of harvesting – requires many hours of human labor.

As the Sinhalese traditionally farm their own land, it was understandable that they didn't want to work on British plantations, especially in parts of the country that were damper and colder than their own regions. Even in the days of the coffee plantations, therefore, migrant workers from southern India streamed into Sri Lanka at harvest time. The tea plantations, however, required a year-round labor force; and the result was that hundreds of thousands of Tamil families from southern India settled down in Sri Lanka. The men took over the work of cultivation, while the women picked the tea leaves. Whole families were housed in primitive rows of huts or simple houses which belonged to the plantation.

Basically, nothing has changed over the years. If you occasionally spot a man picking tea leaves, he's certain to be one of the 152,000 Sinhalese small farmers who operate their own small tea plantations, each less than four hectares. Three-quarters of the tea-cultivating land is owned by large enterprises; the best economic results are booked by plantations measuring 200 hectares or more. From the mid-1970s to the early 1990s,

the largest plantations were state-owned, and there was a lot of corruption and nepotism going around. The ensuing privatization process was a new broom sweeping the dust from the operation of the larger enterprises.

Several times a day, groups of tea pickers in bright saris head out into the fields, with sacks or baskets bound to their foreheads and hanging down over their backs; long, straight, thin sticks in their hands; and usually an apron made of an old plastic bag bound around their waists.

A foreman assigns them their workplaces for the day. Most of them are barefoot. The aprons provide a little extra warmth from the damp, cool air and prevent their clothing from catching in the tea branches. A woman uses her stick to mark the area around the hedge she's about to pick from, and pushes the stick before her as she works on. Quickly and dexterously, she pulls off the bud and the first two leaves of every new tea shoot, and when both hands are full she throws

her harvest with a practiced motion into the container on her back. When their work is done, the women leave the field in their groups and move on to the collection points, where they're awaited by an overseer with the scales. They line up and wait patiently until their own basket or sack has been emptied, the contents weighed, and the sum written down. A tea picker's daily wage amounts to the value of about three kilograms of rice.

The harvest is sent directly to one of the country's 700 tea factories. Large enterprises have their own, while small farmers generally deliver to the one located closest at hand. The fresh green leaves and buds have to wither so that they lose a part of their water content. This takes about 24 hours, although one can speed up the process by strewing the leaves over a huge wire mesh through which powerful bellows blow a strong stream of air. This process is generally based on the second floor of the multistory factory buildings, while the rest of the processing takes place within a few hours on the ground floor.

Above: In the processing plant, the tea leaves are dried, cut and fermented. Right: Tea testers control quality.

The withered tea leaves slip through a kind of funnel down to a lower story onto a circular rotating table, where the leaves are crushed. In the process, they gradually lose their green color, as the contents of the leaves, exposed to the air, begin to oxidize. When the leaves have been cut so small that they're no longer recognizable as such, the process moves onto a large cement or tile surface; the leaves, packed only a few inches high, are subjected to a stream of fresh air, which is sometimes humidified with a water atomizer. This last fermentation process, which often lasts less than half an hour, has a decisive effect on the tea's flavor. To preserve the desired condition once it's been attained, the red-brown morsels are immediately brought to a drying kiln, where they're roasted for another half an hour at a temperature of at

least 85°C. After this, the black tea is basically ready to go.

All that's left to do now is the sorting and packaging. After the tea has been put on a sifting conveyor belt, it is classified according to its quality, with terms such as pekoe, souchong or flowery. This sieving process also sorts out the tea according to the size of the particles: the finest called dust, then fannings, then various "broken" types and finally leaf tea. The teas with a high proportion of leaves – and therefore with a better aroma – are darker in color; lighter colors are the result of a higher proportion of stems. Dark-colored tea dust, the highest quality, is ideal for tea bags, as it steeps very quickly.

Tea plants need plenty of regular moisture, a minimum of around 1,250 mm a year, but they don't respond well to frost. Sri Lanka therefore provides the ideal climatic conditions, apart from its very highest mountain regions. Just like wine, the region where a tea is grown affects its taste. In Sri Lanka, there are three categories: high-grown tea, produced above 1,200 meters, which takes up 40 percent of the land used for tea cultivation; mid-grown tea (25 percent); and low-grown tea, below 600 meters, which accounts for the remaining 35 percent.

Tea grows most quickly in the humid lowlands and slowest in the relatively dry air at higher altitudes. The frequency with which tea is harvested therefore varies according to the altitude and the climate; in the lowlands, tea is picked every five to seven days; on higher ground, every nine to twelve days. Slower- growing teas have finer aromas; high-grown teas, therefore, go for the highest prices at auction in Colombo.

With an annual production of more than 200,000 tons, Sri Lanka is, after India and China, the world's third-largest tea exporter. Some six million people work in the tea industry, and are responsible for between 20 and 25 percent of the total export revenue. Main customers are the Middle Eastern countries, which account for more than half of the export.

CINNAMON AND CARDAMOM

There are a number of tropical plants which flourish in Sri Lanka, but which are not actually indigenous to the island. But Sri Lanka has given two of its local, native spices to the world: Ceylon cinnamon (*Cinnamonum verum*) and cardamom (*Elettaria cardamomum*).

When the Portuguese first encountered the island of Ceylon in 1505, they quickly grasped the magnitude of the treasure they had discovered in the warm and humid coastal forests: the wild cinnamon tree, the bark of which had an exceptionally fine aroma. In the 16th century, the Portuguese still had no competitors in the cinnamon trade, but the Dutch East India Company secured the monopoly on cinnamon export in 1636; Great Britain took it over in 1796, and was able to hold on to it until 1832. In 1668, the Dutch started successfully to cultivate cinnamon on plantations, tilling the whole area between Colombo and Negombo, and ultimately extending their "caneel lands" south as far as Matara.

Above: Spices, especially cinnamon and cardamom, are among the island's most important exports. Right: Fresh nutmeg.

Today, due to the increased urbanization of the area around Colombo, the focus of cinnamon cultivation has shifted to the inland regions near the southern coast. These plantations, however, no longer have anything like the importance they did at the beginning of the 19th century. Nowadays they are generally run by small farmers.

Peeling cinnamon is an art. And the *chaliyas*, members of the cinnamon-peeling caste, see themselves as artists, removing the bark from twigs two to three meters long. When the bark dries after a twofold process of fermentation, it rolls up; the *chaliyas* then dexterously slide these long, narrow rolls one within another, making them take up less space and at the same time keeping them better for transport. Known as *quills*, these rolls of bark, more than three feet long, are

collected into bundles; it's these that get the highest market prices, although even broken rolls, called *quillings*, as well as the less valuable bark from bent twigs, called *featherings*, and *chips* all manage to find buyers. Chips are also used in the manufacture of valuable cinnamon oil.

The Sri Lankans tend to keep their cardamom for their own cuisine; only five to ten percent of it is exported. In Arabian countries, people use it to flavor coffee; in Europe, it's often an ingredient in Christmas cookies.

Nearly every commercial or homemade blend of curry powder also contains cardamom, and there's a widespread view that if you use this spice in a meal that contains garlic, it defuses that condiment's unpleasant smell on the breath. It is a fact that garlic is extensively used in Sri Lankan cooking, and one is seldom aware of the odor.

Cardamom grows wild in mountainous regions, and tends to flourish at altitudes of between about 900 and 1,500 meters. The original forests of Sri Lanka are therefore an ideal habitat; the plant, which actually belongs to the ginger family, needs plenty of shade and grows in forest undergrowth. It would be very difficult to harvest this plant exclusively in the wild, and there wouldn't be nearly enough to meet the demand; therefore, people also cultivate it by planting it in existing forests, or at the shady edges of tea plantations, where you can get at it and harvest it all year round. The Knuckles and the area around the Sinharaja Forest are particularly lucrative cardamom-growing spots.

Growing larger than a man, like many other members of the ginger family, the cardamom plant has long, narrow leaves. Just above ground, it sends out flower clusters with white blooms flecked with red, which look a bit like small orchids. From these grow tripartite capsules, or pods, about half an inch long, which contain the plant's small, aromatic, sweet-sour seeds. These are gathered, dried, sometimes ground, and brought onto the market.

CURRY, CURRIES, COCONUT

The term "curry" can be as confusing as the various aromas wafting up from a spice-vendor's stall. Curry is not the product of a single plant; rather, it is a mixture of spices which can change depending on the individual taste and whims of a chef or housewife. And it's this spice that is an integral component of the dishes known as "curries," generally presented as side dishes arranged around a large bowl of rice, the centerpiece of any dinner in Sri Lanka. There's a spoon in each bowl so that people can help themselves to as much curry as they want, spooned over the rice. You may notice the lack of other utensils; take heart, you've got yours with you. It's customary to use the right hand to mix rice and curry and carry it to your mouth.

Above: Chili peppers add spice to local curries. Right: In Sri Lanka, people don't always marry for love alone. Far right: Wedding outfits in Kandy.

The following recipe yields a curry powder ideal for fish and poultry dishes:
80 g coriander
50 g fennel seeds
30 g cumin
10 cloves
10 cardamom pods
a 2 cm cinnamon stick
5 bay leaves (in Sri Lanka, the finer "curry leaves" are used)
50 g rice
2 teaspoons of mustard seed
20 g pepper
20 g chili powder
1 teaspoon turmeric (the yellow root of the plant *curcuma longa*, often wrongly called "saffron," but not related to real saffron. It's this spice that gives curry its characteristic color).

In a frying pan, without oil, roast all the ingredients except for the chili and turmeric. Mix this blend, still warm, with the chili and turmeric and grind to a fine powder in a coffee grinder.

Coconuts are part of everyday life in Sri Lanka. Every kitchen contains one of the serrated peelers used to extract the white meat from the nut. And anyone who's worried about too-hot curries should take note: grated fresh coconut is actually one of the best ways to ameliorate the fire, and you can always have a bowl of this ubiquitous substance served along with your curries.

Coconut is even used as an ingredient in many curries, and the thick, slightly sweet coconut milk rounds off some dishes with a rich, nutty flavor. This milk is made by soaking freshly grated coconut in a little water, and then squeezing out this mass. The thin, watery "milk" found within the nut can also be used for cooking.

Coconut oil has a wide variety of uses: not only for frying and cooking, but also for hair and body care, not to mention for the thousands upon thousands of oil lamps in the country's temples or on house altars.

MARRIAGE PROPOSALS

On Sunday, Sri Lanka's newspapers, like those in many other countries, are especially thick and especially entertaining. Foreign visitors may find the minutiae of various social events rather dull, not being acquainted with the names of the people involved. But keep reading. A bit further on, in the magazine section of the *Sunday Observer*, for example, are the "Marriage Proposals," a section of personal ads.

Of course, you won't know the names of the Sri Lankans printed here, either, and these ads aren't really representative of the country's 18 million residents. But the variety within even this limited selection does reflect a very real facet of modern, and yet traditional, Sri Lankan society.

Who places these ads? Generally, it's parents who want to find a partner for their daughters or sons, but sometimes other family members embark on the search: brothers, sisters, aunts or grandmothers. In rare cases, where no family member is mentioned, one can assume that the marriage candidate has placed the ad him- or herself. In such cases, the person in question will generally be a bit older, such as an "unmarried, well-educated 46-year-old woman looking for a Buddhist widower, with or without children"; or a "45-year-old divorced Sinhalese Catholic, educated abroad, who would like to make the acquaintance of an attractive, tall, simple, and home-loving woman, not employed, from a good English-speaking family."

But these are the exceptions. Weddings are generally a family affair. Such things are simply not left to the chance happening of two young people meeting and falling in love. In such a lifetime pairing, all the elements that are essential to the formation of a new union must correspond, such as education, place of residence, caste, economic standing, astrological sign, and a host of other contingencies – every family has its own specific set of requirements.

So what do people placing such personal ads tell about themselves to introduce themselves and their families? Most of them mention their caste, although many of the ads specifically state that the caste of their prospective partner is unimportant. This information will also indicate to which of the countless ethnic and social groups the family of the candidate belongs: Sinhalese castes include Govigama, Karava, Salagama, Durava, Vishvakula and Radala, while the highest Tamil caste is Vellala.

These categories are further differentiated through religious affiliation; thus, ads will be placed by "Vellala Roman Catholic parents," people belonging to the highest land-owning Tamil class; "Govigama Buddhist mother," a mother from the Sinhalese land-owning class; "Karava Catholic mother," a mother from the Sinhalese class of fishermen. There's a wide variety of possible combinations, which makes the choice easier for anyone who's looking.

If a family doesn't care about caste, they can merely state "Anglican Tamil" parents, mentioning their ethnic group but not their caste. An ad placed by "Govigama/Velalla" parents makes clear that the bride is the offspring of a mixed marriage between Sinhalese and Tamil parents. Moors, Malays and Burghers can express themselves more concisely, as the caste system doesn't apply, and religious affiliations are generally immediately evident.

Parents are especially fond of listing their place of residence. It may be important to them to keep their child close to them. The educational status of the family member placing the ad may also be a clue as to whether a partner is potentially compatible: "Ceylon Moor engineer brother seeks..." Listings of possessions and money may also help steer the search in the right direction: "Govigama Catholic wealthy Colombo 7 business parents" are wealthy Sinhalese parents in the land-owning class, living in Colombo 7, Cinnamon Gardens, which is Colombo's most exclusive neighborhood, and want to emphasize that they're rich business people.

Right: A good education increases a bride's value – important if the dowry is small.

As to descriptions of the hopeful bride-to-be: you can almost always read her height and age, and often her astrological sign as well. Not much is said about her appearance; it's far more important to mention her domesticity, education, diplomas, profession, salary and dowry, depending on which applies. The last two of these are often given explicitly: "Salary 6,500, dowry 5 lakhs cash and 15 lakhs worth of objects" (lakh = 100,000, in this case denoting rupees); or "a fortune in investments, car, furnished apartment, property holdings"; or "monthly income 15,000 from rentals"; or "dowry includes cash, property, and jewels worth one million." If no dowry is mentioned, the prospective marriage candidate generally has a secure, well-paid job and a good education, or has at least been to a reputable school.

In cases of prospective bridegrooms, the descriptions tend to be a bit different. Appearance is never mentioned, but the ads often list the desirable age range of the prospective bridegroom. Frequent requests for non-smokers and especially for teetotallers reflect – or mask – the fact that Sri Lanka has the highest per capita alcohol consumption in the world. As in many countries, doctor and engineer are the jobs of choice: in Sri Lanka, accountants are also very much sought after. If a bride has an academic education, one hopes that the bridegroom does as well. And nearly every ad requests applicants to list their astrological signs.

It is notable that the number of men who place ads is far smaller than the number of women: only about a third of the ads have been placed by men search-

ing for brides. Many of these ads seek brides for Sri Lankans living abroad, generally in other countries of the British Commonwealth.

This calls for a brave woman, as hardly any young Sri Lankan girls have had a chance to travel to Europe, Australia or America, and it takes courage to up and marry a stranger in one of these places. On the other hand, a Sri Lankan man living in a wealthy industrialized country has something of the aura of a fairy-tale prince, and is generally looked on as a good match. Even if a man looking for a wife doesn't himself live abroad, but has siblings in other countries, this puts him in a good light and is generally mentioned in the ad: "Parents seek educated partner with means for second son. Two brothers in Australia." Such people can expect to find an educated bride with a respectable dowry.

Desirable characteristics in a prospective bride include such attributes as pretty, non-working, religious – all of which are frequently mentioned, as is the waiver "caste/dowry immaterial." Also important to nearly everyone is the astrological sign.

One thing that you will not find not mentioned in any ad, because everyone takes it for granted, is that the bride must be a virgin.

Although young people in Sri Lanka today don't have any problem meeting and going out together, it's extremely uncommon for anyone to appear in public as a couple. Only in dark corners of expansive public parks may you glimpse two young people walking hand in hand. Love woes, and especially unwanted pregnancies, are generally grounds for suicide; and in its suicide rate, as well, Sri Lanka has a high position in worldwide standings.

To answer an ad, you generally write to a box number. And anyone who places such an ad usually wants to know everything about the prospective family member right from the beginning; most of the ads end with the line "full details in first letter."

METRIC CONVERSION

Metric Unit	US Equivalent
Meter (m)	39.37 in.
Kilometer (km)	0.6241 mi.
Square Meter (sq m)	10.76 sq. ft.
Hectare (ha)	2.471 acres
Square Kilometer (sq km)	0.386 sq. mi.
Kilogram (kg)	2.2 lbs.
Liter (l)	1.05 qt.

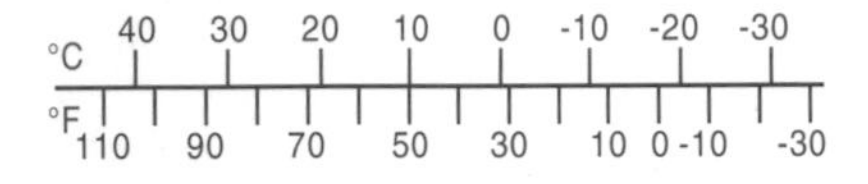

TRAVEL PREPARATIONS

Getting There and Away

Visitors from over 50 countries around the world (including all of Europe except Iceland) may stay in Sri Lanka for up to 30 days without a visa. A passport, valid for at least six months past your date of arrival, is required. In the plane you are given an immigration form, with sections for incoming and outgoing visitors; the immigration authorities keep the former after arrival, and you must keep the latter yourself to present when leaving the country. Visitors may also have to show their return ticket, as well as foreign currency amounting to US $30 per person per day, or an international credit card.

If you plan to stay in the country for longer than 30 days, you can get a 90-day visa before you go (for a small fee) upon presentation of a confirmation of your trip, from a travel agent or airline, to your local Sri Lankan embassy. You can also get extensions from the Department of Immigration, Station Road, Colombo 4 (tel. 01-597510-3). Here too, importance is placed on your having the financial means to pay for your stay and being able to prove your departure.

If you are bringing anything valuable into the country that might normally require you to pay import duty, such as a bicycle or lots of jewelry, you have to declare it upon entering the country and show it again on your way home.

Sri Lankan Airlines insists on carrying out intensive security checks before departure. This may be annoying, but you shouldn't forget that such strict measures are for the benefit of everyone on board. There are also meticulous baggage checks when you leave Sri Lanka.

It is very important to confirm your return flight as soon as possible after arrival, and at the very latest 72 hours before departure. Plan to be at the airport three hours before you leave. There are a number of security checks before you even get to the airport, and you have to show your passport and ticket every time.

Money

You must arrive in Sri Lanka without any local rupees and may not bring more than 250 Rs. (about US $5) out of the country. You can bring in as much foreign currency as you want, although if you bring in more than US $10,000 you have to declare it. Currency can be exchanged quickly at the airport, day or night; once you're in the country, even at many banks in Colombo's city center, exchanging money can sometimes become a lengthy procedure. It's far quicker in the hotels, but you should check the exchange rates beforehand.

Save all of receipts from exchange transactions, if you want to exchange leftover rupees back into your own currency when leaving the country. Many travelers find ready takers for their remaining money in needy local citizens. Note, however, that you'll need 500 Rs. for the airport tax on leaving the country, if your travel agent hasn't already taken care of this. Many large hotels and shops catering to foreign customers accept major credit cards without a murmur; but Eurochecks are seldom accepted.

It's a good idea to keep plenty of coins and 10 and 20 rupee bills on hand as tips for services or for beggars.

Health Precautions

People live healthily in Sri Lanka. The food is varied and nutritious; locals drink water from springs or the tap (but they boil it first) and you can buy bottles or cans of drinking water, tea, beer, or other beverages virtually everywhere. If a dry season sets in, there's a risk in some areas, particularly in the dry zone, of cholera epidemics. Don't panic, but inform yourself upon arrival (ask your hotel doctor or read the paper), and avoid the affected areas altogether or be very careful what you eat and drink when you're there.

It's a good idea in any case to get inoculated against typhus, polio, hepatitis and tetanus beforehand; precautions against malaria are wise if you're staying in regions other than the densely-populated west coast or the hill country.

If you're the cautious type, you can also take steps to protect yourself from the anopheles mosquito by doing as the locals do: keep covered, sleep under a mosquito net, burn incense sticks or coils or use an electric insect killer, and anoint yourself abundantly with insect repellent. Don't underestimate the danger of catching cold in overly air-conditioned rooms.

Many people find that stomach medicine, salt tablets, sun cream and throat lozenges are all useful components of a travel kit. But even small towns and villages in Sri Lanka have their own doctors or at least a small pharmacy (dispensary), and any reasonably-sized town will have at least one fully-equipped pharmacy. If you've left anything out of your travel kit, you'll find you can buy it in Sri Lanka more cheaply than at home. However, you should make sure to bring with you any special medicines which you depend on.

The country boasts thousands of years of traditional Ayurvedic medicine (see p. 243) and there are plenty of Western-trained doctors throughout the country.

Climate / Travel Season

Sri Lanka is in the tropics: temperatures are generally high and vary little between day and night, except in the mountain regions. In the lowlands, average temperatures in the shade are between 24°C and 32°C. The higher up in the mountains you get, the cooler it is. In Nuwara Eliya, the highest town in the country, temperatures average between 12°C und 20°C. "Rainy season" sounds off-putting to many travelers, but in Sri Lanka, flexible visitors can manage to avoid it: during the southwest monsoon, when it's raining on the west side of the island, it will be dry on the east side; while if the northeast monsoon is blowing, it will be dryer on the west side. The strongest rains fall at the start of their respective monsoon: in April/May on the west side, and in November/December on the east side. After this, the rain falls in occasional, heavy showers that are warm and refreshing. Beach-goers should note that during the southwest monsoon, from April to September/October, the ocean along the south and west coasts will be turbulent and not very good for swimming. During the northeast monsoon, from November to March, the breakers crash against the east coast. When the wind changes between the monsoons, in April or in October, the weather can be calm all over the country.

In the hill country you're aware of the monsoons on the west or east side of the mountains. The best hiking and pilgrimages (Horton Plains, Adam's Peak) are in the south and west, and are at their best between January and March.

Clothing / What to Pack

The weather is hot, so visitors from cooler climes tend to strip down. Locals, however, have more experience with sun and heat: men often wear long pants or ankle-length sarongs with their shirts, while women sport skirts below the knee or long saris, and carry umbrellas against the strong sun, not just to preserve their elegant pale skin. Field workers seldom go out without a head covering. If traveling truly educates, perhaps the visitor should learn from them. Clothing reflects local standards of appropriate behavior. In this densely-populated country, private things such as daily ablutions often occur in public places; at roadside pumps, river banks, or irrigation ditches. Yet no one, apart from small children, ever appears naked at such places. The men tie a sarong around their hips, the women a long cloth or sarong around their breasts, before they soap up, scrub and rinse off. Sri Lankans are very tolerant toward their visitors, even when tourists behave ridiculously, but have no understanding at all for nude or topless bathing, and hotel guards or even the police will be quick to step in if this is ignored.

So what to wear? It should be airy yet presentable; cotton is an ideal fabric for this heat. Even if the Sri Lankans have gotten used to shorts by now, it's more appropriate, and more comfortable, to wear skirts, long, wide pants, or sarongs. Clothing that covers more of the body is also the best protection against biting insects. With this strong sun, a hat is advised. Many people in Sri Lanka go barefoot; you don't have to conform to this custom, but you'll have to if you want to enter any sacred sites, where it's also necessary to bare your head. Some temple areas are strewn with gravel, or the pavement becomes so hot in the burning sun that it threatens to burn the soles of your feet: socks are a useful precaution, and they're allowed in any temple. The best protection against tropical cloudbursts is to find shelter and wait it out; umbrellas are generally of little use. Rain gear is only really useful in the hill country. Here, you'll also need warmer clothing, especially on cloudy days or after sunset. Warmer clothing is also essential in air-conditioned restaurants and hotels. As hotel laundry service is generally quick, cheap and reliable, you can keep your packing down to a minimum.

Sri Lanka in Statistics

Area: 65,610 sq km; agricultural area: 20 000 sq km, of which 8,000 are plantations (coconut, tea, rubber), 5,600 sq km rice (irrigated rice: 4,950 sq km); nature reserves and national parks: 8,000 sq km. Population: 19 million. Popuation density: just under 300 per sq km for the whole country; over 3,000 per sq km in the district of Colombo; ca. 30 inhabitants per sq km in the Mullaitivu district (northeastern Sri Lanka); the southwest quarter of the island is the most densely populated. Population under 25 years of age: 56 percent. Life expectancy: Men 69; women 74. Workforce employed in agriculture: 37 percent. Unemployment: 10 percent. Illiteracy for people over 15: 10 percent. Foreign tourists annually: over 400,000; in 1999 there were 81,000 tourists from the U.K., 77,000 Germans and 34,500 French. It is also a popular destination for Japanese and Indians; it is gaining in popularity with other Far Eastern countries and eastern Europeans.

TRAVELING TO SRI LANKA

By Plane

Travelers to Sri Lanka generally arrive by plane. Sri Lankan Airlines serves cities in central and western Europe, which is where the majority of tourists come from; Saudi Arabia and the Gulf states, where many Sri Lankans work as laborers; India, especially southern India, where the Tamil population has many ties; and southern and eastern Asia, with its growing potential of tourists and business partners. There are also daily connections to the Maldive Islands.

Other national and charter airlines help to transport tourists from the main target areas of Sri Lankan Airlines. The flight time from Central Europe to Sri Lanka is about 10 hours; the time difference is five hours (four in summer). There is only one national airport in Sri Lanka, Katunayake, 35 kilometers north of Colombo. From there, you can reach all of the main tourist destinations along the west coast in less than three hours by car.

By Boat

The few hundred tourists every year who come to Sri Lanka by boat arrive in Colombo harbor and are generally cruise ship passengers. Until 1984, there was regular ferry service several times a week between Sri Lanka and India (Talaimannar-Rameswaram), but this has been suspended since the political conflict began.

TRAVELING IN SRI LANKA

By Plane

The airport for domestic flights is Ratmalana, 15 kilometers south of downtown Colombo and 50 kilometers from Katunayake. In addition to Ratmalana, civil air traffic uses the airports of Jaffna, Ampara, Anuradhapura, Batticaloa, Sigiriya, Trincomalee, Vavuniya, Wirawila. Scheduled flights carried out by the Lionair company until the mid-1990s, as well as other domestic civil flights, have been cancelled until further notice as a result of LTTE attacks on Sri Lankan military aircraft. Since 1997, scheduled flights operate on the Ratmala-Jaffna route, but as a rule only for residents of the Jaffna district and authorized personnel. A political thaw should revive many domestic air routes and helicopter sightseeing routes. For information about current domestic flights, contact the Ceylon Tourist Board (see page 247) or the Sri Lanka Tourist Board (see page 70).

By Train

Of the nearly 1,500 kilometers of railway lines, the mountain stretches (past Kandy and Badulla) offer particularly marvelous views. To best enjoy the breathtaking scenery make sure you take plenty of time and travel in the best seasons. For the 120 kilometers from Colombo to Kandy, normal passenger trains take about four hours, the *Inter-City Express* about two hours; a second-class ticket for the latter, even with reserved seats, costs less than US $2. The mountain route (Colombo-Kandy/Peradeniya-Badulla) takes over 10 hours. The following stops lead to special tourist attractions: Hatton for Adam's Peak; Nanu Oya for Nuwara Eliya; Pattipola or Ohiya for Horton Plains. The west coast trip (Colombo-Galle-Matara) is a nice alternative to the congested A2. Old steam engines are sometimes used on this route, and many cars date back to colonial times. Large train stations, such as Colombo Fort, sell tickets at special counters depending on which direction you want to travel. There is presently no service to Jaffna or Mannar. Terminus in the north is Vavuniya. Train travel to the east coast is sometimes limited. Train information: Colombo-Fort, *Railway Tourist Office*, tel. 01-435838.

By Bus

State buses run on a specific schedules, and private ones, generally mini-buses, run irregularly; fares are, however, regulated. As these fares are very low, private bus companies have to get as many passengers as possible on board and drive as fast as possible, to cover costs. Fortunately for them, there are always lots of people traveling in Sri Lanka, and most of them are prepared to squeeze into a bus that's already chock-full in order to zoom through the country at breakneck speed. Traveling with luggage under these conditions, however, can be difficult. Still, tourists on a tight budget can get all over the country by bus; even the more comfortable express buses routes don't cost much more.

For information on state buses, contact: *Central Transport Board*, tel. 01-329604/5.

By Three-Wheeler Taxi

In Sri Lanka motorized *three-wheeler taxis* are more expensive than buses, but are a viable alternative for city or local trips, even for locals. You have to negotiate the fare. Besides the driver, there's room for two passengers in these small, wobbly vehicles, which are far superior to cars or buses in slow-moving traffic.

By Taxi

The most pleasant way to travel Sri Lanka is also the most expensive. Rates are fixed; check at your hotel before you leave to ascertain a reasonable price, and negotiate with the driver. Prices for radio taxis with meters: 25-30 Rs./km.

One popular option is to rent a taxi for private tours, which is a great way to travel comfortably, safely and with a local guide. Depending on the type of car, you pay a flat rate per kilometer (in 2001, 15-20 Rs./km) and pay the driver a flat-rate fee (100-200 Rs./day). Larger hotels have accommodations for drivers; in smaller hotels you sometimes have to pay separately for the driver's room, but given the low prices, this option may actually be cheaper. Usually, drivers know the country well and provide a truly valuable service that should be acknowledged with an appropriate tip.

By Rental Car or Motorcycle

For about the same price per kilometer you pay for taxis, you can also rent a car. Anyone who's driven in the hectic local traffic, with legion trucks and buses zooming by, together with a full complement of ox-carts, work elephants, cyclists (without lights at night) and pedestrians – there are no sidewalks – will be sensible and decide on a taxi. Anyone who insists on driving himself needs a Sri Lankan driver's license; the rental firm can tell you how to get one. A more popular option is to travel with a rented motorcycle. You'll find the largest selection in Hikkaduwa; the best prices in the off season.

Traffic / Cycling

Sri Lanka's road network extends some 26,000 kilometers, only a few hundred of which are free of potholes. Driving is on the left side of the road, or wherever your chances of getting through seem best. The road is there for everyone, from work elephants to funeral processions; from pedestrians to buses racing blindly along their merry way. In less-frequented areas with lower population density, the roads, while perhaps in poor condition, are quiet and inviting, especially for motorcyclists and bicyclists (cycling tours see this page: Activities).

Restricted Areas

As long as the conflict remains unresolved between the Sri Lankan government and the Tamil Eelam movement, which demands its own independent state in the north (and partly in the east), you can't travel farther north than Vavuniya. The military also prevents travel to the island of Mannar, as well as to Wilpattu National Park. The east coast south of Pulmoddai is either open or closed to travelers, depending on the political situation. Countless military checkpoints as well as poor road conditions can slow or prevent further travel on this route. Tourists get preferential treatment at checkpoints. Some sights are located in military zones; in general, a friendly, patient conversation with the people guarding the area will get you through unhindered.

PRACTICAL TIPS FROM A TO Z

Accommodation

Hotels are categorized from one to five stars; there are also unclassified hotels. Those described as guest houses are simple, with only a few rooms. You can also rent a room in small private facilities (Paying Guest Accommodation). Hotels designated as Rest Houses don't fall into any specific category; these are accommodations originally built for colonial officials making tours of inspection through the country. Depending on the management, they may be either marvelous or dubious. Many of them are in particularly lovely locations; those in small villages have only a few rooms. The food (rice and curry) is generally good.

The tourist board's *Accommodation Guide* comes out every six months; while not complete, it gives a good overview of the prices and facilities of the places it does list. In surveying the prices, keep in mind that there's a 10 percent service charge and 5-10 percent so-called Business Turnover Tax (B.T.T.). And take note: The indication "hotel" on some small storefronts actually means "restaurant."

Activities

Canoeing, rafting: Depending on the waterway, guided trips along the Mahaweli Ganga, Kalu Ganga and further rivers are offered. Equipment and extensive range of trips available at: Adventure Sports Lanka, 1/1 Deanstone House, 337 Galle Road, Colombo 3, tel. 074-713334, 01-575425. For Lahugala National Park and Arugam Bay see p. 157.

Ornithological tours and nature observations: Many popular tour organizers offer trips for the individual traveler (see page 70), as do the hotels near the suitable nature reserves as well as TASK Safari camping (see page 141).

Cycling: Subject to comments already made about traffic (page 242), the bicycle is an ideal mode of transportation in Sri Lanka. In mountainous regions, good gear shifts and brakes are an absolute must. Instead of only using the following busy roads, do plan in some detours: Colombo-Katunayake (A3), Colombo-Kandy (A1), Colombo-Galle (A2). Adventure Sports (see above) and other organizers offer mountain bike tours.

Hiking: Hiking is especially satisfying in the beautiful highland regions, but the suitable infrastructure is lacking. Nevertheless, it's possible when visiting Horton Plains National Park or ascending Adam's Peak. Some hotels organize experienced guides for individual tours.

Water sports: Available at all the main tourist resorts along the coast. Also at: Lanka Sports Tours, 211 Hospital Rd., Kalubowila, tel. 01-824500.

Diving: Diving schools can also be found in Beruwala, Hikkaduwa, Weligama, Brown's Safari Beach Hotel/Yala (in peak season).

Admission Fees

It's not uncommon for tourists to be charged tenfold what locals have to pay for entrance fees. Where locals enter a temple free of charge, foreigners are often requested to give donations and pay for permission to take photographs. If there's an official sign posting charges, heed it; if someone makes excessive demands, be friendly but pay less and ask for a receipt.

For the most important sights of the Cultural Triangle between Anuradhapura, Polonnaruwa and Kandy, you can buy a booklet of tickets (enter your name and passport number) for all the sights that is good for two weeks and usually also includes permission to take photos. You can get this at the Cultural Ministry from the *Central Cultural Fund*, 212/1 Bauddhaloka Mw., Colombo 7, tel. 01-500731/2, -587912. It is also available at the museums in Anuradhapura and Polonnaruwa, among others.

Alcohol

The word *arrack* marks licensed stores, which sell not only local brandy specialties made of palmyra flower or coconut palm juice, but also various other local and foreign alcohols. On *poya* (full moon) days, alcohol is sold neither here nor in any hotels. If you need to, stock up beforehand and drink in your room. Alcoholic beverages are very cheap, and alcoholism is rampant.

Ayurveda

Ayurveda is a holistic method of treatment which has been tried and tested for thousands of years. It is becoming ever more popular and more widely available in hotels, where it is carried out by trained practitioners. A list of Ayurveda facilities is available from Tourist Information Offices (see page 247).

Begging

Only a few Sri Lankans enjoy the luxury of an old-age pension. Many elderly people therefore have no choice but to go out and beg. Locals generally give them a couple of rupees and it is expected that tourists wealthy enough to afford such a long trip will be able to do the same.

A popular children's "sport," often played in groups, is to see what they can get off of hapless tourists who happen to come along. The stranger is greeted with cries of: *School pen*? *Rupees*? *Money?*, etc. Some kids have achieved remarkable proficiency in collecting ballpoint pens and money. But bear in mind that if such a junior "champ" manages to collect 100 Rs. in only a few hours, he's quite possibly earned more than his father. This could lead to his skipping school, scorning his parents and wasting money.

However, if you ask for the help or cooperation of children or adults (asking for directions, posing for a photo and the like), you should show your thanks in tangible form for their services. Foreign ballpoint pens are, in fact, a popular gift, and small change never goes amiss.

Business Hours

Larger shops in big cities often don't open until 10 a.m., but smaller ones open earlier. Occasionally, stores will close for lunch. City stores close at 6 or 7 p.m.; supermarkets and small shops at 8:30 or 9 p.m. Some offices are only open in the morning. Banks are open Monday through Friday at least from 9 a.m. to 1 p.m., and many stay open longer. Take note of the holidays! Many small shops are open daily except New Year's Day.

Drinking

In hot countries, drinking is very important. You shouldn't drink tap water, though. You can buy bottled water and tea all over the place, as well as countless other beverages. Many small stands and restaurants serve tea, usually with a lot of milk (Sinhalese *kiri*, Tamil *paal*) and sugar (Sinhalese and Tamil *sini*). If you order plain tea, you'll get sweetened tea without milk. To make it clear that you want neither milk nor sugar, say *kiri sini epa* or *paal sini woundaam*.

A refreshing alternative to bottled drinks is the juice of the king coconut (Sinhalese *tambili*, Tamil *ulani*), available at many stands. Before the eyes of the purchaser, the tip of the orange-red nut is skillfully opened with a long, sharp knife, and the nut is handed over – usually, for foreigners, with a straw.

Eating

Tourist hotels take pains to present their guests with familiar international specialties, but generally also offer samplings of local fare. You can, therefore, often get things like *appa* for breakfast (in English, this has been corrupted to *hopper*); these are semi-spherical pancakes of rice flour and coconut milk, fried in special pans. Fried with an egg, they're called *egg-hoppers*. *String-hoppers* are small pancakes of steamed noodles, eaten with various *sambols* (grated coconut with spices and a little lime) or curries, the wide variety of side dishes that are often served with rice. *Kiribath* is a thick rice pudding made with coconut milk. The standard main dish is rice and curry; a plate is heaped with rice surrounded by smaller bowls with various side dishes, mainly spicy curries. "White curry" is a milder curry. If you still find the meal too hot (spicy), add more rice or sprinkle it with freshly-grated coconut (*pol*). *Pappadam*, crispy cracker-like bread fried in oil, are only crispy as long as they're fresh. People eat with the fingers of their right hand, but foreigners are generally provided with utensils. In smaller local restaurants, the plates are often wet as a sign that they're freshly washed; sometimes, they are even covered with hygienic plastic wrap. Fingerbowls are provided. And you often see neat squares of newspaper which are meant to serve as napkins.

Electricity

Electrical current is 230-240 volts.

Emergencies

Police (Colombo): 433333; **Fire Department** and **Ambulance**: 422222; **Emergency Hospital** (Colombo General Hospital): 691111; **Colombo Tourist Police** 327711 or 421111. For local emergency pharmacy service, doctor or hospital, ask at your hotel. Some of the more isolated hotels often keep their own on-duty nurse and/or doctor, who's always on call. You won't always find telephones easily in the provinces, but the locals are generally friendly and helpful.

Etiquette

Sri Lankans attach a lot of importance to polite behavior and proper appearance. Although there are many minor conflicts every day, you'll seldom witness a full-scale public argument. Anyone who can't control himself loses face. A loud-mouthed tourist complaining about minor difficulties and dressed sloppily is a figure of fun (not only in Sri Lanka) and this may lead to a certain degree of secret scorn for such foreigners, which sometimes extends to foreigners in general. However, Sri Lankans also enjoy the open, friendly way foreigners treat other people, since in their own society they're bound by the rules of their caste and class systems. It's not uncommon for locals to invite tourists home; anyone with genuine interest should certainly go along. But a foreign friend is also sometimes seen as a potential sugar daddy, and it's not always easy to figure out the motivation right from the start. Attention: Shaking your head means "Yes" !

Festivals, Holidays, Pilgrimages

Fixed Holidays: February 4 (National Holiday); April 12 / 13 (Buddhist and Hindu New Year); May 1 (Int. Workers' Day); December 25 (Christmas).

Flexible Holidays: These include all *poya* (full moon) days; in *Vesak* (May), the day after the full moon is also a holiday. Additional holidays: In January, *Thai Pongal*, the Tamil thanksgiving festival; in February, *Maha Shivarathri*, the wedding of the god Shiva and the goddess Parvati; usually in April, Good Friday; *Id-Ul-Fitr*, the end of *Ramadan*, the Muslim month of fasting, according to the lunar calendar; then *Id-Ul-Alha* (or *Azha*), the day when Muslims pilgrim to Mecca; in August, *Milad-Un-Nabi*, the birthday of the Prophet Mohammed; in October, *Dipavali*, the Hindu festival of lights. Furthermore, the government sometimes announces holidays for special occasions; elections, state visits, etc.

Buddhist Pilgrimages and Processions (*peraheras*): These include the *Duruthu* (January) *perahera* in Kelaniya; January to April: Pilgrimage season to Adam's Peak; *Poson* (June): Many pilgrims go to Mihintale; July/August: Season of the 14-day *Kandy Perahera* and pilgrimages to Kataragama. **Hindu Festivals**: In addition to pilgrimages, there's the spectacular *vel* (spear, trident) procession from Skanda and Pillaiyar (Ganesha) *kovil* (Hindu temple) in the Pettah quarter of Colombo to *kovils* on Galle Road and back; several festivals in Munnesvaram *kovil* near Chilaw in August and September/October; August sees countless festival processions on the Jaffna Peninsula, the most famous being that in Nallur, near Jaffna.

Christian Festivals: Passion plays in the Negombo area; Christmas is commercialized here much as it is elsewhere. Places of pilgrimage include Madhu, two weeks in late June to July 2, and Talawila for the festival of St. Anne on July 26. Moslem festivals are less spectacular.

Photography

Colorful and multi-faceted, Sri Lanka offers a wealth of images, and people are generally willing to be subjects. But it is polite to ask first. Your subject will often ask to have the picture sent to him or her, and this seems a reasonable courtesy.

In light of the country's widespread poverty, it is understandable that many people expect a token recompense for allowing themselves to be photographed. On the route between Polonnaruwa and Anuradhapura, which gets many tourists, some families have set up whole exhibitions of giant rag dolls, a kind of scarecrow, along the roadside. Of course, the motivation behind this service is to improve one's income.

Photography is prohibited in some museums and temples: you may a permit.

Shopping

Prices in department and self-service stores are fixed. On the street, or in smaller stores, haggling is common, as long as you're not trying to buy basic daily staples, such as bread, rice, etc.

Telephones, Internet

Four mobile phone companies (Hutchinson 078-661111, 663333; Celltel 541541, 0722-43333; Dialogue GSM 077-678678; and Mobitel 071-755777) have been able to establish a foothold in Sri Lanka within a short time, which is an indication of the weaknesses in the regular public phone network. Some remote areas have no phone lines at all.

Various phone companies are installing ever more public card phones, from which you can also place international calls. You can generally buy phone cards in the shop nearest the phone booth. Some hotels now offer Internet access. Internet café: Speed, 57 Galle Road, 1st floor, Colombo 4, tel. 01-597737, -305360, open daily 9 am to 9 pm.

Theft

"Do not take anything that was not given to you" was Buddha's simple commandment; to make it easier to keep, many windows in Sri Lanka are fitted out with bars. Valuables belong in the hotel safe or be worn in such a way that no one can snatch them off your body.

In crowds accompanying *peraheras*, processions, or in packed buses, pickpockets have an easy time, so be careful.

Tipping

Many Sri Lankans working in the tourist industry live mainly not from their salary, but from tips. Pains taken by the service sector should be incentive enough for guests to make appropriate acknowledgement. No proud and well brought up Sri Lankan will blatantly hold out his hand for money – although there are exceptions to any rule.

Touts

Tourists traveling alone will often encounter them: Polite Sri Lankans offering their services to help find a house, a shop, see the sights. Tourists may feel pestered, and hotel or shop proprietors aren't thrilled either, as these people generally request a small payment.

Friendly refusal and then determined ignoring is the most elegant way of getting rid of them. Sometimes the Sinhalese word *Epa*! / Tamil: *Woundaam*! ("I don't want to!") can work wonders.

Women Traveling Alone

Foreign women won't encounter any problems traveling alone; you may even feel like an especially valued guest, particularly in areas of low tourism.

In the more crowded resort centers on the coast, the precedent set by other woman tourists may lead to undesirable invitations; try to decline these in such a way that the man doesn't lose face. Dress unobtrusively.

ADDRESSES

Foreign Consulates in Colombo

Belgium: Consulate, 22 Palm Grove, Colombo 4, tel. 576403; **Denmark**: General Consulate, 36 D.R. Wijewardene Mw., Colombo 10, tel. 447806; **Finland**: Embassy, 81 Barnes Place, Colombo 7, tel. 698819; **France**: Embassy, 89 Rosmead Place, Colombo 7, tel. 698115; **Germany**: Embassy, 40 Alfred House Avenue; Colombo 3, tel. 580431; **Great Britain**: High Commissioner, 190 Galle Road, Colombo 3, tel. 437336; **India**: High Commissioner, 36-38 Galle Road, Colombo 3, tel. 421605; **Italy**: Embassy, 55 Jawatte Road, Colombo 5, tel. 588905; **Maldives**: High Commissioner, 25 Melbourne Avenue, Colombo 4, tel. 500943; **The Netherlands**: Embassy, 25 Torrington Avenue, Colombo 7, tel. 589626; **Norway**: Embassy, 34 Ward Place, Colombo 7, tel. 687534; **Sweden**: Embassy, 47/1 Horton Place, Colombo 7, tel. 688452; **Switzerland**: Embassy, 63 Gregory's Road, Colombo 7, tel. 695117; **Thailand**: Embassy, 43 Dr. C.W.W. Kannangara Mw., Colombo 7, tel. 697406; **U.S.**: Embassy, 210 Galle Road, Colombo 3, tel. 448007.

Airlines

Sri Lankan Airlines: 21st floor, East Tower, World Trade Centre, Colombo 1, tel. 421161, 073-5555. **British Airways**: Trans Asia House, 115 Sir Chittampalam A. Gardiner Mw., Colombo 2, tel. 320231-3. **Emirates**: Hemas House, 75 Braybrooke Place, Colombo 2, tel. 074-716565-9. **Indian Airlines**: Bristol Complex, 4 Bristol Street, Colombo 1, tel. 326844. **KLM/Martinair**: 29 Braybrooke St., Colombo 2, tel. 439747. **LTU**: 11A York Street, Colombo 1, tel. 424483-6. **Singapore Airlines**: 315 Vauxhall St., Colombo 2, tel. 300757. **Swissair**: Taj Samudra Hotel Shopping Arcade, 25 Galle Face Centre Rd., Colombo 3, tel. 435403-5. **Thai Airways**: Hotel Ceylon Intercontinental, 48 Janadhipathi Mw., Colombo 1, tel. 331166-9.

Tourist Information Offices

Colombo: Travel Information Center, 80 Galle Rd., Colombo 3, tel. 01-437059/60 (opposite the Lanka Oberoi Hotel). **Kandy**: Travel Information Center, "Headman's Lodge," 3 Deva Vidiya, Kandy, tel. 08-22661 (by the parking lot opposite Queen's Hotel).

Representatives Overseas

Canada: Ceylon Tourist Board, Cathedral Place, 925 West George Street, Vancouver, BC, V6C 3L2, tel./fax: (604) 688-8528.

France: Office de Tourisme de Ceylan, 19 Rue de Quatre Septembre, 75002 Paris, tel. 0033-1-4260.

U.K.: Ceylon Tourist Board, 22 Regent Street, London SW1Y 4QD, tel. 0171-9302627.

U.S.: c/o Sri Lankan Mission to the U.N., 7630 Third Avenue, New York, NY, 10017, tel. (212) 986-7040.

GLOSSARY

Both Sinhalese and Tamil use many English words, such as good morning, good evening, excuse me, bus stop, etc.

Sinhalese

How are you? . . . . *kohómede säppe sannìppe*
Thank you . . . . *istúti*
Give me . . . . *matte denewádde*
yes / no . . . . *öu / nä*
I want . . . . *matte one*
I don't want . . . . *epa*
money . . . . *salli*

how much	*kíyede*
too much	*wädi*
Go away!	*yande!*
Careful!	*awadánai*
Where is ... ?	*kohédde?*
Is it far ?	*ätede?*
It is near	*lange*
right / left	*dakuna / wam*
straight ahead	*kellin*
back, backwards	*passe*
I want to get off	*báhinawa*
Get out!	*bahínde!*
milk	*kiri*
sugar	*sini*
salt	*lunu*
water	*watturu*
coffee / tea	*kopi* / tee
bread	*paan*
fish	*malu*
meat	*mas*
chicken	*kukul mas*
egg	*bíttärä*
vegetable	*eläwalu*

	Tamil
How are you?	*éppedi suhém*
Thank you	*nandri*
Give me	*edäi taruvírhala*
yes / no	*aam / illäi*
I want	*enaku wööndum*
I don't want	*enaku wööndaam*
money	*kaasi*
How much?	*öwélawö?*
too much	*kúde*
Go away!	*poo!*
Careful!	*káwanam*
Where is ... ?	*enge?*
Is it far?	*túrama?*
it is near	*kutte*
right / left	*wälädu / udádu*
straight ahead	*nadu*
back, backwards	*pin*
I want to get out	*irakám*
Get out!	*irangu!*
milk	*paal*
sugar	*sini*
salt	*uppu*
water	*tanni*
coffee / tea	*koopi / teetanni*
bread	*paan*
fish	*miin*
meat	*iráchi*
chicken	*koolirachi*
egg	*muttäi*
vegetable	*marákkari*

Numbers	Sinhala	Tamil
1	*éka*	*óndru*
2	*déka*	*irándu*
3	*toona*	*múndru*
4	*háttara*	*nalu*
5	*páha*	*áindu*
6	*háya*	*áaru*
7	*hátta*	*ölu*
8	*átta*	*öttu*
9	*námaya*	*onbádu*
10	*dáya*	*páttu*
11	*ekólaha*	*pádinondru*
12	*dólaha*	*pánirandu*
13	*datúna*	*pádinmundru*
100	*eka siya*	*núru*
1,000	*dáhak*	*áayiram*

Days	Sinhala	Tamil
Monday	*Sánduda*	*Tingal*
Tuesday	*Hangáruwada*	*Sewai*
Wednesday	*Baddáda*	*Puden*
Thursday	*Braasbedínda*	*Wiálen*
Friday	*Sikuráda*	*Wolli*
Saturday	*Senasuráda*	*Sani*
Sunday	*Irida*	*Niyairu*

AUTHORS

Elke Frey is a freelance tour guide; through her studies of geography and geology she developed a keen interest in getting to know countries and people, and she made traveling and writing about her experiences her profession. She finds leisurely travel on foot or by bicycle the best approach to a country. Her love of nature and knowledge of crafts, music and languages open up conversation and work opportunities wherever she goes. Since she bought a bicycle in Sri Lanka in 1983, she's cycled and hiked through thousands of kilometers of this country's varied landscapes on her frequent visits. She is the Project Editor of this book, and also authored *Nelles Guide Tanzania*.

Gerhard Lemmer is a freelance tour guide for study groups. He studied sociology, politics, history and art history; both during and after his studies he traveled extensively around the world, until he finally made his hobby into his job in 1983. Since then, he has kept changing the focus of the trips he leads, from Europe's Mediterranean countries (France, Spain, Italy, etc.) to Scandinavia, America, South and East Asia. Sri Lanka's archeological highlights and the legends associated with them are a particular interest of his. For this book, he worte the chapter "Rajarata."

Jayanthi Namasivayam has for many years been the secretary at the Board of Investment of Sri Lanka, and is fluent in all three of the languages used in Sri Lanka. She compiled the *Glossary*, and advised the authors on questions relating to the Sinhalese and Tamil languages.

PHOTOGRAPHERS

Aitken, Kevin (Silvestris) 12
AKG, Berlin 22, 29, 32
Arvidsson, Fredrik 24, 92
Beck, Josef 8/9, 42, 120, 126, 142/143, 172, 178, 184, 188, 194, 203, 218, 229
Beck, Roland (Silvestris) 20, 94, 139
Begsteiger, A. M. cover, 199
Braunger, Manfred 235R
Dani, C. / **Jeske**, J. (Silvestris) 108
dpa 34
Eifler, Klaus 15, 95
Ender, Klaus 58, 79, 84
Frangenberg, Johannes 181
Frey, Elke 16, 46/47, 74, 78, 104, 144, 146, 152, 155, 234
Helbig, Konrad (Mainbild) 41, 122, 160, 167, 168, 190
Hellige, Wolfgang 189
Helms, Bernd 153, 186
Hinze, Peter 10/11, 68, 80, 90/91, 134, 177, 233
Höricht, Ingo 59, 98
Hoffmann, Per-André 133, 206/207
Holzbach, R. / **Bénet**, P. 52, 62, 83, 230, 231
Janicke, Volkmar E. 111, 112, 196
Jennerich, Herbert 25, 36, 57L, 57R, 64, 65, 136, 170/171, 183, 185, 235L
Karl, Roland F. 150, 214, 224/225
Kißling, Volker 131, 200
Lange, Harald (Silvestris) 19, 67
Lieber, Dr. Werner 121
Lughofer, Josef (Silvestris) 39
Müller, Kai Ulrich 77
Pavenzinger, Josef (Silvestris) 149
Postl, Leo (Silvestris) 102
Purmann, H. und L. 14, 116,148, 182
Riethmüller, Robert 17, 18, 23, 26, 30, 35, 38, 40, 43, 44/45, 48, 53, 54, 61, 72/73, 81, 82, 114/115, 135, 137, 158/159, 179, 187,192, 198, 208, 212, 213, 215,219, 220, 221, 228, 237
Roth, Hans-Georg 110, 124/125, 151, 191, 226/227
Schmidt, Friedrich 100/101, 107, 132
Schug, Bruno (Silvestris) 165
Schwarz, Berthold 130
Schweitzer, U. (Photo-Press) 28, 60, 195
Skupy-Pesek, Jitka 106
Stankiewicz, Thomas 85, 109
Stuhler, W. 63, 162, 164, 193, 201, 232
Vahl, Wolfgang (Photo-Press) 176
Wisniewski, W. (Silvestris) 66

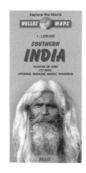